God and Mammon and
What Was Lost

God and Mammon and What Was Lost

François Mauriac

Translation, introduction, and notes by
Raymond N. MacKenzie

A SHEED & WARD BOOK

ROWMAN & LITTLEFIELD PUBLISHERS, INC.
Lanham • Boulder • New York • Toronto • Oxford

A SHEED & WARD BOOK

ROWMAN & LITTLEFIELD PUBLISHERS, INC.

Published in the United States of America
by Rowman & Littlefield Publishers, Inc.
A wholly owned subsidary of The Rowman & Littlefield Publishing Group, Inc.
4501 Forbes Boulevard, Suite 200, Lanham, Maryland 20706
www.rowmanlittlefield.com

PO Box 317
Oxford
OX2 9RU, UK

British Library Cataloguing in Publication Information Available

Library of Congress Cataloging-in-Publication Data

Mauriac, François, 1885–1970.
  [Dieu et Mammon. English]
  God and Mammon; and, What was lost / François Mauriac; translation, introduction,
and notes by Raymond N. MacKenzie.
    p. cm.
  ISBN 0-7425-3168-6 (alk. paper) – ISBN 0-7425-3169-4 (pbk.: alk. paper)
  I. Title: God and Mammon; and, What was lost. II. Title: What was lost.
III. MacKenzie, Raymond N. IV. Mauriac, François, 1885–1970. Ce qui était perdu.
English. V. Title: What was lost. VI. Title.

PQ2625.A93D513 2003
843'.912—dc21   2003046751

Printed in the United States of America

☉™ The paper used in this publication meets the minimum requirements of American
National Standard for Information Sciences—Permanence of Paper for Printed Library
Materials, ANSI/NISO Z39.48-1992.

Contents

Acknowledgements

I wish to express my gratitude to the individuals who have helped me in bringing this book to fruition. First is Jean Mauriac, who kindly arranged for me to read his father's manuscripts in the Bibliothèque Jacques Doucet in Paris. I am also grateful to the staff there, and at the Bibliothèque Nationale, for their patient assistance with my many questions.

Any student of François Mauriac is greatly indebted to Jacques Petit, whose magisterial edition of Mauriac's works is a sure guide through many editorial and textual complexities. My own debts to Petit, and to many other Mauriac scholars who have come before me, will be evident in the notes to this book.

Colleagues and friends who read the manuscript in whole or in part, and who offered many suggestions, include Rick Holton, Michael Lackey, Barrett Newhall, Keith Palka, David Rathbun, and Martin Warren. I have benefited greatly from their responses; any weaknesses that remain in the text are, of course, my own responsibility.

Two grants from the Aquinas Foundation at the University of St. Thomas provided me with the time and the means to do the research for this book. Michael Mikolajczak, chair of the English Department at UST, granted me valuable released time from my teaching in order to finalize the manuscript. The enthusiasm and commitment of Jeremy Langford at Sheed & Ward has made the final stages of this project a pleasure.

My greatest debt is to my wife, Laraine, who not only supported this project with seemingly infinite patience and encouragement from beginning to end, but even took upon herself the task of laying out and formatting the final text. Some acknowledgements are simply too great for words.

Introduction

$\mathbf{W}\text{HAT}$ is the relationship between what an author believes and what he or she writes? The question is a great deal more complex than it appears at first. If we believe the relationship ought to be a very close one, as, for example, Soviet Marxists did, then literature has one primary goal: to be ideologically pure. A good story, even a true story, might need to be radically changed and even falsified in order to reflect the beliefs of the author. Most of us in the West today find such an idea repugnant, and insist that there must be a thick line drawn between literature and propaganda. But most of us are uncomfortable with the opposite extreme—the idea that literature ought to have no traffic at all with belief systems. This line of thought leads us uncomfortably close to saying that literature has nothing to do but entertain. We have a sense, most of us, that literature has some moral function, though we will disagree violently about what that moral function ought to be and how blatant an author ought to be about it. While issues such as these have occupied readers at least since the time of Plato, the issues take on an even greater urgency for authors, especially authors who do feel a profound allegiance to a belief system—such as Catholicism.

This volume brings together two key texts from a critical period in the life of the great Catholic novelist François Mauriac: the 1929 essay, *God and Mammon* (*Dieu et Mammon*), and the 1930 novel, *What Was Lost* (*Ce qui était perdu*). They date from a time when Mauriac, in mid-career, turned to examine the topic of the Catholic novel—what it was, what it should be—and the more urgent topic for him of what it means to be a Catholic novelist. But the importance of these texts lies not just in what they can tell us about Mauriac himself, interesting and valuable as that may be. The two texts also have a great deal to suggest about some of the most fundamental questions regarding aesthetics and ethics, questions that continue to be of pressing importance today. For in these two works—one a theoretical discussion, the other an attempt to put the theory into novelistic practice—Mauriac grapples with questions of artistic responsibility, questions that are just as difficult and as imperious for imaginative writers today as they were for Mauriac in his period of crisis.

The Background

A brief sketch of Mauriac's life and work up until 1929 is necessary for seeing the two works in context. He was born in Bordeaux on October 11, 1885, into a devoutly Catholic family dominated by his mother, Claire. His father, Jean-Paul, died suddenly of a brain abscess when François was only twenty months old, and the family went to live with Claire's mother. While Mauriac frequently wrote in later life of his childhood as happy and even idyllic, his novels—such as *Genitrix*, *What Was Lost*, and *La Pharisienne* (*Woman of the Pharisees*) among others—depict strong mothers as being very much a mixed blessing, particularly when that strength is mixed with pronounced piety. And while Mauriac spoke of his own mother with reverence and real love, it is natural to assume that some of the suffocating mothers in his novels have something of Claire Mauriac in them. In *God and Mammon*, he quotes Rimbaud in regard to his own pious and formidable mother: "I sweated obedience," Rimbaud said. Mauriac, one feels, had some sympathy for the sentiment.

Mauriac's biographer, Jean Lacouture, depicts a family composed of two antithetical strains: the mother's side of the family was monarchist, conservative, and deeply attached to the Catholic Church as both a temporal and a spiritual power.[1] But the father's side was republican, anti-clerical, and even anti-religious (Mauriac's father had lost his faith, and demonstrated it whenever possible, insisting on being served a cutlet every Friday). One need not invoke genetics to suppose that François grew up with a sense that both sides lived on in him, and that he was subject to the demands of both God and Mammon. This conflict was in his case sharpened by the almost Jansenist quality of his mother's Catholicism, which inculcated in him a sense of the ever-present mortal peril of sin. Some of this atmosphere is evoked in *God and Mammon*, when he describes the fear of swallowing some water while brushing his teeth just before going to Communion: an inadvertent drop of water would turn the sacrament into sacrilege.

His schooldays, after some initial miseries, became a happy time for him. He had written his first novel by the time he was thirteen, and, typical of an intellectually inclined adolescent, he became interested in religious controversy and in the movement that had come to be called Modernism. In 1905—the year in which Church and state were officially separated in France—he joined a democratic reformist group known as the Sillon, led by the charismatic Marc Sangnier, whose aim was for the Church to become more progressive, to accept the Republic and its newly official secularity, and work within it for social justice.[2] Such goals were immensely appealing to the young Mauriac, and he enthusiastically supported Sangnier's Sillon; he published his first piece—a short story—in the Sillon journal, *La Vie fraternelle*. After about a year, he came to distrust both the movement and its founder, however, and thereafter he usually kept his distance from political movements. The experience gave him the material, though, for his first published novel, *L'Enfant chargé de chaînes* (1913, translated as the *Young Man in Chains*), and it also taught him to separate matters of faith from politics. (Such a separation was in any case quite orthodox: Pope Pius X condemned and disbanded the Sillon group in 1910, and popes through the 1930s usually discouraged French Catholic political groups of both the left and the right.) For Mauriac, leaving the Sillon movement behind was an early experience of choosing between God and Mammon.[3]

Thus, even from this brief overview of Mauriac's early years, we can see that life presented itself as a series of dichotomies to him, dichotomies that seemed to have their roots in the makeup of his family. On the mother's side are religious conservatism and intense private devotion to God, while on the father's is the anticlerical rebellion of post-Revolutionary France and with it the spirit of personal independence and of political reform. Mauriac's adolescence, his identity-forming years, played out within such oppositions, including a fidelity to the Church and an attraction to what the Church was condemning as Modernism.[4] Charles Taylor's work on the modern self defines our sense of identity as profoundly moral: "Our identity is what allows us to define what is important to us and what is not,"[5] he says, arguing that we define ourselves in terms of a framework of moral values. Our moral values are no something we "have"; rather, they are what we *are*. Whether conscious of it or not, our identities are not just shaped by our moral frameworks, but in fact consist of those very frameworks. From a perspective like Taylor's, Mauriac's early years will seem particularly turbulent, for both sides of the dichotomies are heavily laden with moral implications, violently opposed in terms of what is to be valued in life, in terms of what it is to live a good life. This inner turbulence—to anticipate a bit—no doubt helped greatly in Mauriac's success as a novelist, letting him imaginatively identify with a wide range of characters, many of them deeply disturbed, some of them overtly evil. His outer life remained relatively placid and bourgeois (with a major exception in the late 1920s, which will be discussed below), while he was able to sublimate his other "self," the nonreligious, nonbourgeois self, into his characters. But this divided self would continue to simmer below the surface; and understanding this is crucial for seeing what motivates him in *God and Mammon* and *What Was Lost*.

To return to our chronology: in 1907, he convinced his mother to allow him to move to Paris. His ostensible reason was to study at the École des Chartes, and his stated intent was to research and write a thesis on the origins of the Franciscans in France. But both he and his mother knew the real reason for the move was his desire to become a writer. He dropped out of school in 1909 and devoted himself to writing full time. In November of that year he published his first book, at his own expense, a collection of poems titled *Les Mains jointes* [Clasped Hands]. He came to dislike these poems, but the book came to the attention of Maurice Barrès, perhaps the most eminent writer of the day, and Barrès published an article in 1910 praising the volume. The importance of this for a young unknown writer cannot be overestimated, and later in life Mauriac repeatedly wrote about Barrès and his importance to him.[6] The two never became close—their temperaments were too different, Barrès being deeply political—though in some ways a sort of father-son relationship developed, in part because Barrès was grieving for the recent suicide of a nephew (a suicide that Mauriac would later adapt in his novel, *Le Chair et le sang* [Flesh and Blood]). The suicide had brought Barrès back to Christianity, which no doubt accounts for his having been moved by the religious sentiments in the young Mauriac's poems.

Barrès' notice contributed not only to Mauriac's stature as a writer but also to his self-confidence. He soon had completed and published two largely autobiographical novels, *L'Enfant chargé de chaînes* (1913) and *La Robe prétexte* (1914, translated as *The Stuff of Youth*); both were received with some respect, but neither was especially successful, and neither is widely read today. In 1913 he married Jeanne Lafon, and their first child was born the next year—Claude, who would grow up to become a novelist and critic of significance himself. When World War I broke out, Mauriac was declared unfit for service, due to a bout of pleurisy he had suffered back in 1903; unwilling to sit the war out, he volunteered as a stretcher bearer for the Red Cross, and he later served in a hospital in Salonika. His third novel, *Le Chair et le sang*, was begun in 1914 but not completed and published until 1920; this was his first nonautobiographical work and, though the novel feels rather derivative and unconvincing, it was a major step forward in his maturation as a writer. Another step was taken with the following novel, the 1921 *Préséances* (translated as *Questions of Precedence*). *Préséances* owes too much, undoubtedly, to Balzac, but its satire on the rigid class system in Bordeaux makes it very much worth reading today, and in its attempt to graft something of a religious theme onto the satire, it anticipates his maturer works.

Mauriac's novels up through *Préséances* can be seen as the products of an apprenticeship period: each seems something of an improvement on the preceding one, but taken as a whole they show promise rather than achievement. But the apprenticeship abruptly ended and the achievement came suddenly with his very next book, *Le Baiser au lépreux* [A Kiss for the Leper] (1922). This was Mauriac's first real masterpiece, as well as his first bestseller. As in *Préséances*, Mauriac again drew on his memories of life in the Bordeaux region, but now the atmosphere was not satiric—rather it is intensely claustrophobic, tormented, and tragic. It was quickly followed by *Le Fleuve de feu* [The River of Fire] (1923)—which in fact he was writing at the same time as *Le Baiser au lépreux*. While this novel is rarely classed among Mauriac's best today, it was also highly successful—and it both landed him a generous contract with the publisher Grasset and allowed him to break into the prestigious *Nouvelle Revue Française* [New French Review] circle, led by Jacques Rivière and André Gide. He later wrote about this period that "in literary terms, *La Nouvelle*

Revue Française was my gospel. . . . It took me twelve years . . . to join this literary group with which I felt I had so much in common. It was not so much that I was excluded from them, but I felt they despised me."[7] With the approval of such men, Mauriac could feel he had arrived. His next book, *Genitrix* (1923), confirmed their judgment of him. It was another immense success, both critically and commercially. The story of a poisonous mother-son relationship (the mother having a few touches of Claire Mauriac in her), it is nearly nightmarish, an effect Mauriac accomplishes chiefly through his masterful manipulation of the story's setting, an old house so near to a railroad track that the trains rattle it like anonymous angry spirits.

Le *Baiser au lépreux* and *Genitrix* would alone suffice for us to call Mauriac a major novelist, but in this period, success only fueled further success for him. His next major novel was *Le Désert de l'amour* [The Desert of Love] (1925), which won the French Academy's prestigious grand prize. It is another tale of tormented family relationships, with father and son both in love with the same woman, the enigmatic Maria Cross. And this was followed by what remains Mauriac's best-known novel, *Thérèse Desqueyroux* (1927), the powerful story of a young wife whose repressed lesbianism leads to sexual alienation from her husband, an alienation that soon leads her to plan his murder. The character of Thérèse continued to fascinate Mauriac; he wrote two further short stories about her and one more complete novel—and, most importantly for our purposes, she also makes a brief appearance in the novel *What Was Lost*. While this is not the place for extensive discussion of these great novels from the 1920s, we should note that all of them have a certain tone, which is of great significance for understanding the crisis Mauriac was about to undergo in 1926-1928. To put the matter in Catholic terms, all these novels deal extensively with sin and sinners, and the sinners are presented sympathetically. Thérèse, for instance, is never judged, still less condemned by the novelist; on the contrary, the people around her, especially her husband, are shown to be narrow-minded, materialistic in the crudest way, and deeply hypocritical. It would be a rare reader who did not sympathize with Thérèse in her plight, and most will even cheer her on in her desperate bid to change her situation. The sinner becomes the moral norm, while those who are outwardly respectable are shown to be by far the more corrupt. In this respect, of course, Mauriac's novels of this period are well within the mainstream of twentieth-century fiction, the literature of the anti-hero (indeed, their moral stance in general is not radically different from those of Balzac, Flaubert, or Stendhal). But it is natural to ask also, in what sense are these "Catholic novels"? How are these novels different from those of a nonbeliever? To put it another way, are these the novels of Claire Mauriac's son?

Such questions were being raised as early as 1923, and Mauriac responded to them in an often-quoted interview with Frédéric Lefèvre. Lefèvre began by asking, "Monsieur François Mauriac, Catholic novelist?" And Mauriac responded, "I am a novelist; I am a Catholic—and there is the conflict!"[8] Catholicism, he admits, gives the novelist certain advantages, but he adds: "I believe, in fact, that it is fortunate for a novelist to be a Catholic, but I am also quite sure that it is very dangerous for a Catholic to be a novelist" (217). Mauriac sees the issue in terms of a dichotomous conflict: the novelist must deal with the miseries of the flesh, but the Catholic must not lead his readers into moral danger. He concludes, a little too lightly, that "People do not sympathize sufficiently with the Catholic novelists, caught between human truth and the duty to do good" (223). It would be wrong to say that Mauriac treated such issues quite without seriousness in the 1923 interview, but in fact he would come to see their real depth and complexity in the years ahead. The interview reveals him as intellectually interested in the problem, but by 1928-1929 he would become personally, spiritually involved with it.

Whether Mauriac could be called a true Catholic novelist became an even more urgent question with his next novel, the 1928 *Destins* (translated as *Lines of Life*). The story of *Destins* again presents the sinner as the moral norm—in this case, the forty-eight-year-old Elisabeth Gornac who, like Racine's great heroine Phaedra, succumbs to an all-consuming love for a man young enough to be her son. But the novel goes even further in one important respect: the one character who represents a Catholic point of view is hypocritical, pharisaical, and morally stunted. This is Elisabeth's son, Pierre, who is about to enter the priesthood; his oily piety causes havoc with two other characters, and indirectly leads to the despair and destruction of one of them, Bob Lagave. Insofar as Pierre Gornac represents religion in this novel, the story seems to imply that religion is like a snake in the garden of human relationships. The novel is set in the vine country outside Bordeaux, and again Mauriac orchestrates his setting poetically, with hot days and nights and storms that slowly approach across the plains. A fatalistic tone pervades the story (underlined by the title), and the myth of Phaedra hovers in the background so insistently that the novel feels not only non-Catholic but very nearly pagan—indeed, David O'Connell calls the book "one of Mauriac's most ardent expressions of the power of Cybele and the pagan rites of the flesh."[9]

The Racinian tone of *Destins* is explicable enough when we know that Mauriac was working on a biography of Racine at the same time. But the "pagan" or antireligious note is the result of something else, a spiritual crisis that Mauriac was undergoing. Earlier we saw a set of dichotomies at play within Mauriac's family, two opposed moral frameworks, and it is fair to say that one of those frameworks dominates his novels of the 1920s. The Mauriac of these novels believes in sin, certainly, but sees it sympathetically, sees its drama and its pathos; this Mauriac distrusts avowed religiosity and piety, and usually finds it masking greed and egotism. And this is the Mauriac who had grown into a highly successful and celebrated man of letters, the Mauriac who had put behind him his provincialism and his parochialism, the Mauriac who was read and admired not only by a wide public but by prestigious literary heroes like André Gide. The Catholic Mauriac was slipping into the shade, while the independent thinker, the humanist, the modernist was stepping into the sunlight.

Moreover, this had been noticed by the Catholic press, which had been viewing these novels of the 1920s with increasing distaste. Indeed, these works were all but condemned in the popular work of the Abbé Louis Bethléem. Something of a self-appointed watchdog over literature and its potential immoral effects on the reader, he published a series of works intended to give guidance to the Catholic family's reading habits, the most popular of which was *Romans à lire et romans à proscrire* [Novels to Read and Novels to Ban], which in 1928 had reached its tenth edition.[10] The book orders novels into four categories, from the very most immoral works (*Madame Bovary* is in this category, being "gravely dangerous") on down to those that even children may be allowed to read (Jane Austen and Dickens are listed here). The third category—worldly novels that mature people might be allowed to have in their libraries— includes an entry on Mauriac, and quite a damning one. Mauriac, Bethléem says, has "the soul of a Catholic Girondin, which he does not adequately defend against certain intrusions." There follows a list of

Mauriac's novels, each with a contemptuous parenthetical description. *Le Désert de l'amour*, for example, is called a "novel with wicked morals, very pernicious," and *Destins* is said to be about "the guilty passion of a forty-year-old woman for a kept lover [which is, incidentally, inaccurate on both counts]; a fatalistic and very unhealthy novel" (304-305). Mauriac made a quip about the officious Abbé in *God and Mammon*, but clearly this sort of criticism wounded him, because it suggests that he was not only a wicked writer but a bad Catholic. And it was not just Bethléem making such charges: the Abbé Calvet, for example, in his 1927 book, *Le Renouveau catholique dans la littérature contemporaine* [Catholic Renewal in Contemporary Literature], refused him the title of Catholic writer, and the Catholic press in general was coming to see him as a renegade.[11]

Along with the jibes of the Abbés Bethléem and Calvet, other things were happening in Mauriac's life during the 1926-1928 period that raised the question for him also: was he in fact a bad Catholic? Was he really a Catholic at all anymore? The non-Catholic literary world had embraced him warmly, while the Catholics seemed to be closing ranks against him. In such a bind, it would have been understandable if Mauriac had simply chosen to go where he was welcome, so to speak, and to carry on with his work—even if this meant coming to see his Catholicism as a hindrance to it. Instead, and characteristically, he began to think about the matter more deeply, and to think about himself with humility and insight. But it was not only the Catholic press that brought him to this introspection; quite independently of his critics, he was going through a period of crisis. He later wrote of the years around 1925-1929 that "it was as if I was mad," with a madness that arose "at the intersection of the flesh and the soul."[12] The flesh and the soul—another dichotomy, or rather a new formulation of the old ones. Mauriac had been brought to think seriously about the demands of the flesh because of a love affair he had been engaged in, about which we unfortunately know very little. O'Connell refers to this as "a sentimental attachment to a younger person" (19), and perhaps it was as innocent as that phrase suggests; but that it contributed to Mauriac's sense of "madness" in these years suggests that, to him at any rate, it was not at all innocent. In the absence of any further facts, speculation is pointless—but the importance of the affair to Mauriac's sense of personal crisis seems likely to have been very great.[13]

Events in 1928 brought all these matters to a head. *Destins* was published in book form in February. In the spring, he attended a conference on the Catholic novelist, giving a talk which was published as "La Responsabilité du romancier"[14] (The Novelist's Responsibility; this talk would be incorporated into *God and Mammon*). In May, Gide read *Destins* and the biography of Racine, and he sent Mauriac a letter about them. The letter was then published in the June *Nouvelle Revue Française*; the letter thus became something of a public challenge, and it became the catalyst, or one of the catalysts, for what would become *God and Mammon*. But over the summer of 1928, the letter must have occupied Mauriac a great deal, for in it Gide accuses him—in a friendly but provocative manner—of having it both ways: Mauriac's works are all about Mammon, but he considers himself to be on the side of God. Finally, Gide says what must have stung worst of all: if Mauriac were a better Christian, he would be a worse novelist.

While all these issues were simmering inside Mauriac, he contracted with the author and editor, André Billy, to write a commentary on the seventeenth-century cleric Bossuet's *Traité de la concupiscence* [Treatise on Concupiscence] for a series Billy was editing. This was strictly a commissioned task, a way of picking up a little money, but the project also forced Mauriac to confront Bossuet's severe Christianity, with its condemnation of physical love as sinful. Mauriac wrote the piece, which was published in Billy's collection, and then he also published it, in substantially the same form, in the *Nouvelle Revue Française* for October 1, 1928. Here it was given the title, "Souffrances du chrétien" (The Christian's Anguish). The Christian's anguish stems from God's impossible demands on fleshly creatures, as the opening paragraph makes clear:

> Christianity has no part in the flesh; in fact, it suppresses the flesh. "God wants *everything*," says Bossuet. And Pascal: "Lord, I give you *everything*."[15]

The essay is an extended lament concerning the weaknesses of the flesh and sexual weaknesses in particular:

> Is there one single man anywhere in the world who, delivered from all the delights of the flesh, lives in union with God? Is spiritual life, even apart from all defined religions, compatible with the carnal life? (127)

The delights of the flesh, we should note, also include literature itself. Racine is the supreme example of the writer who put literature behind him in order to follow the God who demands we rise above all the corrupted things of this world. Racine was of course a Jansenist, a follower of an extremist sect (seeing the Jansenists as Catholicism's version of puritans would not be entirely wrong) condemned by the church. But Mauriac's personal crisis was driving him more closely toward the Jansenist outlook—an outlook that, after all, was not foreign to the brand of Catholicism he grew up with. Gide's open letter to Mauriac was taunting on this very point, and implied that if he really believed Racine was morally right to abandon writing, Mauriac himself was either not a real Christian—or he was a hypocrite. The essay "Souffrances du chrétien" seemed to say that Racine and Bossuet were right—but that he, Mauriac, could not follow their lead. Did this mean that Mauriac was about to abandon Christianity?

This is exactly what it seemed to mean to one of its readers, Charles Du Bos. A critic and man of letters, Du Bos (1882-1939) had in 1927 returned to the Catholicism he had abandoned since his youth, and he admired Mauriac's work greatly (he had written an excellent study of *Le Désert de l'amour* in the *Nouvelle Revue Française*). Now, the "Souffrances" essay alarmed him—he saw in it clear signs that Mauriac was in danger of losing his faith. Du Bos was perhaps the ideal person for the moment, a person for whom the word "sympathetic" is far too weak. In his journals and his criticism, he developed the notion that the self only exists when it is fully open to an other: on the literary level, this meant that the poet, novelist, or critic had to be in a state of emptiness and openness, and that intellectual "creation" was not so much creation as reception, acceptance of something freely given. Georges Poulet wrote of Du Bos in terms of his having a sense of inner incompletion, and he quotes from a journal entry from 1926:

> If, as the etymology of the word indicates, the poem is the thing which is made (par excellence), then the poet, before being he who makes, and in order to become that, is he who receives, or rather, he who undergoes. The poet is a point of intersection rather than a center. . . . The poet is penetrated by things *more than he originates them*.[16]

Du Bos, following his conversion, applied this idea of reception to the Christian awaiting divine grace, so that, as Poulet puts it, "the psychology of literary life does not differ fundamentally from the psychology of grace" (174). Both are a matter of waiting, of remaining open, and finally of receiving. Given this orientation, then, it is not surprising that when Du Bos read Mauriac's "Souffrances" essay, he took it with the greatest seriousness, and resolved to try to intervene and help.

He arranged to have dinner with Mauriac on November 6. On that day, Du Bos first attended Mass, and then spent the day reading texts by the Catholic philosopher Jacques Maritain: he approached the dinner with the serious intent of saving Mauriac's soul.[17] He convinced Mauriac to see his own spiritual advisor, Father Jean-Marie Altermann. Within weeks, Mauriac's conflicts were dissipating, chiefly due to Du Bos and Alterman[18] reminding him that, through the Incarnation, Christianity does indeed have a great deal to do with the flesh. It was a message he needed to hear. He went on a retreat to Solesmes in December, and there began drafting a second part of his essay, which would be titled "Le Bonheur du chrétien" (The Christian's Joy)—whose title suggests that it is in effect an answer to "Souffrances," putting the balance right. At this time, he was also working on *God and Mammon*. "Le Bonheur du chrétien" was published in April of 1929 in the *Nouvelle Revue Française*, and soon after, *God and Mammon* was published. The crisis was over: Mauriac had made his choice. He was recommitted now as a Catholic, and he would henceforth strive to integrate his faith with his work. He would become truly a Catholic novelist. The question remained, however, as to exactly what that entailed.

God and Mammon

As we have seen, Gide's open letter to Mauriac was one of the catalysts for Mauriac's thinking about the issue of Catholicism and the novel, thinking which was to result in *God and Mammon*. Gide taunts Mauriac for admiring Racine but not having the courage to be Racine—that is, Mauriac admires Racine's ability to give up sinful, fleshly literature because he felt called by God to do so, while Mauriac himself continues to write. Gide never uses the word "hypocrisy," but that is essentially the charge. Authors have shrugged off far worse charges than this, but it is a sign of Mauriac's essential sincerity, as well as of the seriousness of the crisis he found himself in during this period, that he felt compelled not simply to answer Gide—to justify himself—but to examine the issues more completely than he ever had before. And we should note that the nearly despairing essay, "Souffrances du chrétien," was in fact written and published *after* Gide's provocative letter. If the choice had to be between, on the one hand, the demands of the flesh and the literary life, and on the other the Christian faith, it would appear that Mauriac's decision was made in favor of the flesh—or so it would appear with the October 1928 publication of "Souffrances." But then came the intervention of Du Bos.

Thirty years later, Mauriac wrote a series of prefaces for a collection of his complete works. Looking back on *God and Mammon*, he wrote:

> Nearly thirty years have passed over these forgotten pages, pages about which I retain only a confused memory. Now, I rediscover them as if I were finding a forgotten key, and indeed "key" is the proper word. I have never written anything about myself that so deeply pressed into my own inner shadows as chapters II, III, and IV of this book. I have never opened myself up to this degree. And thus an out of print and almost unknown work suddenly reveals itself as being perhaps the most important thing I have ever written regarding my personal story.[19]

God and Mammon is, therefore, a great deal more than a merely theoretical discussion, and more than a response to the goading of André Gide. Mauriac says as much in the 1958 preface:

> If Gide's letter is what put the pen in my hand, it was not responsible for the feelings that emerged in these pages. In truth, Gide's provocation coincided with a state of crisis I had been going through after my fortieth year, midway on life's path. (1341)

The allusion to Dante should be taken with all its force: *God and Mammon* is a reflection of Mauriac's own experience of the Inferno.[20] Du Bos and Father Altermann played the role of Virgil for him, and at the end of *God and Mammon* there is something of a glimpse of Paradise.

The book begins with a discussion of the modern author's plight: the reading public wants to make inferences from the book to the man. While the author labors to create a work of fiction, the reader wants to unravel the fiction and get at the truth of the person who wrote it. These opening pages contain some fine grumbling on Mauriac's part, but in fact there is nothing particularly twentieth-century about the problem he describes: since the emergence of the author as a public figure in eighteenth-century Europe, and in some cases well before that, readers have been just as fascinated by the writer as by the book. But the modern phenomenon of literary journalism, of the reviewer who sees no difference between gossip and literary criticism—this is Mauriac's chief annoyance. He is careful to distinguish between such deadline-driven journalism and the work of genuine critics, though even with the former he finds that they sometimes point him toward some truth about himself.

On the list of critics Mauriac excepts from condemnation is Ramon Fernandez, and Fernandez contributed a prefatory essay to *God and Mammon*, titled "François Mauriac et le roman moderne" [François Mauriac and the Modern Novel]. The essay is a generous appreciation of Mauriac's achievements. But interestingly enough, Fernandez puts great emphasis on what he sees as the author's presence within the novels: he says the reader can sense Mauriac present inside one of his novels as a person is present inside a suit of clothes, and ultimately the greatest pleasure in reading him is this happy alliance of the author's personal presence with fully dramatized events and characters.[21] On the subject of Catholicism, Fernandez—tellingly—sees Mauriac as having a double vision, both Catholic and simply human. He sees the humanity of Mauriac's work as arising from a tension between the rigidity and narrowness of his religious education, and the human possibilities revealed to him by sensation and experience. But Fernandez also sees Mauriac's Catholicism in a positive light: it has allowed him to reintroduce the human conscience into the novel, an element missing in Proust, the greatest modern novelist (57). Having Fernandez' essay prefacing *God and Mammon* is an interesting choice, for it adds an outsider's secular perspective (a highly respectable outsider) to the book's discussion of Catholicism, placing it within a wider context. And Fernandez' insistence on the presence of the author in the novels adds something of a dissenting voice to Mauriac's insistence in chapter I on his purely fictional, nonpersonal intent in his fiction.

This discussion in chapter I sets the stage for some autobiography. chapter II concerns Mauriac's upbringing in Catholicism. There are details here about his adolescent rebellion against what he saw as superfi-

cial pieties enforced by the Church, but these are placed within the framework of an important thesis: some people—Mauriac himself, at any
rate—simply cannot leave the Church, any more than they could take
leave of their essential selves. He uses the metaphor of an inoculation:
some people are resistant to it, but others, once inoculated, stay inoculated. And with this realization, that Catholicism is part of his own fundamental identity, he revisits those once-detested pieties and finds that, petty
as they are, they have a real importance to the Christian. To be Christian is
to live the faith, every moment, in every detail, no matter how mundane,
of one's life. And thus even the prohibitions against letting a drop of
water get down one's throat before Communion make sense because they
concretize the reality of the Sacrament. Mauriac's acceptance of this
aspect of the faith sounds confident and measured in these pages, but the
confidence is of course a new-found one; one can only imagine how he
would have treated this subject if it had not been for the intervention of
Du Bos. And the chapter concludes with a much larger acceptance, the
acceptance of a certain suffering that each person must undergo, a cross
designed for every human being. Even more importantly for the newly
recommitted Mauriac, this cross is also seen now as our greatest comfort,
the place we come to rest.

Chapter III seems at first digressive, as it is a meditation on the life
and death of Arthur Rimbaud (1854-1891). Rimbaud would appear to be
the antithesis of a Christian literary hero, the opposite of a Racine. In his
violent rebellion against not only social and moral norms but even against
faith itself, Rimbaud seems an unlikely figure for the context Mauriac has
created. But the tortured poet becomes a symbol of two things. First, he
exemplifies the modern intellectual's flight from faith as a flight from
bondage into freedom; in this respect, Gide himself is one of the direct
heirs of Rimbaud. And secondly, he is an example of how, in Mauriac's
metaphor, our cross follows us wherever we go, and when we finally recognize it for what it is—refuge and consolation rather than bondage—we
accept it gratefully. Whether Mauriac reads Rimbaud accurately is certainly open to question (though Paul Claudel read him the same way); the
testimony Mauriac adduces about the poet's Christian conversion at the
point of his death is highly debatable.[22] But in reclaiming Rimbaud for
Christianity, Mauriac is performing more an act of faith than an act of bio-

graphical criticism; the chapter is richer in implications about Mauriac than it is about Rimbaud.

From the time of *God and Mammon* on, Mauriac had a marked tendency to see Christian truth working its way in even the most non-Christian writers, and the treatment of Rimbaud is an early example of this. His son Claude wrote about this tendency in a journal concerning a visit Gide made to Mauriac's country home, Malagar, in 1939. Mauriac exclaims to Gide that "It is possible to be outside the body of the Church and participate in its soul just as it is possible to be a part of that body and never come near the soul."[23] And while Gide responds warmly to the truth of the point, there is an amusing anecdote that follows, when Gide got up to go to bed early. Claude Mauriac notes:

> I suspect him of having been forced to take that hurried escape by excessive discretion. Or perhaps he ran off to make a few entries in his *Journal* like "Mauriac must at any price prove that the ancient Greeks are Christians . . .". (115)

One can choose to see this tendency as a kind of Christian imperialism, of course, but it is an important element in Mauriac's post-1928 theology, and it represents a breaking down of an important dichotomy: it is no longer a matter of them and us, of nonbelievers and Christians. Rather, God's workings are revealed everywhere we look; grace is operative everywhere.

Chapters IV through VII take on the central question directly: given the author's faith, what is his responsibility in his writing? How is the serious Christian novelist to proceed? The options, as Mauriac develops them, are three. First, of course, is the Racinian option: one can see literature as being so implicated with the sins of the flesh that the only thing to do is to renounce it. This option was not new with Racine, of course: it is traceable from his contemporary seventeenth-century Jansenists back to St. Augustine and ultimately to Plato. Underlying this is the sense of an absolute division between corrupt flesh and pure spirit. A second option is to carry on as before, simply to write about the flesh as the ordinary non-Christian novelist does. But this option is the one that Jacques Maritain (whom Mauriac quotes in *God and Mammon*) calls "connivance." If a Racine throws in his lot with the spirit, the "conniving" novelist throws his in with the flesh. But the third option, the one Mauriac eventually works his way toward, is the one that denies neither flesh nor spirit but rather sees spirit in the flesh. This is the option of seeing God working within our earthly lives, and this is the lesson Mauriac is taught by the discourse of the unnamed man in chapter VII. The metaphor of warfare—of a fundamental distinction if not enmity between spirit and flesh—is retained, but the crucial Christian doctrine of the Incarnation transforms that warfare altogether. God Himself shared this flesh, and continues to do so within the Eucharist. The Eucharist, Mauriac learns, is a symbol of this sharing, of the uniting of flesh and spirit. The unnamed man tells Mauriac that "the Real Presence [in the Eucharist] is the real occupying army of our flesh guarding all the gates and keeping surveillance over all the weak points." If flesh and spirit are antithetical, the Incarnation effected a mysterious but profoundly real synthesis.

The challenge for the Catholic novelist, then, is to reflect this synthesis, to reveal the workings of God within the world of humanity. The novelist must be true to that human world, but without slipping into "connivance." And the opposite error must also be avoided, that of the superficial piety that falsifies life.

Charles Du Bos wrote what remains one of the best treatments of this idea in his 1933 *François Mauriac et le problème du romancier catholique* [François Mauriac and the Problem of the Catholic Novelist]; certainly no one has ever been better situated than he was for such a study. He notes that those Catholic critics who condemn "impurity" in fiction are wrong to do so. Human life involves impurity, and the novelist's task is to deal with the human. Thus, "a properly Christian love of the holiness of truth commands him to respect impurity."[24] Most Catholic novelists fail in exactly this. But writing so as to reflect this union of spirit and flesh effected by the Incarnation, while of course the great challenge for the Catholic novelist is also the greatest gift. For Catholic novelists, Du Bos writes, have the ability to see their material in all its dimensions, while the nonbeliever only has the human one. He uses a musical analogy, saying that the ordinary novelist only hears the mezzo, while the Catholic novelist hears also the bass and the highest notes (20-21).

For Du Bos, Mauriac's earlier novels, fine as they were, did indeed exhibit something of what Maritain called "connivance." Mauriac did seem to find in the worst, most sinful areas of human experience a certain "irresistible lyric halo" (83). But this all changed, Du Bos argues, with his next novel: *What Was Lost.*

What Was Lost

Mauriac's first novel after his recommitment to his faith in 1928-1929 represented a great challenge: could this theory of the Catholic novelist be put into practice effectively? Du Bos tells us that the work was conceived before the conversion, and was originally to be titled *Pygmalion* (84). As that title suggests, the novel would have focused chiefly on the character Marcel and his tormented imaginings that his young wife and her brother were lovers. But Mauriac's newly clarified view of the novel and of the Catholic novelist's responsibility entailed a complete rethinking of the story. The manuscripts of the novel (deposited in the Bibliothèque Jacques Doucet in Paris) reveal some of the difficulty Mauriac encountered. The manuscripts consist of five separate notebooks and two completely different attempts to write out the story; each notebook is itself so full of false starts and crossings-out that trying to follow Mauriac's creative process is extremely complicated and perhaps impossible. Jacques Petit, in the Pléiade edition, has striven to provide as many of the major variants as he can, but even he has had to omit hundreds of minor changes and revisions—not to mention the numerous drawings and doodlings Mauriac made in the margins, evidence that the writing was not flowing smoothly. The one safe generalization one can make from reading the manuscripts is that *What Was Lost* was one of the most difficult books Mauriac ever wrote.

But of course, in matters of art there is often no correlation between effort and success, and *What Was Lost* remains one of Mauriac's least known novels today. Mauriac himself said of it:

> of all my novels, it is the one which gives me the most regret because it is the draft of what could have become a great book. Abbreviated, hasty, it bespeaks a certain timidity before a fearful subject. . . . Written at the time in my life when I was the most preoccupied with religion, *What Was Lost* visibly suffers from the desire to edify, together with the fear of scandalizing.[25]

This verdict is harsher than it need be, of course. While *What Was Lost* is not a great novel, it has intensity and force, and while it may indeed try to be "edifying," its edification is hardly of the facile or glib variety.

It consists of two interlocking sets of three characters. We first meet the unhappy married couple, Hervé and Irène de Blénauge, and Hervé's mother, Madame de Blénauge. These three characters intersect with the writer Marcel Revaux and his young wife, Tota; soon we also meet Tota's brother, Alain. And herein lies, probably, the novel's real weakness: it tries to do too much too briefly. Mauriac's characterization of the novel as "abbreviated and hasty" is at least half right: if the novel were twice as long, he could have developed all these characters and their conflicts more fully. But Mauriac was never able to write a truly long novel; his genius lies in his very conciseness and the power of his focus. He is a novelist of depth rather than breadth. The reader will find Mauriac's terseness and his intensity of focus in evidence in *What Was Lost*, along with brisk prose and a rapid pace.

Hervé is perhaps Mauriac's most determinedly evil character. He has no satanic grandeur, but is rather a shabbily self-indulgent man-child, and this quality of a spoiled and dangerous childishness makes him loathsome to his friend Marcel and even to his own wife. It is of interest to note that in the novel's early draft, Hervé was clearly homosexual, and it is equally interesting to note that Mauriac came to write that out of him. In that early draft, Hervé's homosexuality is simply a cheap way of coding him as lustful and hence evil—a literary practice common in early twentieth-century fiction, one that even Proust is not entirely free from. In the published version, Hervé indulges in sexual lust, but what is loathsome about him is not his sexuality but the fact that he lets this come between him and his wife, Irène, who is slowly dying and who desperately needs him.[26] Irène herself is a memorable and finely drawn character. On the one hand, she is typical of the twentieth-century agnostic/atheist, desperately seeking some meaning in a world without God, trying even to find it in reading Nietzsche. But on the other hand, her suffering, both physical and mental, raises her almost to the level of sainthood. And it is this suffering, the novel comes to insist, that really matters: when Hervé's abandonment of her leads her finally to commit suicide, we follow her as she slips from life into death—and into the waiting arms of Christ. The passage, one of the more powerful in Mauriac's works, could be construed by the conventionally minded as a validation of suicide. But in fact it is a validation—and a highly effective one—of the idea of an Incarnate God consumed with love for suffering humans.

God is not a judge, but love. This is the message Mauriac so badly needed to hear when he wrote the "Souffrances" essay, and the scene of Irène's suicide is an extraordinary embodiment of it. Another scene—and the novel's other high point—involves Irène's mother-in-law, Madame de Blénauge. She is devastated by the suicide, in part because she had seen it coming. She is a bustling, pious Catholic, and at one point she tries to head off what she knows is coming by hiding Irène's pills—a subterfuge that is so ineffectual as to be almost comical. Now, with her daughter-in-law dead, she is haunted by guilt, and she goes to confession. Her monologue in the confessional reveals that she feels such remorse not so much because she did not prevent Irène's death as by what she represented to the younger woman. She realizes that Irène laughed at her simple-minded Catholicism and her bustling little pieties, and now she feels anguish at having made something so precious appear ridiculous in the eyes of a person who so urgently needed it. When the priest finally replies to her in the confessional, we know he has been given a profound insight not only into the situation but also into its ultimate meaning. He tells her that he is convinced that, when she died, Irène was not alone.

The other set of characters—Marcel, Tota, and her brother Alain—are linked in various ways to the story of the Blénauge family, but probably not linked as firmly and clearly as they might have been. Marcel is a burnt-out, once-famous writer with nothing left to say. He tries to rejuvenate himself by taking a very young bride, whom he has met while taking a cure at a spa in the country. Tota Forcas, the bride, is less deeply etched than one would wish. She is essentially a country girl on the make in Paris: now that she is married and has gotten away from home (and from her abusive monster of a father), she wants a bit of fun out of life, and intends to find it in the nightclubs of Paris. Marcel is not bothered by this as much as by her past: when he confides in Hervé that she comes from a dysfunctional home, and has always been very close only to her brother, Hervé plants a doubt in Marcel's mind. He hints that perhaps there is an incestuous relationship between Tota and Alain—neither of whom he has even met at that point—and the hint takes root within Marcel. Alain's visit to Paris only makes Marcel more uneasy, and soon he is undergoing an agonizing mental torture.

The incest conjecture hovers over the story (it is quite false, though Marcel can never really let it go). This would have been the original *Pygmalion* novel Mauriac had planned, and arguably the Hervé-Irène story is too awkwardly grafted on to it. Even so, Marcel's self-created torments are rendered with the psychological subtlety and force that Mauriac is best at. And this strand of the novel allows Mauriac to introduce a new and vital character, Tota's brother Alain. Alain is at the outset something of a stock type—the innocent country boy in the wicked city for the first time; it is a type that goes back to Marivaux and to Fielding. But Mauriac soon makes him into something much greater than that, simply by taking his innocence seriously. Alain has been raised without religion, due to the wishes of his fiercely anticlerical father. But now, in young manhood, he is experiencing the call to faith on an almost visionary level; at the novel's end, we find he has decided to pursue the priesthood (and in a later novel, *Les Anges noirs* [The Dark Angels], Mauriac reintroduces him as a village priest). But in the meantime, the sin and the sufferings of others bother him obscurely but deeply—not out of some prudishness or sense of moral superiority, but out of a deep identification with others' pain. One night, Tota takes him along to a bar. Eventually he has to flee the noise and the smoke, and he goes out walking around Paris. Near the Champs-Élysées, he hears a woman weeping, and he approaches her. It turns out to be Thérèse Desqueyroux, the heroine of Mauriac's 1927 novel, herself once a country girl, now corrupt and adrift in Paris. The moment, in its conception and the very texture of its execution, is unlike anything else in Mauriac's fiction, as it brings in the themes and the emotional atmosphere of the earlier novel, suddenly enriching the scope of *What Was Lost* immeasurably. And, of course, when reading *What Was Lost* in its biographical context, we can see that the apparition of Thérèse has the force of a ghost from the past, and is a link to that past.

Thus, both *God and Mammon* and *What Was Lost* are products of deep introspection on Mauriac's part; the essay presents a solution to the conflict between art and faith, while the novel tries to embody that solution in its set of characters and events. *What Was Lost* may be a minor work considered in isolation, but it occupies a major place in the career and intellectual development of one of the twentieth century's great novelists. Mauriac's career, and his struggle with these issues, did not of course conclude in 1930. His 1932 novel, *Le Nœud de vipères* (translated as *Viper's Tangle*), can claim to be the greatest Catholic novel of the century. Its story, every bit as harrowing as *Genitrix* or *Destins*, concerns the slow but inevitable operation of grace on its protagonist, an old, embittered, resentful husband whose chief motivation is vengeance on his wife and children. One might see *Le Nœud de vipères* furthering and perfecting what Mauriac first tried to achieve in *What Was Lost*—incorporating, as Charles Du Bos put it, not just the midrange but the bass and the high notes of humanity from a Catholic viewpoint, and doing so in an even more artistically satisfying way.

In 1933, Mauriac was elected to the Académie Française, the highest literary honor France offers. Under the early years of the Nazi occupation, he wrote *La Pharisienne* (1941), which is his most masterful treatment of his old theme of religious hypocrisy and the damage it wreaks on people's lives; but here too, grace breaks in, and the novel offers a vision of redemption quite absent from the books of the 1920s—a vision first attempted with the characters Irène and Alain in *What Was Lost*. Mauriac then abandoned fiction for the duration of the war, writing instead for the Resistance under the pseudonym Forez, and incurring the contempt and threats of collaborationists for daring to speak out against the Nazi persecution of the Jews. His reputation as a writer committed to the cause of morality and civilization no doubt contributed to his being awarded the Nobel Prize in 1952.

The Mauriac of the Resistance can already be glimpsed in the Mauriac who wrote *God and Mammon* and *What Was Lost*: in 1928-1930, under pressure from both conservative Catholics and from liberal nonbelievers, he continued to think for himself, to struggle toward his own solution to some of the most difficult problems a serious novelist can face. The sheer courage it took to do so is by no means the least inspiring aspect of the two works translated here.

Notes

1. Jean Lacouture, *François Mauriac* (Paris: Éditions de Seuil, 1980). My treatment of Mauriac's life is indebted to Lacouture throughout.

2. The most detailed study of Sangnier's early career is J. Caron's *Le Sillon et la démocratie chrétienne, 1894-1910* [The Sillon and Christian Democracy] (Paris: Plon, 1967).

3. Much later in life, he wrote, "The only politics permitted to the Christian is the quest for God's kingdom and His justice." See *Ce que je crois*, [What I Believe], 1962 (in François Durand, ed., *François Mauriac: Oeuvres autobiographiques* [Paris: Gallimard, 1990], 601).

4. See Claude Escallier, "François Mauriac et le modernisme," in *Nouveaux Cahiers François Mauriac*, 1 (1993), 35-59.

5. Charles Taylor, *Sources of the Self: The Making of the Modern Identity* (Cambridge: Harvard University Press, 1989), 30.

6. Mauriac's fullest discussion of Barrès is his *La Rencontre avec Barrès* [The Meeting with Barrès] (Paris: Éditions de la Table ronde, 1945), but he is mentioned countless times in Mauriac's nonfiction. He even makes an appearance in the 1933 novel *Le Mystère Frontenac*, where the young Yves Frontenac, like Mauriac himself, has his literary career deeply affected by a meeting with Barrès.

7. *La Rencontre avec Barrès*, in Durand, 192-193.

8. Frédéric Lefèvre, *Une Heure avec . . .* (Paris: Éditions de la Nouvelle Revue Française, 1924), 217. The interview took place on May 26, 1923.

9. David O'Connell, *François Mauriac Revisited* (New York: Twayne, 1995), 85. O'Connell goes on to read the novel as a step in the direction of the true Catholic novel, but what Catholicism there is in the book is, at the very least, subtle.

10. L'Abbé Louis Bethléem, *Romans à lire et romans à proscrire: essai de classification au point de vue moral des principaux romans et romanciers, 1500-1928, avec notes et indications pratiques* (Paris: Éditions de la Revue des Lectures, 1928), 10th edition. (The full title reads *Novels to Read and Novels to Ban: An Essay in Moral Classification of the Chief Novels and Novelists, 1500-1928, with Notes and Practical Instructions.*)

11. O'Connell, 19. See also Lacouture, 359-363, on some others among the Catholic press who questioned Mauriac's faith and intentions.

12. Cited in Lacouture, 323.

13. It is tempting to read some of Mauriac's fiction from this era as more autobiographical than it otherwise would appear. The 1926 short story, "Un Homme de lettres," for example, concerns a middle-aged writer who has abandoned his lover of fifteen years; he is revealed as a cruel sort of parasite on the lives of others, using their grief for material for his works. Did the affair lead Mauriac to consider leaving his wife, and is the story a way of exorcising such a temptation, complete with vigorous condemnation of the man who would do such a thing?

14. *Revue Hebdomadaire*, June 22, 1928.

15. Durand, 117.

16. Du Bos, journal entry of November 7, 1926, quoted in Georges Poulet, *Entre Moi et moi: Essais critiques sur la conscience de soi* [Between Me and Myself: Critical Essays on Self Consciousness] (Paris: Librairie José Corti, 1976), 172. The words in italics are in English in the original.

17. Lacouture, 338.

18. The strength of Altermann's personality would in the years to come cause some conflict between him and Mauriac: see the treatment in Lacouture, 338 ff.

19. From Mauriac's "Préface" of 1958, rpt. in Jacques Petit, ed., *Mauriac: Oeuvres romanesques et théatrales completes* (Paris: Gallimard, 1979), volume 2, 1340.

20. The phrase "midway on life's path" echoes the opening line of Dante's *Inferno*, "Nel mezzo del camin di nostra vita . . .".

21. Ramon Fernandez, "François Mauriac et le roman moderne" in Mauriac's *Dieu et Mammon* (Paris: Éditions du Capitole, 1929), 20.

22. The question of deathbed conversions was in the air following the untimely death of Jacques Rivière in 1925. Rivière, who like Mauriac had his origins in Bordeaux, had been one of the founders of the *Nouvelle Revue Française* and its director from 1919 up to his death from typhoid fever. His last words were widely reported, in widely divergent forms, and many Catholic writers were convinced Rivière had been

touched by God's grace at the last moment. On the controversy that ensued, see Lacouture, 275-278. See also the fuller treatment in Lacouture's *Une Adolescence du siècle: Jacques Rivière et la "NRF"* [The Century's Adolescence: Jacques Rivière and the NRF] (Paris: Gallimard, 1994), 885 ff.

23. Claude Mauriac, *Conversations with André Gide*, trans. Michael Lebeck (New York: George Braziller, 1965), 114.

24. Charles Du Bos, *François Mauriac et le problème du romancier catholique* (Paris: Éditions R.-A. Corrêa, 1933), 14.

25. Mauriac, "Préface" to 1958 collected works edition, in Petit, 883.

26. Mauriac does indulge in some of this cheap homosexual coding in the 1924 novel *Le Mal* (translated as *The Enemy*), in which a character's flamboyance is meant to stand for homosexuality, which in turn is meant to stand for moral decadence. One of his most interesting statements on the subject concerns his gay friend and adversary, André Gide. In a volume published at Gide's death, Mauriac notes that Gide's homosexual predilections would in no way have affronted Christ as such, for we all have sinful predilections. What matters to God is the extent to which we resist them. "The world's reprobation of homosexuality is simply a social issue, and it has nothing whatever in common with Christ's condemnation of all our sins, nor with the benediction he gave to those who keep themselves pure: Blessed are the pure in heart, for they shall see God" ("Les Catholiques autour d'André Gide," in *Hommage à André Gide, 1869-1951* [Paris: Nouvelle Revue Française, 1951], 106). Mauriac's attitude toward Gide and his homosexuality is even clearer in Chapter XII of his 1959 spiritual autobiography, *Mémoires Intérieurs*, where he says that Christ's "commandment is the same for all of us—that we make ourselves pure, that we renounce our lusts, *whatever their object may be*" (François Durand, ed., *François Mauriac: Oeuvres autobiographiques* [Paris: Gallimard, 1990], 513. (The italics are in the original.)

God and Mammon

I

TO write is to reveal oneself. With my first book, I hadn't yet learned this, and in those days I found Claudel's line scandalous:

The man of letters, the assassin, and the brothel girl[1]

A young author, of course, is not really unaware that he is in fact the subject matter of his books. But he believes that the true aim of art is invention, is making of this earth and this heaven new heavens, new earths, the original substance of which will remain unknowable. He imagines that, as author, he is somehow not present but immanent in the work. Certainly, he finds it possible that some readers will discover him in his work, but this does not disturb him; because, in his view, only sympathy, charity, love will let a reader discover the face of the inventor intermixed with his invention—just as only mystics are able to see an image, a shadow, a vestige of God in the visible universe.

In fact, at the point when the writer is no longer content simply to paint reality but to provide an impression of reality; at the point when he is not intent on communicating facts to us but his feeling about those facts—at that point, it is no longer just facts that he opens up for our curiosity, but himself.

Now, today, it is precisely the writer himself that most readers search for in his work. Baudelaire's gentle taunt to the reader—"Hypocrite reader, my likeness, my brother"[2]—is today applied by the reader to the author. The reader wants to discover his likeness, his brother behind the book. He wants this likeness, this author, to teach him what his own attitude ought to be toward life and toward death—yes, an attitude rather than principles. He can find principles in the philosophers. But the reader is most often a poor creature who is accustomed to knowing nothing beyond what he can see and touch. He loses his footing in the abstract; he doesn't know how to navigate there. "But I can learn how to manage this," he says. Undoubtedly true—but the philosophical vocabulary feels harsh to him; moreover, most philosophy proceeds by allusion, and each system seems to require that one already know all the systems that preceded it. The average reader finds that the effort required is overwhelming, and one cannot afford to become entangled in an uninterrupted sequence of research: the web is endless, with no way out. The difficulty, in philosophy, is knowing where to begin.

And in any case, time is short, and the real issue is to know how to live. The difficulties I have to surmount are mine, as unique and singular as the outlines of my face; no general law has foreseen them. But while the philosophers only know the universal, every literary work reflects an individual. Literature is a collection of types; a single book expresses an autonomous sensibility. Since people write these books, surely I will find among this crowd a half-brother, a sort of likeness?

Of course, in certain wise epochs, literary people also avoided the particular. But the "man in general" of the classics can no longer help the pagans of today. The Christian era saw likewise a universal agreement on the moral law, and thus literature too was universal. Anything that fell outside the boundaries of this universal human nature—the eccentric, the strange, the repugnant—was the business of the confessor and the casuist, who quickly subsumed it under the heading of one of the seven deadly sins, and accorded it its preordained sanction.

According to Christian teaching, the great classic writers, even the libertines among them, were able to distinguish good from evil, and through this distinction they could understand and judge the character of man. But when we have arrived at the point of having abolished within us, as Bossuet says, the holy truth of God, when we have "overturned that august tribunal that condemns all sins"[3]—then it is that writers, each with his own panacea, take on importance, swell themselves up proudly, and grow larger than that diminished faith.

The Christian distinction between good and evil obliges writers to adopt a uniform point of view with regard to humanity. But once this distinction is abolished, everything is called into question: man no longer exists, only innumerable men; not truth, but individual truths. The examination of conscience, pursued in the light of Christ, incites us to reject, repress, or sublimate our vicious tendencies. But today, wrong-headed sages substitute self-creation for that examination of conscience; and self-creation is a process that involves rejecting and repressing nothing.

Thus, every book now tends to be no longer an objective creation, detached from the artist; readers want the author to show his hand: what has he found in himself, now that they have begun to get to know him? What obstacles has he had to overcome? Has he had difficulties with sex? Have his actions conformed to his desires? Has he taken account of those like him? Has he attained a harmony between the general interest and his own particular needs? Does any residue of religion subsist in him? Has he assimilated it—or has it got in the way of his efforts to become an authentic person? And thus even the most modest author, however small his field of influence, becomes the object of a perpetual clamor to reveal himself.

We, even more than the romantics, are the children and heirs of Rousseau. Corrupted children of Christ, the romantics nonetheless held firmly to the ancient distinction between good and evil, even when they made a divinity of evil and played at being fallen angels. Today, many of us labor to accept ourselves, just as Rousseau did; but while the great Genevan failed to create a correspondence between his cherished inner self and his social self (shot through with moralism as that self was), many moderns have succeeded in quelling their fear of how they will look to the world, even when they reveal what would have been traditionally regarded as perverted and shameful instincts.

This requires, to be sure, some courage, but of a less admirable sort than they believe: one observes how they first hesitate, then risk a few partial avowals, then retract them, and only then take the plunge. And in order to get to that point, they need the secret complicity of readers, of admirers who demand an example to follow, a justification for themselves.[4]

We might say that the man who has lost the distinction between good and evil finds himself on an endless quest among the writers, endlessly soliciting answers from them. He needs to persuade himself that he is not a monster, and finding his likeness in books will reassure him. And his quest is not limited only to the writers. Since the war, one encounters many people nibbling and sniffing about with anxious curiosity. And when they have found some connection between their personal failures and those of postwar society, they can tell themselves that the same causes must have produced similar effects among their contemporaries. The strange need to proselytize that one sees among these half-mad people of our time is, after all, only the result of a need to feel they belong to the majority. They don't want so much to change others as to persuade them that, as children of the same decadence, they must all possess common traits. When the fox had his tail cut off, he said to his companions, "You have no tails either. You know you don't." Provoked by all this, even the most private author, the one most determined not to bare his soul in his books, eventually finds himself having to, as the police say, lay it all out on the table.

Vainly he reminds himself not to do this, not to reveal what he knows ought to be kept private—his religious opinions, for example. If his works reveal some of that sort of preoccupation, he will be labeled a Christian novelist. But the freedom he employs in his descriptions will soon land him in trouble with the pious critics. What a temptation it is to say, off-handedly, in an interview, "I am not a Catholic novelist."[5] And he doesn't need to say much more to find himself considered a renegade. Then it surely is his duty to protest that in fact he had denied nothing having to do with his faith and his hopes. So he starts off down a path that has no end.

A writer, unless sustained by some friendships and some admirers, will quickly attain a state of indifference. It is so easy to persuade ourselves that those we don't like do not exist! Apart from those few we love, those few whose hearts are one with our own, we soon come to feel, quite without effort, what Caligula said in his ferocity: the rest of humanity is a single anonymous, grimacing head that we cut off with our indifference.

But the danger comes from the response we start making to even the slightest criticism. The idea the journalist has of me keeps me constantly upset. If this image he has created of me from my work shocks me, how can I restrain myself from trying to find how he came by it? In vain I repeat to myself that this image corresponds to no reality, because nevertheless this image now exists, and it is just as irrefutable as the photograph that needs to be retouched before the client consents to recognize himself in it. Exactly how does the real me differ from the created one? The day the writer starts measuring that difference is the day he loses forever that state of grace that is the state of indifference. And it is on precisely this point that the role of the critic—especially the hostile critic—becomes important to us. The critic forces the artist into a perpetual confrontation between the person he is or thinks he is, and his reflection as it appears to other, adverse minds. That which I take to be an alteration or a deformation of my real self—is it not, in truth, an unknown aspect of myself, one I need to slowly get used to?

An author is at least partly aware of his own dissimulations: he has secrets, ruses, subterfuges which he more or less avows; he makes much of his instinct for disguising himself. He is everywhere and nowhere in his work[6]; but he is unaware that, seen from the outside, certain traits that seem insignificant to him are revelatory to others. We can only view our play from our vantage point in the wings; the author is rarely in the theater seats. Whatever the author wanted to reveal of himself, doubtless the public will fail to see it; but in return, the critic will often discover something that the author had not bothered to dissimulate, thinking it unimportant, or being quite unaware of its presence. That person we try to be, the one who receives honors, with all our declarations of principle, with our social situation, with the home we have established—this person is constantly in combat with another person much more confused, less well defined. We try to keep this other person in the shadows, but sooner or later he is well known and clearly outlined. Because this person is stubborn, and thanks to his continued demands, his monotonous tenacity, eventually we ourselves can see him, distinct and detached from our apparent self (despite the innumerable ties that unite the two). These two parts of our selves are both reflected in our work, and they thus create a third self, proceeding from the two others—but a self that, due to its dual origins, is full of maddening contradictions; this irritates the critics exceedingly.[7]

Now, many critics want to know just what they're dealing with; they only like writers they can easily classify. Of course, not only critics but anyone of lively intelligence has a certain curiosity: who made this? The reader who is only a reader, able to abandon himself entirely to a book, to be taken up by it, to look for nothing beyond what the story gives him—this sort of reader is only found among the masses, and among the majority of women. And there is a specific kind of literature devoted to such readers. We might call this the pure reader, the kind of reader we all were in our childhood, when Jules Verne's characters swept us up in themselves, when we had no interest in who Verne was, nor in the methods he employed to seduce us so entirely. But our reading public stands ready to ferret out, beyond the book we give them, facts about our inner life. They are made eager for this not so much by professional critics as by the literary journalists, who are only too numerous. We spend our time opening ourselves up to each other. We know the details of the seraglios in which we grew up, and we reveal the least objectionable aspects of them to each other. Thanks be to God, even the subtlest author doesn't go very deeply when he talks about others—because he is really only interested in talking about himself. As for the professional critics, they are even less dangerous in this regard.

Anyway, it bears repeating with regard to some of them what Malebranche said of his dog: "It doesn't feel anything"; or rather, "it doesn't feel anymore."[8] Except for a few—such as a Bidou, a Gabriel Marcel, a Jaloux, a Thibaudet, a Fernandez, a Du Bos[9]—most critics, force-fed with all the new books they must somehow digest, seem like the very people least likely to be able to discuss a book's real value and importance. The best of them are aware of this, and they content themselves with simply classifying the book, which they can neither feel nor understand. Or they point out its influences, whether from the past or the contemporary scene. And these are the peaceable critics. The others are more concerned with classifying the author: is he on the left or the right? And this is the most annoying type. When a book is labeled, it doesn't mind anymore than does a flower in a garden: but an author balks at being labeled. Just when you have him classified as a radical, he publishes something that outrages the radicals.[10] You can't categorize the author or set him once and for all in this or that camp: he is always cropping up in the opposing camp. Such contradictions irritate the critic, who likes his lists and tables, and condemns these hybrid authors—having neither the taste, nor the leisure, nor probably the intelligence to enter into their complexity. Hence the critic's hasty judgments and his unjust rulings—which exasperate the writer, though he affects indifference.

And he is indifferent, but he cannot keep himself from continually chewing it over; even if the conclusions of Zoilus[11] strike him as grossly unjust, he cannot bring himself to dispute the basic premises. These reveal to him his own deep-seated contradictions, and even the most trivial of critical articles can bring him back to his own inner obstacles. And perhaps we should ask our judges to do no more than that.

If the critics were subtler thinkers, they would lose interest in us and, I suspect, expend their energies elsewhere. So it is with André Gide, who is so interested in his own personal drama that he keeps a journal of his journals, and who did me the honor of showing some interest in me. He saw me as having to ask permission to write *Destins* and still remain a Catholic.[12] My religious inquietude—an inquietude that Gide boasts he has never felt (though in this he libels himself: on the day Gide feels no inquietude, what we will do with his corpse?)—do my religious difficulties stem from the fact that I am a man split between God and Mammon, and who pretends he can enjoy both the freedoms of the novelist and the hopes of the Christian?

After serious examination, I find the question is not so simple; but still I must thank Gide, as well as other, lesser men, who have made me the target of their bile often enough, for leading me to meditate on this topic. It cannot be avoided any longer; there is no escape route. I have given up the privileges of modesty: to write is to reveal oneself. However small may be the circle of my readers, I have given them certain rights to myself. It's not a matter of giving up my soul to them. There are Catholics, Mauriac, who have faith in you; are they wrong? Others consider you a renegade; are they wrong? Try, therefore, to see the issue clearly. Try to articulate your position with regard to Catholicism, or even (God willing!) within Catholicism. You may not succeed: if ever the term "essay" was justified, it certainly is for this book.

II

ONE of Pascal's *Pensées* illuminates the issue in question: "Whatever people say, it must be admitted that the Christian religion has something astonishing in it. Some will reply, "That is because you were born into it." But just for that very reason I harden myself against it, for fear of being blinded by my prejudice. But even so, even being born into it, I find it astonishing."[13]

"Because you were born into it . . ." Here is my own drama. I was born into it; I did not choose it; this religion has been imposed on me since my birth. Many others who were also born into it have quickly abandoned it. But that is because this faith with which they were inoculated did not *take* with them. As for me, I belong to that race who, born into Catholicism, have learned from early manhood that we simply cannot move away from it, that it is not our lot to leave, or to re-enter. We are Catholics deep within ourselves, and we can never change that. Our race is flooded with the light; we know that it is true.

Once I became aware of this certitude, as an adolescent, I set loose all my critical impulses at once; this was my first sin, for which I have paid dearly. All the difficulties there are about the faith, all the apparent impossibilities of it, all the superficial objections to it—all these rose up inside me then. When I was about sixteen, I revolted against all the pious practices of my family, of my schoolmasters, of the priests who frequented our house. One of my friends from those days, who has since become a priest,[14] could testify to the ugly frenzy with which I attacked them all. It was the only time in my life when I delighted in the works of Anatole France; I sought out the clerical caricatures in his books.[15]

But the harder I shook the bars of my cell, the more I found them unbreakable. It was not my fate to lose my faith (lose it and then regain it, as I secretly wanted to be able to do). I already knew that I could never leave Catholicism; it was inside of me. Wherever I went, I found it there with me. And instead of accepting this for what it was, a special grace, I often felt a secret envy, when I frequented the chapel of the Benedictines, for people like Psichari and Maritain[16]: for them, Catholicism had been a choice. They had examined it from the outside, took its exact measure, compared it to other religions. As for me, who had never left the faith, who would never be able to leave it, I went constantly from one extreme to another: sometimes I believed that Christianity was the most important preoccupation for the whole world, and sometimes I believed that I was a lifelong prisoner of a tiny Mediterranean sect. But, like it or not, one has to get on with things; it's impossible not to live; I had to work things out as best I could. And thus at sixteen, I found myself passionately involved in proving the truth of my religion to myself—this religion to which I knew I was attached for all eternity. The Brunschvicg edition of Pascal, which is on my table today, battered and heavily annotated, bears witness to my passion.

In those first years of the century, the French Catholic church was undergoing a terrible crisis. But the so-called laity laws, even with all their virulence, moved me less than the drama of modernism. The church seemed to me to be rejected by the modern world, and out of stubbornness (which I was fool enough to think I could judge) was withdrawing from modern thought. I was only a pretentious child, ignorant of so many things, but I lived through this drama with a certain feverish intensity that, today, makes me smile tenderly when I think of it. The grand old eternal ship was detaching itself from the world of men, and sailing into confused shadows—but I was on board, I was on my way too, I was part of it.

I loved the church ardently, proudly, never missing a chance to testify as to my faith. For example, one day at school, in my second year of philosophy at the *lycée*, our teacher, dear Monsieur Drouin (brother-in-law of André Gide) asked if we would suggest a manual for the next day's lesson. I ostentatiously proposed to him the absurd manual by Father Lahr,[17] which was then in use among the Marianists—and for my pains, I was jeered by the whole class.

This is not the place to explore the human reasons that made me such a favorable soil for Catholic culture. To do so would make me go into too many considerations, involving people other than myself. I would have to discuss my family, and above all I would have to discuss God's will with regard to my life. But the fact is that I was so possessed by God in those years that all my uncertainties and anxieties took on the form of religious scruples; everything crystallized for me around the ideas of purity, of sin, of the state of grace. And then, excited by reading Huysmans,[18] I abandoned myself to the delights of liturgy and music—and, dare I say, the Sacraments.

I ask the pardon of those Marianists who taught me, but I will say that with them around 1905, religious instruction was just about nonexistent. Just two hours a week were devoted to it, and no one—masters or boys—gave it any importance. Further, I'll say that not a single student in my class would have been able to answer, even in the most general way, any of the objections to which a Catholic ought to have been able to respond in those early years of the century. Instead, our masters excelled in bathing us in a heavenly atmosphere that covered every minute of the day: they were not forming Catholic intellects, but Catholic sensibilities.

I can still recall the details of how we spent our Sundays: at 7, Mass with communion; at 9, High Mass; at 10:30, Catechism and Congregation of the Holy Virgin; 1:30, vespers and benediction of the Blessed Sacrament. No doubt many of us could have said, later in life, that attending this school dispensed us from attending church for the rest of our lives. But I was disposed otherwise: everything about the liturgy, even the simplest of songs, enchanted me. Whether exquisite or ordinary, this wine intoxicated me daily. And even during this daily intoxication, I remembered that I had not *chosen* this.

I remember how important Pascal's successive conversions were to me: it's thus, I said to myself, that one converts *within* Christianity. I would say, humorously, to a friend who shared my mania, "Well, that was between my second and my third conversions." But above all what I loved about Pascal was that he assured me that the quest was always possible, that one could go on a voyage of discovery from within revealed truth. The reader will see that this is where I too felt the Modernist unrest—though for me it was only a spiritual sort of attitude, my ignorance in matters of philosophy being profound.

However, I accustomed myself to the idea of being a Catholic for all eternity: I no longer shook my bars. The easy delights of a religious sensibility led me to my book of poems, *Mains jointes*.[19] I entered into literature like a cherubim from the sacristy, pressing the keys of my little organ. If Barrès was at all moved by this tired canticle, it was because he had, by some power of divination, discovered in it "a mad and voluptuous note," as he wrote in his review article in the *Echo de Paris*.

I cultivated my garden, my monastic garden. Anyway I pretended to cultivate it: I played with the chalice on the altar and sniffed at the

incense. But already, in secret, I was coming to feel disgust for this sensu-
alist brand of devotion, this delight that occupied the sort of person who
would never take any risks. In the depths of the so-called spiritual
literature[20] I was steeping myself in, the terrible demand of Christianity
came clear to me. I knew that the Christian God demanded everything.
That He had no part in the flesh, that nature and grace are enemies—this
Pascal taught me, with that excessive and unjust rigor that in itself seemed
to me to be a terrifying proof.

During the same time, below the surface of my pious posturings, a
powerful spring began to well up in me. At first there was little more than
a trickle, but soon I saw it spread itself out over all my practices and atti-
tudes, my acts and my words. This inner water rose up and began to flow.
I discovered that I was a being every bit as passionate as anyone else my
age; twenty years of piety had only dammed up the flood for a while. It
was as if my family and my schoolmasters had piled rocks up over the
source; but the water soon broke out, finding its own way. Slowly, nature
began to overtake grace; I despaired of finding an equilibrium between
them, and turned now to the one, now to the other, as toward two equally
powerful enemies. My God didn't want me to dwell for a second on what
my passionate nature was demanding of me. Then my impure spirit said,
but who around you really practices this pitiless doctrine? Almost no one.
And among those who had embraced the madness of the cross, I found
some dying of thirst for that water which, it is written, takes away all
thirst. And as for the others, who seemed content, I was sure they had
never known the thirst. Today, having attained the age where one can look
back over the long road, I realize that I have become acquainted with so
many who have lost their faith because a troubled conscience, as mine
was, attracts similar sorts of people. Some secret instinct made me turn
away from those who could have given me a vision of the Sacred Joy. A
secret instinct—or rather a perverted will, because the impure spirit fears
nothing so much as one of his own meeting up with a holy person. Still, I
never asked myself whether the time had not come for me to renounce
Christianity: this was never even a question. Only one issue dominated
my thinking: I felt I had to resolve to give myself either to God or to the
lower power. There was no hope at all of escaping from the Christian vise,
no possibility of seeing things in anything other than the Christian way.
That, certainly, would have changed everything. All around me, some
were slipping away on tiptoe, and others were noisily beating on the door,
and they would go on to remake themselves in some other moral shape.
But as for me, I remained as attached to the Church as a man is to the

planet: running away from the Church is as mad as pretending to change planets.

Equally foreign to me is the attitude of those who feel they can reshape Christianity to accommodate themselves; they seek out texts and authorities that will allow them to accommodate Christianity to their passions. They may protest against this, but some of their books make the most dangerous alterations to the Gospel that any Christian has ever had the audacity to try.[21] But I, at the age of twenty, *I knew* that God would not let my conscience become twisted—though this was not through any merit of my own. The heaviest of my passions were not enough to alter the precision of the scale, and the needle always pointed implacably at the exact name and gravity of my error. What was the good of reasoning about it? God's needs were always clear to me: He wanted to be loved (which would be easy enough), but He also wanted to be the only one I loved—or at least, if I loved others, I would love them only for Him and in Him. And this is not the destruction of human love, but its sublimation.[22]

All that remained for me was to hurl myself entirely into my literary work: to express, to make concrete this monster that I had conquered. My future work took shape in my eyes. But then I was assailed by another difficulty. The label of "Catholic" brought my work to the attention of certain people; already, I began to hear some complaints. Inoffensive as my writings were, they tended to shock people—not just timid people, as I might have expected—but people of a delicate insight who were able to detect my secret poison, my monster. Very quickly I experienced the conflict between the artist's disinterestedness and what I called the apostles' sense of utility—an antagonism that I believed to be insoluble and that I hope today to be able to surmount. It is true that he who defends a sacred cause, the soldier of God, demands that everyone serve: write nothing unless it is of immediate utility. Looking at a novel, he asks, "What good will that do?" For him, what I called the artist's disinterestedness is inconceivable. If you try to tell him, to take an obvious example, that certain things he sees as useless are only apparently so, and that ultimately if you deprived humanity of Shakespeare, Racine, and Dostoevsky, you would impoverish our race, he will only reply: "You are neither Shakespeare nor Racine!" But even the humblest among us is persuaded that he deserves the name of artist if he undertakes his work in a spirit of purity, of detachment, of indifference to everything else. The deep innocence and candor of a writer, even if he is the most corrupt, so long as he is a real writer—of all this the Christian soldier knows nothing. But there is no need to insist upon this point now; I will return to it later. The strange thing is that I

have never even thought of evading this issue, even though such an eva-
sion might have given me, as a writer, some elbow room. Often enough, I
have even taken the part of my enemy-brothers against myself! For if I
can readily absolve a book for being useless, I cannot be similarly indulgent if it is morally harmful: all anybody ever had to do was speak to me
about some soul in peril in order to soften my stance.

And thus I have continued to work from within Catholicism, an object
of suspicion and even of disgust and reprobation for my fellows. I have
sometimes thought that they only continue to see me as one of theirs in
order to have the right to judge and condemn me. And here is the worst: I
have observed certain of my judges with an ugly malice. I end up telling
myself that there is a certain kind of stupidity that only they possess, a
certain method of lying, a lowness that is theirs alone. Yes, I'll confess to
the feelings I've had about them. But let it be clearly understood that,
even at the height of my exasperation and in the worst throes of my revolt,
I have never ceased to believe, or rather to see, the most startling thing:
that Catholicism can get something out of the human being that no other
doctrine can. I have always felt stupefied by the crowd's indifference to
the beat-up black carriage and the old horse of the Little Sisters of the
Poor, drawn up by the curb. Thanks be to God, I have never ceased to
venerate the heroes and saints who continue to testify for the Church; but
they aren't the ones a miserable writer comes up against. We should
notice that the pious adversaries from the "good press" can sometimes
distill a venom whose formula I believed I came to understand: these people, I said to myself, allow themselves to do anything so long as they see
it as something they don't have to mention in the confessional. And I said
to myself, oh, if only they'd take it just a bit further! But in truth this was
merely an ingenious sort of duplicity on my part, because Christ, who is
Justice, hates injustice, and everyone rightly condemns in this world what
has been eternally condemned by God. Has Catholic criticism been profoundly unjust toward my work? That scent of corruption it detected in
my works—can I pretend it really isn't there, that my works don't in fact
hover around cemeteries—cemeteries that, nonetheless, are in the shadow
of the Cross?

Although hostile toward my brothers, at least I have not blasphemed
against the Eternal Church. But, it has seemed to me, this Church, this
mother of humanity, even if she loves humanity, the ephemeral individual
is never very important to her. Individuals are as dust to her, and this is
why this mother can sometimes seem to lack heart and feelings. Nonetheless I remain in her hands; if she were to judge me, I would not appeal
against her sentence. I cannot leave the Church; her net is too strong. If I

tried to leave, I would only find myself with her elsewhere. So in this sense I can say that the kingdom of God is within me, and that "Wherever Rome is, I am."[23]

No doubt some will say, well, there is nothing so surprising in all this, for it is simply another example of what M. Estaunié has called "imprinting."[24] They would add that, in me, the power of religion is greater because of my own particular weaknesses; that my story is like those of many weak personalities; I simply provided fertile soil for the propagation of the faith. But no—it's not that simple. I have subjected all my previous enthusiasms to rigorous analysis. I have guarded myself especially against all the esthetic and emotional elements of Catholicism—especially the emotional appeals. With all my heart I can call them "the consolations of religion," but I now know at what price one must purchase them. I now know that true peace that is within suffering, and I now know the bitterness with which my past sins remain alive within the grace of the present.

Just as great rivers are put into motion by the ocean's tides long before they reach their mouths, so death is mixed into the life of the Christian long before it actually approaches. Now, the deepest instinct of man is to escape the vision of himself as a future corpse. Is there anything stronger in me than this instinct? I have said little about my own difficulties, as doing so would lay me open to ridicule, so little of a philosopher that I am. But the drama of the Christian metaphysic—as Pierre Lasserre called it, speaking of Renan—this drama has taken me up in itself powerfully enough. I will only sketch it generally here.

All the moorings had been thrown off—yet the ship scarcely moved, and the tide did not carry it forward. In the middle of that frightful garden whose gates were broken down, the maddened soul remained—a little apart from all the others, but it remained.

People will say this is only the ancient fear, this fear of gods which itself created the gods—this hideous fear which outlives even faith. Am I that sort of animal, tamed and trained since birth for certain kinds of worship, tamed by fear? I must make myself remember that this God of my childhood, who reigned within my family, controlled not only my smallest gestures and my most furtive thoughts, but even entered into the details of my nutrition: We had to watch out on Holy Friday that the little crust of bread allowed us at four o'clock had not been even slightly yellowed by butter. And eggs, of course, were forbidden, even for children. Let yourself swallow a bit of water while brushing your teeth, and your communion became a sacrilege. Thus you knew your soul much better than you knew your body. Are you sure that this God of your childhood, who amused Himself with all these details, isn't still spying on you in the dark? Still, I do not deny this God. I have exaggerated a bit here, but exaggerations like this are common property for all Christian educators. Would any confessor criticize these excesses of prudence? Being educated into purity allows for no half-measures. As the Abbey Perreyve wrote on the eve of his ordination, "I want to be ignorant, like a child with regard to certain things."[25] And you have to have the courage to admit that, if you replace this detail-obsessed God with one who is less concerned with the trivia of your life, you will not have gained spiritually; rather, you will have regressed. You will become less scrupulous as you become less pure. Concede nothing to the flesh: this is the true Christian law, the law you learned since you were old enough to understand at all. Our teachers said, "In this area, everything is grave." Everything is grave, and everything has implications for your eternity. And experience has proven to you the extent to which they were right. It is the spirit that reaches out to God, and the sated flesh that separates us from Him infinitely. Unimaginably petty as these little prudences are, they conform to the essence of Christianity. Truly, when the real Christian reawakens in me, it's always the adolescent that I was, with a conscience insanely fearful of the slightest specks of dust. And then that adolescent comes up against the man I have since become, and the contrast between them is painful; and I wonder whether I can ever go back to the source, to find again the candor and openness of my youth.

But none of this, anyway, has anything to do with real doubt. For me, doubt was never anything but a slight disturbance on the surface of my soul; deep inside, there was always a calm certainty. All my passions could not corrode that foundation—though they did spatter it with their mud. The foundation remained secure.

How can I define this incorruptible element in my faith? It's a matter of evidence: the evidence of the Cross. We only have to open our eyes to see it nearby: *our* cross, waiting for us. Who would have imagined that two pieces of wood, one placed over the other, could take on as many different forms as there are individual destinies? But that's how it is: yours is made to your exact measurements, and you will have to stretch out on it—whether willingly or by force, whether through revolt and hatred or submission and love. How mysterious that man should have lived for so long before he discovered this sign over the charnel house, the leafless tree, the naked tree on which, one day in human history, God Himself came to hang. "Oh God who loves all suffering bodies, that you chose for yourself the body that was to suffer more than any other in the world's history."[26]

And even if our diminished, feeble faith can only see the supernatural distantly, we are given this wood that we can touch, against which our flesh is nailed. The specific elements that make up your own cross come from a common patrimony. I have never understood the frightful cry of Michelet, as reported by Daniel Halévy: "At the entry into this great agony called old age . . ."[27] Old age: long before it reaches us, we begin to breathe the air of death, and only this agony awaits. But above the depths of this misery we all share is our own individual sorrow, made to fit our individual heart and our body, unique to each of us. Artists are given the privilege of expressing their own in all its particularities and differences, and it is this which creates the artist's style, giving him a unique voice, a singular and inimitable resonance.

I cannot detach myself from my cross. "If you are the son of God," said those who insulted the crucified Christ, "come down from your cross."[28] He could have if he had wanted to. But we, His creatures, we cannot descend from this gibbet on which we are born, this cross that has grown along with our bodies, stretched along with our arms and legs. We scarcely feel it in our youth, but the body develops, growing heavier; the flesh expands and hangs heavily on the nails. How long it takes us to realize that we are all born crucified!

The soul I am describing is to be found below the level of the worst, because it understands while they do not. Still, it retains, even in the midst of their unholy sabbaths, a sharp clarity: it can see the others' crosses as clearly as its own, and sees they are abandoned, misunderstood, unknown. All these destinies, spread out and unraveled at random, all are unaware of their center, of that which would give them order. The world's chief occupation is in fleeing its sorrow, avoiding its cross, not recognizing it: but at the same time, one flees oneself, and one is lost. It is our sorrow which gives us our unique face; it is our cross which fixes and stabilizes our individual contours.

I am no longer concerned, as I used to be, by the small place Christianity holds in our world. Outside of the mystical city of those who know their cross and thus know themselves, who carry their cross and thus support themselves—outside of that group swirls the crowd of those determined to live in ignorance of themselves, to become lost, to become annihilated. For me, the gaze of an Arab, a Hindu, or a Chinese is unbearable, because I can see in it the absence of the cross, and a deliberate, pursued, willed ignorance of the suffering of the individual.[29] They rip off this armor Christ has given us, and they tear themselves off the cross, the gibbet that hovers over nothingness, and sleep delightedly. The contemporary mania for drugs is tragic in that drugs open up dreams which seem to promise an escape from the cross. Opiates are the frontier that the deserters of the cross traverse, beyond which they will only find a cheap version of the true, the unique Peace: *Pax Dei quae exsuperat omne sensum* (Paul to the Philippians).[30]

What does it mean to lose one's faith? I can only tell you what I see, and I cannot help but see it. Those who are born Christians and abandon their faith, living in peace with their defection, are those who have never understood the fact of their cross.

We are born prisoners of our crosses. Nothing can tear us from them. But a peculiarity of Christians in my country is to believe that they can descend from their crosses, and in effect they do. They are free to refuse their cross, to distance themselves from it, to lose awareness of the mysterious threads that tie them to it, to move away from it so far that when they turn back they can no longer see it hovering in the sky. And they can continue on even further until, stopped suddenly by some obstacle, by some wound in the heart, they stumble and collapse. Then, no matter how lost they have become, once again the threads pull them back with a surprising force, and again they find themselves there, mercifully leaning against the wood. Instinctively, they stretch out their hands and their feet, which were already pierced in their infancy.

III

NOW imagine a being of my sort, but gifted with far greater powers of resistance than I am, and one who hates this servitude. Imagine one who is frenzied and exasperated by this mysterious enslavement, and who finally liberates himself through a profound hatred of the cross. He spits on this symbol, trailing it behind him, believing that the threads connecting it to him must be broken if he willfully, methodically degrades his soul. He cultivates blasphemy, bringing it to the level of an art, and strengthens his hatred of holy things with contempt. But then suddenly, above all this desecration, a song is heard, a cry, an appeal—but it is scarcely a cry, and scarcely has the sky opened to hear it when suddenly its echo is drowned out by the ugly and scornful laughter of a demon. No matter how strong this man is, he will continue to trail his cross behind him, like a convict's ball and chain, without ever accepting it; he will persevere in dragging it behind him down every path in the world. He will seek out the countries of fire and ash, the countries most likely to consume it. But however heavy the cross becomes, it will never be enough to exhaust his hatred—until the appointed day arrives, when at the turning point of his destiny he finally collapses under the weight of the tree. He struggles some more, gets back up, and falls once more, and is carried to his hospital bed by nuns, whom he curses. He insults his angelic sister as a fool and an idiot—and then suddenly interrupts himself. Now is the moment marked out from all eternity: the cross he has trailed behind him for thirty-seven years, the cross he has denied, stretches out its arms to him—dying, he hurls himself against it, holds it tightly, espouses it. He is serenely sad; heaven is in his eyes. He speaks: "Everything in the room must be made ready and set out. The chaplain will be coming back with the Sacraments. You'll see him. They'll be bringing the candles and the lace. Everything must be covered with white linen . . ."[31]

Such is the mystery of Arthur Rimbaud. He was not simply the mystic in a state of nature, as Claudel saw him,[32] nor the brilliant hoodlum hero as seen by so many disaffected youth of today. He was crucified despite himself, hating his cross, tormented by it; and he was in agony when it won out in the end.

If we want to comprehend Rimbaud, we have to comprehend his terrible mother. A Christian, she wanted her children to be Christians— wanted it with a will of iron. Arthur became one, whether he wanted to or not. As he put it, he sweated obedience. On Sundays, the little boy, pomaded and dignified, leaned his elbows on a mahogany card table and read the Bible. Was this hypocrisy? We should recall his holy furor when he saw some older boys joking around a holy water font: he threw himself against them with all the power of his being. And undoubtedly he would have soon enough renounced this obscure law which he had not chosen, and which he would come to curse. *A Season in Hell* is marked both by this subjection and this hatred. He hated the yoke, but the yoke was upon him. Rimbaud's blasphemy is unbounded because it is willed, and yet it seems torn from his throat with pain. His natural note, the one that arises out of him without effort, is the one described by Claudel as "the note of Edenic purity, of an infinite sweetness, of a heart-rending sadness." Claudel misses the fact that Rimbaud's "heart had heard the *coup de grace*," and that he heard the songs of the angels: "Reason is born to me. The world is good. I will bless life. I will love my brothers."[33] Suddenly, astonished by this unknown purity that manifests itself in him, seemingly coming from elsewhere, he turns and insults Christ horribly. We watch him walking through London, drunken, like a criminal. And then, after he has terrified Verlaine mortally, he improvises and speaks in a tender patois: "of death that brings repentance, of all the miserable wretches there must be, of painful toil, of partings that lacerate the heart. In low dives where we'd get drunk, he used to weep for those around us, cattle of misery. He would lift up drunkards in the dark street."[34]

And yet he pursued this same Christ with hatred, the Christ who was in that Verlaine who had returned to God. When Verlaine later set up a meeting with him in Germany, Rimbaud saw the older poet approaching him "with a rosary in his claws," hoping to convert him. And he took great joy in getting Verlaine drunk and making him renounce God, the Virgin, and the saints. He attacked Verlaine with his fists, like a madman. But while he was hammering that lamentable face, could he recognize therein that Other? Couldn't he recognize that bloody sweat, that expression of both suffering and love? Likewise, couldn't he hear that it was with another voice that Verlaine addressed him when he sent him the poems from *Sagesse* at Roche? But Isabelle Rimbaud found Verlaine's manuscript in the latrine, an example of Rimbaud's tenacious determination to dishonor the living Christ in his friend.

Between the day when the adolescent, ashamed of having spoken and of having betrayed himself, vowed himself to silence, and the day of his last agony when he was surrounded by angels, can we find a single sign of this presence of Christ, of this invincible possession? Nothing—except for a single phrase in a letter addressed to his mother, from Harare on May 25, 1881: "If I am forced to continue fatiguing myself as I am now, and to nourish myself on miseries that are as vehement as they are absurd, in atrocious climates, I fear I will shorten my existence. . . . If only we could enjoy a few years of true rest in this life—and, fortunately, this life is the only one, the proof being that we cannot imagine another life so full of such intense boredom as this one."

The adolescent Rimbaud had burned his manuscripts and had chosen to be silent for the rest of his life. But this little phrase in a hastily written letter is enough to reveal the inner groans of a hunted soul. If ever a human word signified the exact opposite of what it seems to say, it is in this small, enraged affirmation: "Fortunately, this life is the only one."

Then the current of grace dried up, and did not flow again until the last days of his life, when he was in his hospital bed. Do you object that the fear of death makes these deathbed conversions meaningless? If so, remember the surprise of the chaplain after he had confessed Rimbaud: he said that not only did this dying man have faith, but it was of a very rare quality, a quality which he had rarely encountered.[35]

IV

THE elder son[36] and the early morning laborer have a malady in common. Whatever the elder son does, he can never return because he has never left; he has never seen the world outside of the paternal house. Thus he can never take the exact measure of that house's importance in the larger world. Because he has felt the love of the Father, he fears he may lose that consolation forever. Because he has so often taken his place at the table, he no longer can discern clearly the taste of its bread and its wine.

The early morning laborer is similar, in that he feels no lightness in his work, no eager pursuit of a goal. He cannot recall why he began working. He will never go on strike: why should he quit his task before receiving his salary? No love comes to his aid: the Master and he know each other too well, he tells himself; they hardly ever see each other anymore. The early morning laborer cheats a bit, doing the least he can get away with, knowing he will be paid at day's end just the same.

But even the Prodigal Son and the strayed sheep can only be prodigal and can only become lost within the house of the father, within native pastures. When they imagine that they have strayed far away and seen foreign lands, they have only to turn around to see that they have never left.

Such is the power of religion over those who possess it: everything is situated within it, even things that seem to be diametrically opposed to it. The Christian of the type I am describing cannot accomplish any act that will deliver him from it, because every act always has meaning within the religious scheme. Certainly, he can manage to escape from grace; but falling into sin is hardly escaping Christianity—on the contrary, doing so only strengthens religion's ties. Giving in to the flesh, nourishing one's doubt with various doctrines, sacrificing to idols—none of this, for the

Christian, is leaving Christianity. Péguy explains it: "The sinner belongs to Christianity. The sinner can make the best prayer. The sinner is an integral part of the mechanism of Christianity. The sinner is at the very heart of Christianity. . . . The sinner and the saint are as it were equally integral parts of Christianity's mechanism. They are both indispensable to each other, two mutually complementary pieces. They are both complementary but not interchangeable—though they are interchangeable with each other—both parts of that unique mechanism that is Christianity . . ."[36]

There is a certain sort of person who, once installed within the mechanism, will never exit from it. The only exit, sin, is in no way a real exit, but only a door that does not open outward. Such people move from grace to sin, from sin to grace; they are free to testify or to refuse to. But neither doubt, nor negation, nor even denial can remove the tunic that has, in effect, adhered to their skin.

We are now a long way from "this soothing compromise that allows you to love God without losing sight of Mammon"! I refuse Gide's reproach, but not in order to prove myself innocent. Indeed, I may be more guilty than a fellow who is tugged by temptation, who wants to write his books without failing heaven, and who wants to attain heaven without failing his books. It's saying little enough to claim I haven't lost sight of Mammon; the whole world can see I'm at the head of the Mammon crowd. But though one cannot serve two masters, still one does not necessarily lose sight of the neglected master, or lose awareness of the power the Abandoned One retains over one, or lose the sense of His presence. And even if this awareness and this sense were abolished, it remains true that the Master has clothed us in His livery, and that we cannot remove it, and that wherever we go we carry with us this mysterious heraldry. Thus no matter how distantly we roam, there will always be someone who says to us, "But you too were with that man—you were one of his followers."[38]

And even our freest writings will always reveal a certain marking, a particular accent, a taste of the land—of that land whose wheat and vines contain something infinitely more powerful than ordinary bread and wine.

Are writers like us prisoners? Yes, but prisoners who refuse the world's pity, who do not merit it, because such a fate, fearful as it may seem, can only be part of the supernatural order. For such writers, their drama only has reality if the universe and our destinies all have a single direction, a single goal. So it is first a matter of salvation. For those who do not believe in salvation, who only believe in appearances, why should they pity such an artist? If those believers who cherish us have deep reasons to feel alarm for us, the nonbelievers would be wiser to envy us—

especially those among them who are professional writers, for they know the real peril of complete liberty.

Look at them: they're all in search of some fixed reference point, some scale of values. I'm not referring to the philosophers; they all have their criteria. But I mean the artists and writers who stake their all on feelings and sensations. Shifting terrain, confused forces, everything quickly destroyed and dispersed, swarming over nothingness. Nothingness—they all hate it, they all fear it. Look at the external life of Barrès as an example: his political views, the League of Patriots, the Chamber, the *Echo de Paris*: all defenses against nothingness. He placed the Palais-Bourbon between himself and nothingness.[39]

And the poor children of our century, look at them. Two titles chosen at random from the best works of recent years reveal their state of disarray: *Nothing but the Earth*, proclaims the first; *Hunted Travellers*, responds the second.[40] Nothing but the world, nothing but that, at least for those who only live with their senses. Our ancient planet is quickly traversed, a poor fruit that is soon peeled, squeezed, and tossed away! Look at Montherlant's character on his quest for some "supports": he leaves school, goes through the war, moves on to sports, then to bullfighting . . . What's next? Do we dare guess? He bounces from one continent to another like a rubber ball.

But don't imagine that the bad Christian triumphs, or thinks himself any stronger. It's a given that for him, everything takes its place, even the smallest sensation has its specific worth and its place. For him, all human loves form a united front, ranged up against the one, unique Love. Every desire, pleasure, or sorrow forms part of his great work—the statue of himself that he is sculpting. Everything he does, even the smallest act, modifies the statue somewhat; everything is added to this work, which is watched over either by eternal reprobation or eternal love.

You might object, "Of course, if you contrast the Christian and the libertine, you see the issue of values clearly, and values are of great use to the writer. But what are the advantages outside of literature? "Nothing but the earth" is sad enough, but "nothing but heaven" isn't going to be of much help to the doubting Christian who has lost his desire and ability to renounce the ephemeral life."

This ephemeral life is in fact the most tenacious obsession of the bad Christian, owing to his lengthy familiarity with the supernatural. Even as a child, he shivered at religious retreats where the priests tried to give him a whiff of his future corpse. But these priests, whether too simple or too pure, couldn't see that the ephemeral seduces us at heart just because it is ephemeral. They couldn't keep the child from loving the things that pass; they only succeeded in making his love all the more vivid.

Above all, the libertine pities the lukewarm Catholic for having to renounce the morality (if that is the right word for it) which gives us the illusion of ennobling youth by virtue of its joy—the ethic initiated by Stendhal, even before Nietzsche. But the Christian recognizes that this ethic is only attractive to young people, and only to those among them who are indifferent to metaphysics and immune to the thought of death. It is a morality adapted solely to the young. This is both its seductive quality and its great weakness, for it only appears valid at that moment of life when our pulses tell us that every power is at our disposal, that we are called to greatness, and that our days are not numbered.

True, Julien Sorel and Fabrice[41] think about death from time to time, but only as a risk they are free to run, an honorable risk when it's a matter of love or of adventure. Everything is allowed to the young, or rather the young think it is, even death. The young contemplate suicide far more often than the old, because to them death is a choice, and they believe themselves free to choose not to die. But when they come to that age that is in the midst of this life's path,[42] death ceases to seem a glorious peril or the playing field of love and adventure. Instead, it is the inevitable doorway opening on to darkness. One can still play the hero, shake one's fists and declaim against it, insist on one's mastery and dominance—but now this is little more than a sham, a pose. And where both libertine and Christian tremble when they face the unknown shadows, the Christian's fear is at least tempered by some small sense of love, of the beginnings of a great love.

The anti-Christian will object that the dying libertine retains the value of the illusions from his youth: in those days, the thought of death never paralyzed him, and he was able to cultivate the human, worldly virtues: strength, bravery, a taste for amorous conquests, pride in domination. He can console himself from "that horrible agony called old age"[43] with the memory of having played his game dangerously, in his powerful years, of having risked everything, and solely for the pleasure of sensing his young heart beat more strongly. Thus the aged libertine consoles himself—condemned to death because he no longer has the strength to play a game he's already lost.

Are we not all condemned to death? Will you tell me that the libertine learns of his condemnation only in his old age, while the Christian knows of it since his childhood? It is true that, since I was ten, I have been bent under the weight of *Ecclesiastes*. But a child with a heroic spirit can find plenty of uses, within the Christian scheme of things, for what I have called the human virtues. The cause of Christ has need of the bold and of would-be conquerors. The saints were of this type. Compare the ephemeral victories of an Alexander or a Bonaparte with the mystical empires of St. Francis or St. Theresa. The motto "live dangerously" takes on a more profound meaning within Christianity.

But this seems to imply that Christianity has no place for mediocre personalities. A mediocre libertine can follow Beyle's[44] precepts—live a decorative sort of life, moderate his delicate appetites, be faithful to honor in the worldly sense of the term, and ultimately be praised for his pleasant nature. But a mediocre Christian has only a negative kind of virtue—he avoids what is forbidden, and is always in a position of retreat, of refusal. Or if he is in fact guilty of something, he is good at hiding it, good at wearing a mask. Fortunate is he who can leap over the abyss with a single bound and land on the other side as a saint. But being in the middle is worthless. The world is justified in its contempt for these Christians despite themselves—but the world doesn't know their struggle, which is to be unable to make a choice, to be stuck halfway up Mount Tabor, incapable of either running away or going forward.

A man can be the prisoner of a metaphysic with which he is in disagreement, body and soul. If such a wretch has the faculty of self-expression, he can use his work to pour out the story of his life. He can tell himself that what the artist really needs is not really a domain but simply his own patch of ground. Vigny said that the human race constitutes a discourse of which each man of genius represents a single idea.[45] But in truth, any given discourse is not only composed of large ideas, but of millions of nuances, and it is up to the humblest writers to express these. The large themes of a Pascal, a Rousseau, a Chateaubriand, a Barrès leave room for the subtlest and minutest variations to accompany them.

We have to express our own individual drama, express it as it is—but with art. What matters is not us but the work of which we are the substance. The work—our work. Who, then, is this new God, whose prerogatives I grant, and to whom I apparently owe everything? Did I ask someone, in Gide's words, for "permission to write *Destins*"? Did someone give me permission? If so, how did I ever begin to dream up such a dependency?

I need to be careful not to repeat Cain's error: yes, I am responsible for my brother. I don't want to die without having given expression to my own particular drama, my own vision of the world and of people—without having left behind me a written, arrested, fixed expression of it in the hearts of people, the greatest number of people possible. I want to reach them, to touch them. But one cannot touch without wounding. A book is a violent act—sometimes even a violation. How deeply one can enter into certain souls! (For example, I think of all the letters I received after publishing my *Sufferings of the Christian Life* in the *Nouvelle Revue Française*—an essay in which I only wanted to say how this religion is both true and impracticable, in order to excuse my inability to conform my life to it.) No question is closer to my heart than this one, concerning the writer's responsibility.

V[46]

FOR many, this question of responsibilities never gets posed. If there is any dogma to which most writers of the nineteenth and twentieth centuries have adhered, it is that of the artist's absolute independence. It would appear to be settled, once and for all, that the work of art has no end other than itself. All that matters is the degree to which the work is gratuitous or useless. According to this dogma, anything written to prove something, to argue for something, to serve some cause, is no longer art. Gide has written, "the moral question for the artist is not whether his idea is moral or useful for the greater number: the question is whether he has presented the idea well."[47]

But so many artists wouldn't take the trouble to continue making this point if it were not in fact vigorously contested. Away from the world of letters, we hear a constant protest against this pretension to absolute independence. For example, when Ernest Psichari proclaims that one must write anxiously under the gaze of the Holy Trinity,[48] he becomes the spokesperson for all those who believe in the soul's immortality, who believe in the profound importance of their writings to their readers' immortal destinies.

And there is an immense crowd of novelists who hesitate, drifting back and forth between the two extreme camps. On the one hand, they evaluate their work according to the degree with which it comprehends the entire living human being, with his heights and his abysses, the creature as it really is. They sense profoundly that any intervention into the lives of their characters in order to prove or demonstrate something—even something they hold to be true—is arbitrary. They are entirely sincere in wishing not to falsify life.

But on the other hand, they also know that they are dealing with dangerous matters when they depict any and all passions. They know this can have incalculable effects in the destiny of individuals, and that the effects can be almost infinite.

Every novelist worthy of the name and every playwright born a Christian worries about this. French literature provides us with an illustrious example. Giving in to the fashion of the day, I passed a vacation recently writing a "life"—and I chose that of Jean Racine.[49] Racine is the archetype of the writer torn between two ways of seeing his work and his responsibilities. Writers like him know that their ultimate fate depends on the decision they make. The outlines of Racine's struggle are well known. At the age of twenty, he escaped from Port-Royal, his youthful genius in full revolt against its unbearable constraint. And when Nicole violently attacked novelists and dramatists, in his letter on *Les Imaginaires*,[50] Racine was on fire with rage. Nicole had written: "While the qualities of the novelist and playwright are not very honorable in the eyes of decent people, they are particularly horrible when viewed from the principles of the Christian religion and of the Gospel. A maker of novels and a poet of the theatre is a public poisoner, not of bodies but of the souls of the faithful, and they should see themselves as guilty of an infinite number of spiritual homicides."

Racine responded to this vicious blow in two letters that are not so well known, letters of a verve and a malice quite unequalled. But in our rush to defend Racine and to explain that he was the victim of this oppressive, inhuman doctrine of the Jansenists, let us not forget that Nicole was only developing more fully the ideas of Saint Augustine. When Bossuet wrote about the theatre, he was no gentler. Who could argue with Bossuet when he affirms that the success of a novel or play arises from the audience seeing their own passions depicted in it? In truth, Racine's rage resulted from his sense that Nicole had touched the heart of the matter. And we can observe his carrying on the debate within himself over the following years until, at thirty-eight years of age, he finally renounced this career of depicting the passions.

This is a renunciation of which very few writers are capable. But Racine's renunciation is not quite so simple. When a man carries a work of art within him, is he truly free not to give it to the world? Perhaps a writer renounces writing only when he has nothing left within him—that is, that he can henceforth only go on repeating himself, imitating himself. And this is precisely what most writers do when they have given what they have to give, delivered their message: they keep on laying their eggs out of habit because they have nothing else they can do—and because, in any case, one has to make a living.

But no human force can reduce a writer to silence during his most fertile years; a supernatural force is required for it. I know of no case where grace has won out over a writer determined to write; in fact, when a writer is converted, we usually see his efforts redouble. He now wants the largest print run possible so the whole world can read about his experience. We still await the miracle of God's reducing an author to silence.

In fact, all the best writers are caught in the crossfire between the two camps. On the one hand, they are convinced that their work is worthless unless it is utterly disinterested, that they dare not alter reality out of modesty or the desire to edify. And on the other, they sense their responsibilities toward their readers—whom, of course, they want to be as numerous as possible. And the writer retains one certainty: no work of fiction is of value unless it submits absolutely to its subject, which is the human heart. The writer has to advance in his knowledge of the human, to bend down and inspect all the abysses he encounters without giving in to vertigo, or disgust, or horror. This is a certainty. But there is also something else, a feeling, a vague sense—that is, for the nonChristian writer. But for the Christian, when a single soul is troubled, a single soul exposed to a fall—now we are dealing with matters of eternity. A Christian writer gives himself certain reasons, as we will see shortly, for continuing to depict the passions. But the nonChristian writers cannot keep themselves from feeling vaguely responsible, and they invent a great deal of sophistry to argue that this feeling is not a real one. Here, I would like to point out that in fact this feeling is based on a profound reality, and if the question seems more grave for writers of faith, it is of concern to nonbelievers as well—to the precise degree that they believe only in the human, in no world apart from this one.

A few years back, a magazine asked of a number of writers, "Why do you write?" Most responded with jokes, like Paul Morand who said, "I write in order to be rich and famous." The humor in such replies consists in their confusing immediate motives with deeper ones.

The deeper motive seemed to me to lie in a certain instinct within us, an instinct not to remain alone. A writer is in essence a person who will not resign himself to solitude. Each of us is a desert: a book is a cry in the desert, a carrier pigeon with a message tied to its foot, a bottle thrown into the sea. Writing is an attempt to be heard, even if only by one other person. It is an attempt to have our idea, or, if we are novelists, our characters (which are the most living parts of us) accepted, perhaps understood, perhaps loved, by another intelligence, another heart. The writer who claims,

"I write only for myself, and I don't care whether anyone else ever reads me" is a boaster who is either fooling us or himself. Every one of us suffers from being alone. The artist is the one for whom and in whom this suffering takes bodily form. Baudelaire was right to call artists "beacons": they light a great fire in the darkness; they set themselves alight in order to attract as many of their brothers as possible.[51]

Artists, and writers especially, are the most delicate people in the world, and at the same time the ones most avid for praise. A writer is never overcome by compliments. But this is no despicable trait revealing a low personality: on the contrary, they have this great need for praise because they doubt themselves so much, because they sense so keenly the nothingness of their work. They need to be reassured.

But out of all the compliments you can make to a writer, the one that gives him the greatest possible happiness is to say, "Sir, you are so admired by young people . . .". Then his contentment will positively swell within him. This is because even the most detached writer wants young readers above all else; if he doesn't attract a young audience, he feels he has somehow failed in his destiny.

Yes, nothing counts but this—to attract other people and, among them, those who can still be influenced, dominated, those young hearts that are still uncertain and not fully formed. Nothing matters so much as leaving one's imprint on this living wax, depositing the best of ourselves in the beings who will survive us. Because if we write so as not to be alone, it is not enough simply to attract some others: we have to see our own image imprinted on them, an image that will survive when we are in our tombs.

Don't believe in the false humility of writers: the humblest among us aspires to nothing less than being immortal, the least pretentious still has the pretension of not dying altogether. Those who affect not to care, the sort who write their poems on cigarette papers, do so in the hope that their works, being lighter than others, will be carried farther by the winds, to the most distant shores. The artist wants to escape from his desert during his life, but he also wants to escape from the greater solitude of death. Even if it is only one book, one page, one line, we want something of us not to perish, for one young human, during the centuries to come, to sing the song we have invented. And it is not just themselves that artists want to make immortal, but their loves as well. They have the audacity to think they can impose the vision of the face they have loved on future generations:

Suppose my name were favored by the winds,
My voyage prospered, and the future read
All that I wrote, and marveled . . . Love, they're yours!
I give you poems to make your memory . . .[52]

Now, if the writer's passion is to attract the greatest possible number
of readers in both the present and future, and to mark them as profoundly
as possible—even without being a Christian, he must feel some responsibility toward these people. Even if we set aside this term "responsibility,"
which will mean different things to the Christian and the nonChristian,
can the writer possibly feel no concern for those who have been touched
in this way? In fact I know of no writer worthy of the name, even the least
religious, who is entirely unconcerned. I do not mean that this concern
somehow influences their work, or reins in their curiosity or the intensity
of their descriptions. But they are convinced that every real work of art, so
long as it conforms to the real, cannot help but be good. Flaubert's greatest ambition was to win the title of demoralizer, and today Gide would
welcome the title.[53] Does this mean that such authors want to do evil? Not
at all; but they would disagree with us as to what is good and what is evil.
In their eyes, a work that scandalizes is nearly always a book that liberates. They see the writer as a sort of benevolent demon who tears the bandages binding us, restoring us to freedom and ease in our movements. But
this is not the place to show that, in the eyes of the Christian, these writers
are in error to the extent that they do not take the dogma of the Fall into
account. They do not take proper account of how defiled and corrupted
man really is: they don't see how virulent and terribly contagious these
wounds in man really are, and they rip off the bandages with increasing
audacity.

But this does not alter the fact that the novel is nothing if it is not the
study of man, and that it loses all justification if it does not advance us in
the knowledge of the human heart. Should the novelist, therefore, alter his
object according to his scruples, and if there is the possibility of some
soul being hurt by it, should he falsify the life he studies?

I know that the question can be evaded in more ways than one. But
we should not evade it by saying to ourselves that, after all, we are not
writing for little girls, and we are not in competition with Madame de
Ségur.[54] No, unfortunately it is the readers who have attained the age of
reason who are the ones that my books trouble the most. Often, one is better off if one's books are read by little ones eating their sweets with no
knowledge of evil than by people in the full bloom of young adulthood.
You can scarcely imagine the letters a writer receives. After reading one
of my novels, *Genitrix*, a young man sent me his picture with the dedica-

tion, "to the man who almost made me murder my grandmother." He explained to me in his letter that his grandmother so closely resembled the woman in *Genitrix* that he nearly strangled her in her sleep. How can one protect such readers? Even the Abbé Bethléem himself[55] would have his hands full doing it. If reading novels is to be forbidden, it ought to be forbidden to adults rather than to children.

In truth, those writers who alter reality in order to edify the reader and who paint their characters falsely in order to avoid being immoral rarely attain their ends. Because one must not forget that the writer is not the only author of a novel: the reader is his collaborator and often adds in his own horrors quite unknown to the novelist. We would be astonished if we knew what our characters became in the imagination of the woman who speaks to us about our book. I am not afraid to admit that no book has moved me more deeply than a very chaste novel that I adored when I was fourteen, called *Feet of Clay*. It was the work of an old woman full not only of virtue but also of imagination and sensibility: Zénaïde Fleuriot. The heroine of *Feet of Clay* had the beautiful name of Armelle Trahec. She was a young redhead with freckles on her face—freckles which I have since distributed generously to my own heroines. When a journalist asks me which masters have most influenced me, I always speak of Balzac and Dostoevsky, but I never dare mention Zénaïde Fleuriot.

All this goes to show that the devil never loses his rights, and I can imagine that on the Day of Judgment, while many writers will have to answer for the souls they have injured, some others will be utterly shocked at the unforeseen impact their chastest works had in certain people.

The question of good or bad books becomes insoluble because of this always surprising, always unique collaboration of reader with writer. I suppose that only the novelist is in a position to make the judgment. For my part, I know from experience—from letters and confidences I have received—that those of my books that have been called the most daring, perhaps with good reason, are also those that have had the greatest religious impact on certain people. All books, the best and the worst, are like two-edged swords, and the unknown reader will make use of them in an utterly unpredictable way. We cannot predict if the book will wound the libertine, the debauchee in the reader, or the honest Christian. Each of us makes his honey according to his own recipe: each goes from book to book, from doctrine to doctrine taking what seems good to him. He searches for himself in books, until he believes he has found himself. Consider the young men who killed themselves after reading Goethe's *Werther*: if that book had not existed, wouldn't they have found a reason somewhere else for giving in to that mortal vertigo they felt? Goethe is not responsible for their deaths. Each of us recreates and recomposes our reading into the image of our own hearts, an image and an idea that suits only us. No doubt I am peculiar in this, but from the work of Proust, what most stands out for me is the image of an immense hole, the sensation of an infinite absence. In Proust's vision of humanity, what strikes me is this vast emptiness, the absence of God.[56] I see this because I am a Christian, while others perhaps come away from his work with even more troubling images. And so what remains for writers is the hope that the evil they have done will be pardoned because of the good they have also done, good of which they are probably unaware.

Anyway, so I try to reassure myself. But sincerity with regard to ourselves is the great virtue of our generation; let us dare, therefore, to look evil in the face. Everything I have just said does not remove the fact that we writers consent to this career of depicting passions. The passions are the object of all our study, and we only sell our books because thousands of readers take a disturbed kind of joy in these depictions. Saint Augustine confesses that he found in plays "the image of our unhappiness, love and the nourishment of its fires . . ."[57] There is no need to spread this fire around the world with obscene depictions. "Don't you feel," says Bossuet, "that there are certain things that, while they don't have an obvious effect, nonetheless secretly insinuate evil dispositions into certain souls—even though their malign nature is not overt? Everything that nourishes the passions is of this type. We would have no difficulty in finding things to say in the confessional if we looked within ourselves for the causes of evil." And he adds, "He who could find the secret basis of sensual joy in man, that unquiet, vague disposition to find pleasure in the senses, that disposition tending both to nothing in particular and to everything—he would discover the secret source of the greatest sins."[58]

The secret source of the greatest sins: can we artists deny that this is almost always what we are seeking? Certainly this is no premeditated and hardened strategy on the artist's part, but in the light of this fine text of Bossuet's, we can better understand what André Gide means when he claims that no work of art is created without the collaboration of the devil.[59] The writer always relies on this secret basis of sensual joy in order to touch and move the reader, this vague and unquiet disposition toward sensual pleasure that leads both nowhere and everywhere. The writer colludes with the reader in this—whereas he ought to be seeking to conquer the reader, the adversary. Every man, certainly every young man and every woman, is an accomplice for the writer in feeling this desire for languor, this taste for emotion, this thirst for tears. I repeat, there is no writer deserving of the name who thinks of any of this in writing, and who deliberately strives to trouble his readers' hearts. But the writer has a sure instinct for it; his entire art depends on attaining this secret source of the greatest sins, and the more genius he has, the surer it is that he will get there.

Should one, therefore, give up writing? Even if we feel that writing is our profoundest calling, if literary creation is as natural to us as breathing, that it is our whole life? Perhaps some sage can unlock this enigma, and tell us how the morally scrupulous writer can escape from the dilemma. Evidently we must either falsify life, the object of our observation, or risk spreading scandal and disquiet into our readers' lives.

And let us frankly avow that a writer who is troubled by this debate will find practically no one to take him seriously. On the left, there will be only mockery and a shrug of the shoulders. People will refuse to take seriously something that is not a problem to them. They will deny that the artist has any other goal than those of realizing the beautiful and of coming as close as possible to psychological truth. And on the right, the writer comes in for an even greater misunderstanding. Here, people believe the writer has neither scruples nor noble motives. The first time some pious journalists accuse you of writing pornography with no other aim than making money, you'll find it hard not to feel suffocated. Back when I was still naïve, I wanted to open my heart on this subject to these high and holy people. But after my very first words, I suddenly realized that they saw no difference between me and, say, the author of the Folies-Bergère reviews. And this in no way shocks me: those who have undertaken the care of souls have an infinity of items far more pressing than aesthetic problems. It would be ridiculous of me to expect them to take these matters as seriously as I do.But finally there was a Catholic writer who took the problem seriously and tried to resolve it. Here, I cannot go into all the complexities of Jacques Maritain's thought, but I will extract a few lines from his book, *Art and Scholastics*, in which he seems to sketch precisely the uncertain novelist's responsibilities. He says, "The essential question is not whether the novelist ought to depict a certain aspect of evil. The essential question is on what level he is when he attempts it, and whether his art and his heart are pure and strong enough to carry out the depiction without conniving in the evil. The deeper that the modern novel descends into human misery, the more the novelist needs superhuman abilities. To write Proust's book in the way it ought to have been written would require the inner light of a St. Augustine. Alas, the contrary is the case, and we see the observer and the observed, the novelist and the subject matter, merging in debasement."[60]

So Maritain puts it, and nearly everyone would agree that he poses the question very well—everyone, that is, but novelists themselves.[61] In these lines, he does not take the essential thing into account, for he neglects considering the laws of artistic creation—"the observer and the observed," he says. He likens the novelist bent over the human heart to a physiologist bent over a frog or a guinea pig. For him, the novelist is just as detached from his subject as is the scientist in a laboratory about to open an animal's stomach. Now the novelist and the scientist are of completely different orders. Perhaps Maritain is still absorbed in the naturalists' conception of the novel.[62] In fact this "connivance" of the novelist with his subject, which he warns us against, is the very condition of our art. The novelist is not an observer but a creator of fictional life. He doesn't observe life but creates it, putting living beings into the world. The novelist doesn't dream of getting up on a level above them; he gives in to the temptation of mingling with his creatures, and in a sense annihilating himself in them: he identifies so closely with his creations that he becomes them.

Someone may object that, if the novelist had the superhuman qualities Maritain calls for, his characters could never be abominable: a good tree does not produce bad fruit. Let the novelist work on his own inner reformation, and what comes from him can never be a cause of scandal. No doubt—but let us note in passing that superhuman virtue is not very widespread among people, and certainly not among novelists. And would a deeply virtuous person ever even start writing novels? For if he were truly an artist, he would find himself incapable of creating tediously edifying tales, deprived of all human reality. And he would understand that a living work of art must be inevitably disturbing: this most chaste novelist would risk sometimes finding in himself the desires he has suppressed and the temptations he thought he had conquered. Just as the most admirable people sometimes have unworthy children, our most admirable novelist would have to fear that the worst in him might become incarnated in the sons and daughters of his spirit. This is why the fervent Christian may describe the passions from some higher plane in a sermon or a treatise, but not in a novel where these passions are not to be judged and condemned but to be depicted, to be depicted in their very flesh and blood. Nothing can keep a fire from burning. The Abbé Perreyve, just out of school, wrote in a letter to his friend Charles Perraud about "this vice of voluptuousness whose very name weakened us when we were sixteen years old."[63] If the name alone can weaken an adolescent, what will a depiction do, even a weak one?

    Some will say that the novelist has more material than just vice to
depict, that humanity has its miseries but it also has its greatness: are there
not beautiful souls who would make a good subject for a novel? Certainly,
I am far from sharing Gide's opinion that one never makes good literature
with fine sentiments[64]—one does no better with bad ones. It is more exact
to say that good literature is not easily made with fine sentiments alone,
and we cannot separate the good ones from the bad ones in order to make
an edifying portrait. The modern novelist's ambition is to capture the
entirety of human nature, with all its contradictions and its twists and
turns. In real life, there are no beautiful souls existing in a pure state—
they only exist in novels, and only in bad ones. What we call a beautiful
soul only became so after a battle with itself, and that battle must continue
up to the very end. What the soul has to conquer in itself, that evil from
which it must detach itself, exists, and the novelist must take account of it.
If the novelist has any reason for existing at all, it is precisely in order to
show, among the noblest and the highest, the part that continues to resist
God and to dissimulate and hide its weakness—and to show, among those
who seem to us to be the most fallen, the secret source of purity.

    It is nonetheless true that there are people who have conquered that
part of themselves, and the saints are as proper material for the novelist as
any other living persons. Why haven't I tried to depict saintly men and
women as others have done, or have tried to do—others like Benson and
Fogazzaro, Baumann and Bernanos?[65] It seems to me possible to reply
that on this very point, on the issue of holiness, the novelist is off his
grounds. In order to write a novel about holiness, one not only has to create characters, but one is also tempted to the supreme madness of trying to
imitate God, and acting on men's souls in the way He does. And I think
that with this topic, the novelist will always be outdone by reality, by the
holy people who have actually lived. Francis of Assisi, Catherine of
Siena, the two Saint Theresas—all these great mystics bear witness to a
reality, to an experience that infinitely surpasses the novelist's powers.

    Every time one of us has tried to reinvent in a novel the ways of
Grace, its struggles and its victories, we are always left with the impression that we have been arbitrary and false. Nothing is harder to get down
on the page than the finger of God directing a human life. Not that this is
invisible, but its touches are so delicate that they vanish when we try to
get them fixed. No—God is inimitable; He evades the novelist's grasp. I
remain convinced that what is admirable and successful in a novel like
Sous le soleil de Satan has to do with the very point that the character
depicted is not a true saint: this tormented and unhappy soul wanders
along the extreme border of despair. Or perhaps, if you prefer, this young

Abbé Donissan is a true saint: but in that case, Bernanos follows his novelistic instincts and discovers the secret weaknesses and deviations within the character in order to show that, despite his heroic virtues, he is a member of sinful humanity. Most novelists who have tried to depict saints fail in this respect, in trying to depict sublime, angelic, inhuman characters, whereas their real opportunity was to shed some light on how the saint retains some of the poverty of what it is to be human. And just here is the proper domain of the novelist. In reading the lives of the great saints, I have always been intrigued by what seemed to me their excessive manifestations of humility. It has always seemed to me that a being so elevated and so perfected could not be quite sincere in speaking of his or her unworthiness; they seemed to want to place themselves below the level of ordinary people. But now I am persuaded that saintliness is, above all else, lucidity. "To know oneself is to move forward into horror," Bossuet wrote to the Maréchal de Bellefonds.[66] As the saints advance in their double knowledge, of both God and of their own hearts, they attain so acute a vision of their own unworthiness that they abase themselves—a most natural result. It is not sufficient to say that they believe themselves to be wretches: they really are, and their saintliness is what gives them the clarity of vision to know it. They can see in the light of God what it is to be a human, even a holy one, and they are in a state of horror.[67]

A true novelist who tried to depict only saints would nonetheless himself have to rejoin the ranks of the human—that is, would have to re-enter the state of peril. He cannot avoid encountering certain abysses. At the source of admirable lives, there is often some vice that has been curbed and dominated. One knows this to be true of revolutionaries and of great heretics. But it is also true of people whose lives are saintly and pure.

And so it happens that the novelist, caught in the crossfire of all these difficulties, feels at some times a temptation, one to which he rarely gives in: the temptation to be silent. To be silent, to interrupt all these dark disclosures, to cease giving birth to wicked creatures who go into the world and propagate their evil: the novelist is tempted by the sacrifice we so admire in Jean Racine.

Bossuet said that living according to nature and living according to grace are not so different.[68] The debate between the two troubles all Christians, but it is especially acute and even more tragic for the novelist. How can the novelist consent to silence? If he almost never consents to it, undoubtedly there are simple and crass reasons for why a man is attached to his career, especially when that career flatters his vanity and his wish to wear a kind of halo of glory, and brings various sorts of advantages along with it. But there is another kind of necessity operative with the writer: he cannot *not* write. He obeys a profound and imperious exigency. We cannot resist these creatures stirring within us, who take shape and ask to live. They ask to live, and we cannot decide in advance what sort of souls they will have. Our severest critics ought to consider and try to understand Goncourt's point: "One doesn't write the book one wants to write." No, one does not—but one does write the book one deserves! Our censors reproach us as if our work depended entirely on our free will, as if we deliberately decided to write a good book or a bad one, an edifying or a scandalous one. They seem not to have even the faintest idea of the mysterious, unpredictable, inevitable element in the creation of a novel. The need to write ends up becoming, for the novelist, an almost monstrous function from which he cannot escape. It's rather like the old advertisement for a hat factory: a live rabbit is put into the machine on one end, and out at the other comes a hat. Life takes over the novelist similarly: out of his desires and sorrows a book will be born, and nothing can stop it from happening. Even if he removes himself from life, shuts his mouth and stops his ears, his distant past will continue to ferment within him. For a born novelist, the experience of childhood and youth will be enough to nourish an immense set of books. No, no one is capable of damming this river that flows from us.

Of course, our books resemble us deeply, and the reader has the right to judge us by them, and to condemn us for them. Everyone knows Novalis' phrase, "Character is destiny."[69] Well, just as there is a strong link between a person's character and the events of his life, so the same kind of link exists between the novelist and the characters and events that issue from his imagination. And he is no more the absolute master of these characters and events than he is of the course of his own destiny.

People of my sort do enjoy complicating this question of the "Catholic novelist"! The humblest priest would say to me, following Maritain: "Be pure, become pure, and your work too will reflect heaven. Purify the source first, and then those who drink from its waters will never again be ill . . .". I will let the priest have the last word.

VI

HAS this little book been as sincere as I intended it to be? In rereading it, I find I've taken great pains to complicate the most ordinary situation. The fish muddies the waters so he can make his escape. Why widen the search so? A man doesn't have to discover Christianity if he was born into it, only to recover it. It's a matter of an interrupted current. These difficulties I've been examining can make me forget the facilities that a long acquaintance with my religion have given me. Someone taking his first spiritual steps, if he has never been on his knees, has never talked to God, will perhaps feel some envy in reading me complain about my lifelong familiarity with Christianity and heavenly things.

These pages have certainly not lied insofar as their tone has revealed the irritation of a soul drawn toward God like a plant toward the sun, a plant that has the power to resist its own natural law. But where does such a resistance, such a rejection come from? On the day that a man comes to know the truth about himself—without which he cannot enjoy even temporal salvation—nothing is simpler than to abandon himself, to slip easily into submission, to close his eyes, like a child giving himself up to all-powerful hands.

To understand how a soul can feel at the same time both the great temptation toward God and a vivid desire to escape from the grace that already surrounds it, one should recall the shock I felt when studying the life of Jean Racine. For me, the mystery of Racine was his perseverance. I was not surprised by his sudden change in the very year he wrote *Phaedra*; as the historians tell us, any number of reasons might account for it. But that he never strayed from his spiritual path for the rest of his life, and that he instead became more and more deeply involved in spiritual life—this is what surpasses anything in my experience.

Christianity retained a hold over Racine throughout all the vicissitudes of his life, and the hold was perhaps even stronger the further away he strayed. This is because there is an essential difference between the sinful Christian who resists grace and the nonbeliever who gives in to his corrupted nature. The latter thinks he can make his peace with the corruption, assign limits to it, and integrate it into what the world calls a normal and honorable life. But the sinner knows, through a wisdom given by God, that he is not integrated with his sin, that he can do nothing toward his salvation if he does not cut off the sin at its deepest roots. The godless man never dreams of such an operation, and if he did, it would seem absurd to him or at least wholly beyond human capacity. But the sinner knows it is possible, that God renews us each day, that the raising of Lazarus itself was the most ordinary of miracles, given the thousands of spiritual resurrections God accomplishes every moment.

When he sees it from a distance, the sinner is not at all averse to this total renewal. To start afresh, to begin one's life all over again—who has not felt, at least once, this desire? What flesh has not wished to be cleansed of its stains? Now, the Church asks that we not only hate our sins, that we make sincere repentance of them, but also that we not allow them to weigh us down as we walk forward; the mysterious wisdom of the Church demands of us both expiation and forgetting.

In one of those public letters André Gide has done me the dangerous honor of addressing to me, he professes to be scandalized over this point. One of his converted friends, he says, felt nothing but joy after his conversion and would not even think about certain elements in his past, a past that no longer existed for him.[70] It is believable that this man put it that way to Gide, but I am quite sure he never meant he "was finished with repentance." Repentance is the natural state of the converted sinner, but this state does not require a constant preoccupation with the sins committed. Obsession with such things, an overscrupulousness that leads to spiritual morbidity, retards the soul in its ascent and interrupts spiritual advancement.

Changing one's life, being reborn, becoming a new person—this is the all-powerful attraction of returning to God. And the power of that attraction is increased by our occasional disgust with sinfulness and the sorrow it engenders, and by the world's criminal habit of sometimes ceasing to be so delicious. A given sinner may give in to this attraction once, twice, innumerable times: and this shows that none of his returns was definitive, that he could not persevere, to the extent that he cannot even believe that the grace to persevere could ever be granted him. Then, when he has just given in to the Christian charm and the happiness of having his

burden lifted from him, just when he begins to believe himself worthy of
the peace and joy of Christ—then he sees, surging over the horizon
toward him, the forces that the enemy has waited till now to deploy. A
thousand intellectual objections and difficulties that the sinful soul had
never even dreamed of considering, weighted down as it was by its sins,
unable to think of anything else but the desire for deliverance—everything the human mind can construct to argue against Catholic dogma, all
this assails him at once. And the assault is hurled at the weakest, least
defended point. Then he hears the voice of the tempter: "So now what? Is
it for this hypothesis, this tired metaphysic founded on worn-out ideas,
that you have sacrificed the heart's delights, the caresses, the repose of the
flesh? Are you going to climb aboard this old vessel, abandoned by practically everyone who has ever counted in the human race—the philosophers, the writers, the leaders, and the followers? The boat is leaking, and
you choose this moment to get aboard, in order to throw your immense
riches into the sea. Look around you: you are alone here."

And as the enemy speaks, all the abandoned sensual delights of the
past rise up, renewed and recharged again with mystery. One by one, the
passions awake and begin to prowl, scenting out the object of their lust.
They attack the poor undecided soul from within; he has no chance.

How many times must he be thrown into the ditch and almost smothered by the mud, to grasp at the edges and pull himself again into the
light? How many times must his grip give way, must he fall again back
into the shadows, until he finally submits to the law of spiritual life? That
law is the most misunderstood one in the whole world, the most hated
one, but the one without which the grace of perseverance remains inac-
cessible: he must give up his autonomy. This is what Pascal expressed
perfectly: "The sweet and total renunciation. Total submission to Jesus
Christ *and to my spiritual director.*"[71]

What is this? To give ourselves a master makes us unworthy of being
called free men. And this is a master unlike the one in Epictetus,[72] who
could break his arm but fail to disturb his soul. Not that sort of master—
but rather one who has power over our very thoughts and desires, often
before we even know them ourselves.

Servitude of this sort is, miraculously, liberation. After all, how have
you spent the years of your freedom, if not in forging chains for yourself
and tightening them a bit more each day? You have spent these years of
apparent freedom submitting like an ox to the yoke of your innumerable
hereditary passions. Not one of all your crimes has done anything other
than continue to live, to proliferate, and to close more tightly around you
every day. And the man to whom you are to submit *wants you no longer*

to have the freedom to be a slave. He wants to break the circle of your fatalities, whether inherited or acquired. Against the half-extinguished ash-heap of your passions he wants to ignite the fire of Grace—"because our God," St. Paul wrote to the Hebrews, "is also a consuming fire."[73]

VII

FOR the man who has passed his youth, who looks back over the great length of time he has lived, the greatest anguish lies in discovering that he was really not the master of his life. His inner enemies, many of them unknown, now take off their masks and reveal their presence in him, a presence embodied in the acts they have forced him into. On the framework of the revolving days, he can see his destiny depicted clearly: his acts, the things he has done and those he could not help doing, all that was accomplished, all that has proliferated and that has been perpetuated. And the sin he has committed this night recalls in detail another sin committed twenty years ago—like a hideous old man's features reborn in his grandson. And this new sin will give birth to another tomorrow.

The framework of a life is like a tightly woven web, and no earthly power can cut through it; and as the drama unfolds, not one scene can be cut from it. This is a fatal interdependence: if we go all the way back to the man as an infant, when his features were still indistinct, we will be able to trace there the creases and wrinkles that the forty-year-old will see, with fear and horror, in his mirror.

The unhappinesses on the childhood playground are a prefiguration of all his future sorrows. Even before his blood began to rise, when the heart, which had never beat for someone else, slumbered in peace, that heart was an open space on which indistinct forms began to live: the larval passions, the chrysalises where the anguish and the sins to come were still sleeping. And if the man wants to go back further still, beyond his infancy, to the very source of his destiny, he can see it springing from the entrails of the empoisoned earth. It springs out of the country churchyards, out of the old bones that in their day accomplished the secret acts similar to those the living accomplish today in seeking out their joys. If only things could see and remember, within those old houses where the furniture is passed on from generation to generation: the couches could remember, after half a century, how the various bodies that had stretched out on them committed the same crimes and madnesses.[74]

Now, when the man is no longer young, seeing his fate and its implacable continuity across all his life, he does not fool himself into believing that the future will be any different. Just as his ripened years were contained within his youth, and his youth within his earliest years, so his soiled maturity contains already all the elements of his shameful future decrepitude. The future old man is already present in this baldness, in this shapeless mouth, and his future soul is already present in this one, enslaved by a lifetime of habit. The die is cast—in fact it was long ago, in his infancy. Indeed, it was cast before his birth.

So the man raises up his head, defies his despair, and resolves to cherish his fate. To do this, he shapes his life, since his will is incapable of changing it, and he tries to put together the elements destiny has provided into some sort of order that pleases him aesthetically. The aesthetic is confounded with the ethical: he wants to present artfully his theory of submission to his instincts.

Thus, he no longer looks into the shadows to find some way to justify submitting to the laws of the flesh. Instead, he raises his arms and joyfully rattles his chains, glorying in them, and inviting all others to do the same with their chains.[75] He professes that this law written in his most secret depths comes from God. He professes this with the same authority with which he previously denied that his conscience came from God. Is it true that sin is the thing we cannot not commit? Who will console us for this degeneration, if not those who made us fall? Look, he says, I am no longer anxious; I even laugh at my anxieties. At sixty years of age, my youth sparkles with joy, and everyone in the present generation watches me with admiration.

"I am no longer anxious." Why this need to proclaim something that ought to go without saying? If everything is indeed given, if I only look at myself like an artist, organizing and representing my inheritances and my weaknesses, I can only feel a great calm—unless this calm is a mask of despair. But then, total despair is a great calm.

But is there any man who is not anxious and troubled? And you who have made mock of my own trouble, we all know about yours. You are a writer, which is to say you reveal yourself every moment. Practically nothing in you is hidden. But your boasting of this lack of anguish suggests that it is a new state for you—and just how precarious a state it is, you know better than we do.

The shape of your destiny is designed and unfolded in an uninterrupted manner, today's events being contained in potential within yesterday's. And despite it all, you continue to act as if you could alter that shape, interrupt the flow, or at least make it deviate in some other direction. You have both hoped for and feared some external force operating on you; but whether you feared it or desired it, you never ceased believing that such a force was a possibility. *We all await the hour when a face will emerge against the background of our past—and we hope it will not be the obscene face we expect, but an unknown one, covered with blood, and of a frightening sweetness.*

In the most sovereign manner, Jesus Christ's incarnation made Him a sharer in our human history, and he now seeks out a second chance to enter into our destiny, into each particular life. By doing so, he introduces his will into each apparent determinism, ultimately destroying it. His attempts are sometimes subtle and hidden, and renewed after long intervals; and they are sometimes direct and imperious, pressing upon us in a unique, solemn way. But in all cases, these attempts give even the most enslaved man the sense of actually being master of his own "yes" and his own "no." The man feels sometimes that no earthly force could prevent him from giving in to temptation and to his familiar sins. But then he feels the insistence of this force asking to absorb his weakness—and suddenly he feels astonishingly free. Having been a slave with regard to every chance to do ill, he is a slave no longer when the One who wants to save him arrives. And this One will save him despite himself, asking only for a state of acceptance, of self-abandonment—only for his consent to cease defending himself, to play dead for a time.

Many will say they have never felt the approach of this imperious grace, this force that seeks to overflow its banks and stream out upon them, mixing itself with them. They will say that some people have a religious nature, while others have a repugnance for anything metaphysical, and that neither will ever persuade the other.

However, if we were able to penetrate each life, into its most secret turnings, I am convinced we could always find the place where the appeal can be made. And how many times have we seen religious personalities become carried away by mysticism and actually resist and persecute Christ! On the other side are the "intellectual" types who attach themselves to God in the name of reason; their intellects must first be satisfied, and the reasons of the heart[76] only occur to them much later. Thus both types of person either submit to or resist Grace, each according to its own mode. The heart can find as many pretexts for denying God as the intellect can. The heart is the most easily convinced, but because of that facility, it can quickly grow tired and detach itself just as quickly as it was attracted.

Yet there is a particular sort of intellectualism which rejects grace in advance, closing up all the avenues grace might take: it breaks down all the bridges, and blocks up all the canals. Among our intellectuals today are some who have taken such effective measures that it is difficult to see how grace could possibly prevail with them. But grace can be more inventive than we can possibly imagine.

Still, these two sorts of personalities are separated by an eternal debate. Christ is a fact, his survival in our world is a fact, and the human conscience is a fact—but they tell us that our thirst for the supernatural keeps us from looking at facts objectively. And we reply that their impassioned denial of the supernatural deprives them just as surely of accurate observation.

I can only laugh at those who say we should make everything a mechanical sort of problem, including the history of religions. They accord no value to the conclusions of those whom they see as throwing themselves onto the Gospel with such avidity that, if they had to, they would invent the God for whom they have such hunger and thirst.

I would object that their rejection conceals a certain kind of self-protection: it is not so much the cross of Christ that they reject, but their own crosses. Incapable of resolving to undergo such a renunciation as the cross requires, they deny the One who asks it of them. They must soothe their consciences, and therefore Jesus is not Christ. They protest that real courage consists in regulated, ordered, and reasonable self-indulgence, and that the distinction between good and evil reduces and strips bare one's life, makes it anemic. To hear them speak, it is Christians who fear life, who flee its perilous and sublime disorder; they need eternal promises to comfort them.

No argument makes a Christian more indignant than this one. And here our adversaries give in to a weakness that affects us all when confronted with a doctrine we hate—that is, judging it by its most mediocre expression so as to despise it more easily. In truth, those who seek comfort and ease and consolation in religion crowd up around its entrance without actually going in. The spiritual life, for those who really embrace it, is an adventure, and sometimes a frightening one. You don't play games with the Cross: it makes demands on us that we cannot foresee; its passion burns so intensely that it makes human follies seem harmless. St. John of the Cross says that in the end we will all be judged by love, and we know to what lengths such a belief led the saints. Pascal's "Lord, I give you everything"[77]—if a man says this with real commitment, his friends can hope, or fear, that he will be capable of anything except allowing his life to become a joke.

And of course the adversary will not let the Christian have the last word: the misunderstandings will be endless, the dialogue interminable. There is little point in carrying it on, for what truly has convinced the Christian is most often of value to him alone. If he speaks of some interior influence which has buried the old passion beneath a living silence, they will respond that he has created the atmosphere in which this sort of feeling can occur because his heart has weakened and he needs time to catch his breath. There is no tribunal for judging such spiritual miracles, nothing like the one at Lourdes where cures of the flesh are evaluated. And even if the spiritual change is obvious in the eyes of everyone, it will never appear as definitive as the remission of a cancer or the healing of a lung. Those who have experienced spiritual miracles continue to live, tremblingly, right next to the misery from which eternal mercy has redeemed them.

They tremble, but their testimonies, which have multiplied over the last quarter century,[78] all agree as to the profound peace they have tasted—and of the fear they have of losing that peace. They tell us that Grace is tangible, aware no doubt that they will not be believed. One of them[79] told me that for years he had only lived for the brief interactions with grace that, each week, were given him. He said that he was not exactly happy during these moments of presence, but that only then was he without suffering, and the rest of his time was nothing but sorrow or sickness. He knew that his desires were extreme, for if we cannot expect any corporal creature to be always with us, how can we demand a constant interior spiritual union? He told me that he was quite aware of his folly, that he had no hope of ever attaining his desire, but that time (which he had hoped would cure him) only made the mysterious desire stronger, enriching it with his daily sorrow, giving it the stamp of eternity. Even though he worked prolifically, his days seemed interminable to him, because they were horribly empty of the one thing he desired. Time became his executioner, whom a thousand daily tasks could not kill. The absence of grace made time into a yawning gulf into which he would have thrown anything to achieve his desire. How much did he throw into it? He did not say; perhaps everything would have seemed a reasonable price for filling in this abyss. What dishonors a man is almost never his love, no matter how carnal it may be, but rather what he replaces it with. He does replace it—until the day when he finds that this love itself has taken over a place destined for Another.

If I have interpreted his words correctly, this man has been saved by a miracle, and he now rests his faith on a rigorous conformity between his desire and the God he finally possesses. A little image made of flesh and blood, a sham resembling the Divine, suddenly falls away like a mask, and now the true Face appears along with the true flesh and the true blood.

And this is the miracle, the tangible sign as he described it to me: after a long period of interior uproar, of the sort that makes a soul mad, suddenly a prodigious silence descended, a supernatural calm, a peace above all other peace. The soul was now no longer alone and was waiting for no one—it continued to love, but now it carried its love in prayer as an eagle carries a lamb. He incorporated this eagle and lamb image into his new-found joy, associating it closely with this unhoped-for salvation. As the eagle mounted with the lamb upward into the light, unknown reasons for their encounter, unsuspected perspectives revealed themselves. And finally arose the hope of never being separated, a hope so sweet that the heart can hardly bear to face it. In this sense, then, it is absurd to say that God demands to be the only one we love; what He wants, rather, is for each of our loves to be contained within His love.

I replied to the man that one cannot embrace or hold on to the spirit, and that thus our body seeks out likenesses from our own species and, failing to find that spiritual union, it grows unquiet. And then this body's dead weight quickly becomes terribly live weight, making demands on us, like a beast of prey. This objection led him to talk to me about the Eucharist. An instinctive Jansenism had always kept me from seeing why frequent communion is necessary, particularly for those of a fiery nature. He said to me that the Real Presence is the real occupying army of our flesh, guarding all the gates and keeping surveillance on all the weak points. The creature wants this presence madly—and here it is, granted to us. As this man put it, it is not a matter of nerves, emotions, or effusions. No, it is simply that Someone is there who takes on all the capacities of a person who, otherwise, continues his normal life. He reads, works, chats with a friend. But even amid the world's noisy celebrations a single moment of remembrance is enough—as if, in a crowd, your hand is furtively pressed, as if you suddenly sensed a warm breath, as if you abruptly caught sight of a love that the others cannot see; a sign and symbol of collaboration, a miraculous security. He asked me, "Who was it who dared to write that Christianity has no part in the flesh?"[80] I dared not tell him that it had been me, and I could not help but lower my head.

Notes

1. Paul Claudel, "Saint Jude," in *Corona Benignatatis Anni Dei*: "Jude, with a single hair, saves and draws up to heaven/The man of letters, the assassin, and the brothel girl." Mauriac professes shock here that the writer is classed with the most flagrant sinners; but there is added flavor to the juxtaposition when we recall that Jude is usually regarded as the patron saint of hopeless causes.

2. Charles Baudelaire, "Au Lecteur" [To the Reader], the prefatory poem to *Les Fleurs du mal* [translated as *Flowers of Evil*].

3. Bossuet, "Sermon sur l'endurcissement" [Sermon on Hardening], originally preached on December 1, 1669. Bossuet's sermon is concerned with the sleep of the conscience, with hardening of the heart. In the passage from which Mauriac quotes, Bossuet describes the sinner's conscience as the voice of God within him, keeping him in a state of conflict with sin; but some, he warns, have let this voice be stifled and so have become fully engaged in their sins. These are the ones who have abolished the "august tribunal" of conscience. Mauriac quotes from the same passage in his *Souffrances et bonheur du chrétien* [translated as *Anguish and Joy of the Christian Life*] (published in segments in the *Nouvelle Revue Française* in 1928, 1929, and 1931), which grew out of what was originally intended to be a commentary on Bossuet. Clearly, Bossuet's impassioned call to religious awakening and a new awareness of the immanence of God's judgment had a deep effect on Mauriac in these years. And it is quite relevant to recall that Bossuet came to express a deep distrust of imaginative literature as essentially immoral, and that he lived in an age when such a distrust was very widespread, profoundly troubling even the greatest dramatist of the age, Racine.

4. Jacques Petit (1345) points out that this passage evidently refers to Gide and his sexual confessions in *Corydon* and *Si le grain ne meurt* [trans-

53

lated as *If It Die*], but that Mauriac does not specify Gide in order to
avoid what would seem to be a personal attack. Indeed, Mauriac would
hardly have needed the example of Gide, as the confessional literature he
describes was very widespread, to the point of becoming a hallmark of
modernism not only in France but throughout European literature. Still,
for Mauriac, Gide remained the exemplar of the modern Rousseauistic
obsession with self in his writings: in his *Mémoires intérieurs*, he allows
that "most modern authors find in themselves the matter of their books,"
but that "André Gide never revealed anything but André Gide" (trans.
Gerard Hopkins; New York: Farrar, Straus & Cudahy, 1961; 101-105).

5. Mauriac had essentially said this in a 1924 interview with Frédéric
   Lefèvre in the "An Hour With . . ." series. His exact words—which
   caused him much regret in years to come—were, "I am a novelist and I
   am a Catholic, and there lies the conflict" (quoted in Petit, 1345).

6. A paraphrase of Flaubert's famous dictum, "The author in his book
   should be like God in the universe: Present everywhere, but visible
   nowhere." Flaubert made the statement in a letter to Louise Colet of
   December 9, 1852.

7. Mauriac's humor in this passage derives from his playful use of the sort
   of terms used in discussions of the Holy Trinity, notably of the composite
   self that "proceeds from" the others.

8. The anecdote alluded to is said to have taken place when the philosophers Nicolas Malebranche (1638-1715) and Bernard Le Bovier de Fontenelle (1657-1757) were walking together. Malebranche kicked one of
   his pregnant dogs, and in response to Fontenelle's shock, said, "But don't
   you understand? It can't feel anything." The anecdote demonstrates Malebranche's bizarre (by modern standards) theories of causation and per-
   ception: nothing happens that is not willed by God, and we do not feel or
   perceive things themselves (such as the pregnant dog), but only the idea
   of the things. Mauriac made use of the anecdote again in 1954, in an article on peace in Indochina. There, he tries to rouse the reader out of apathy about the issue, saying that the French public's apathy makes certain
   policymakers see them as like the dog of Malebranche: "They don't feel
   anything." The essay is reprinted in Jacques Touzot, ed., *La Paix des
   cimes* [Peace on the Heights], 449-451.

9. These critics are exempted from the charge Mauriac brings against critics
   and reviewers generally, that they are deadline-driven and thus have no
   time to formulate any valuable insights into the books they discuss. In
   the original manuscript, Mauriac made no exceptions; he added these
   names in his revision.

Henry Bidou (1873-1943) wrote reviews of literature, art and theater. He is best remembered for his popular 1937 history of Paris.

Gabriel Marcel (1889-1973) went on to become a distinguished Christian philosopher and dramatist. He converted to Catholicism in 1929, and his work seeks to blend the Catholic vision of hope with contemporary existentialist thought.

Edmond Jaloux (1878-1949) was a prolific critic and novelist. His reputation for elegance of style and critical insight was well established by the time Mauriac wrote *God and Mammon*. He wrote a thoughtful essay, "François Mauriac, Romancier" which appeared as a preface to Mauriac's *Le Romancier et ses personnages* [The Novelist and his Characters], (Paris: Correa, 1933).

Albert Thibaudet (1874-1936) was the leading literary critic of the *Nouvelle Revue Française* at this time, and probably enjoyed the highest contemporary reputation of all the critics Mauriac lists here, though his work will seem dated to the modern reader.

Ramon Fernandez (1894-1944), Mexican-born, was a novelist and critic of considerable intellectual power; he became an outspoken antifascist in the 1930s. He wrote an important study of *God and Mammon*, which is discussed in the Introduction.

Charles Du Bos (1882-1939), to whom *God and Mammon* is dedicated, was a close friend of Mauriac during the period of his religious crisis, having converted to Catholicism himself in 1927; his book on Mauriac is discussed in the Introduction. His critical essays were collected in a successive series of volumes titled *Approximations*, which are still in print today. His last years were spent teaching at the University of Notre Dame in the United States.

10. Petit points out that, in an early manuscript, Mauriac had written, "Just when you have classified him as a Catholic . . .". Making this revision allows Mauriac to defer his chief subject a bit, and allows him to continue speaking of authors and critics generally.

11. Zoilus is a traditional name for an unreasonable critic. The original Zoilus lived in the 4th century BC, and wrote attacks on major figures such as Plato and Homer. He criticized Homer, in particular, for the insufficiency of his inventiveness—which is rather like criticizing Everest for not being large enough.

12. May 27, 1928

My Dear Mauriac,

You may not have personally sent me the copy of your Jean Racine that I'm reading, as it has no dedication, but I want to thank you for having written the book. It is truly an admirable book (a word I hardly ever use about contemporary works). It may be pointless for me to tell you how it touched me; you have made it clear that you thought of me from time to time in writing it. Ah, how grateful I feel to you for your having cut the great man down to size; anything is better than a plaster idol. Let Souday speak about "calumny," but let us agree that Racine has been greatly diminished, or at any rate deprived of his halo at your hands. Your knowledge of the human is deeper here, I think, than in one of your novels, and I believe I prefer the author of Racine to the disturbing author of Destins.

May I make one small remark? You write (page 132) that "despite the fable, nothing is less criminal than Phaedra's anxiety." But, my dear friend, even as you extenuate the incestuous character of her love (falsely incestuous, true; I agree wholly with you on this point), you must not forget that her passion remains an adulterous one. Is this what you call a bit later "the most ordinary love"? Everything you go on to say on this point is highly interesting, and would be very accurate—if only it were not based on a false premise.

I wrote all this before having finished the book. Your final chapters are no less good. In fact they may be the very best ones, or at any rate the most skilful. But the very last chapter forces me to restrict my praise! When you speak there of my "anxiety," there is some misapprehension. The anxiety is on your side, not on mine. This is precisely what bothered Claudel so much: I am not a tormented being. I never understood this so well until I read your book, which also showed me that what makes you most Christian is your anxiety. But despite the twists and turns of your specious thought, the aging Racine's Christian point of view and yours as a Christian novelist differ to the point of actual opposition. Racine gives thanks to God for having recognized him as one of His own despite the tragedies that he wishes he had not written, that he spoke of burning (because he understood much better than Massis had that startling statement, "There is no work of art without the collaboration of the devil"). But you rejoice that God, before seizing Racine, left him enough time to write the tragedies, to write them despite his conversion. In short, what you were looking for was permission to write Destins, the permission to be a Christian without having to burn your books; and it is this that makes you write them in such a way that, as a Christian, you won't have to disavow them. All this (this soothing compromise that lets you love God without losing sight of Mammon), all this is, for us readers, worth that anguished conscience that makes your face so attractive, that gives such a savor to your works, and that ends up giving so much pleasure to those who, while abhorring sin, would be very sorry to have to give up their preoccupation with it.

You know what this would do to literature, and to your own in particular; and you are not enough of a Christian to cease being a writer. Your great art is making your readers into your accomplices. Your books are less capable of bringing Christianity to the sinner than they are of reminding the Christian that there is something else on the earth besides heaven.

I once wrote, to the great annoyance of some, that "one makes bad literature out of beautiful sentiments." Your literature, dear Mauriac, is excellent. No doubt I would follow you less enthusiastically if I were more of a Christian.

Believe me your good friend,

André Gide [Mauriac's note. See the Introduction for a discussion of Gide's letter and its context and ramifications.]

13. *Pensée 606* in the Brunschvicg edition.

14. Mauriac's childhood friend André Lacaze. Mauriac based the character of Maryan on him in his 1928 short story, "Le Démon de la connaissance" (The Demon of Knowledge), and Lacaze is also the model for the character of André Donzac in the late novel, *Un Adolescent d'autrefois.* Mauriac also describes him affectionately in his autobiography, *Nouveaux Mémoires intérieurs*, as being extremely important in his intellectual development: the young Lacaze, far from being one of the "pious" Catholics, was intellectually adventurous and felt that the Catholic should not dismiss or condemn modernism but understand it and adapt to it.

15. Anatole France (1844-1924), winner of the 1921 Nobel Prize, wrote a great deal of anticlerical satire, the best of which is his 1908 novel, *Penguin Island*, which begins with the tale of a missionary with bad eyesight who inadvertently baptizes a set of penguins.

16. Ernest Psichari (1883-1914) wrote novels, travel writing, and a journal—the latter, *Les Voix qui crient dans le désert* [Voices Crying Out in the Wilderness] chronicles his religious conversion. He was killed in action in the first year of World War I. Jacques Maritain (1882-1973) is of course the great neo-Thomist Catholic philosopher. The Benedictine chapel to which Mauriac refers is in the Rue Monsieur, and in the prewar years was a favorite chapel for many writers, including Huysmans (who lived for a time in its monastery), Claudel, and Jacques Rivière. In *What Was Lost*, Alain hears the chapel's bell ringing.

17. Petit notes that in Mauriac's early novel, *La Robe prétexte* [translated as *The Stuff of Youth*], he refers to this textbook as "simplistic" and "peremptory" (Petit, 1347).

18. The esthete turned convert Huysmans wrote ecstatically of liturgy and music in, for example, the autobiographical novel *En Route* (1895) and in his poetic celebration of Chartres, *La Cathédrale* (1898). The objective modern reader will be struck by the way in which Huysmans seems to be subsuming religion into aesthetics, rather than the other way around. Huysmans eroticizes Catholic liturgy and music so thoroughly that he inadvertently reminds us of Flaubert's confused Emma Bovary. This would be heady reading for an adolescent such as Mauriac describes himself.

19. *Mains jointes* [Clasped Hands, as in prayer] was Mauriac's first publication, in 1909. In later life, he often spoke with distaste of these poems because of what he saw as their too easy, too uncritical tone and content. The eminent writer Maurice Barrès (1862-1923) wrote the review Mauriac alludes to here and, in effect, made a literary life possible for him. Mauriac paid tribute to him and to what he had done for him in his *La Rencontre avec Barrès* [Meeting Barrès], (1945). He also gives the young writer Yves Frontenac, in the novel *Le Mystère Frontenac* (1933), his own encounter with Barrès.

20. *By this I mean the pious aesthetic of the salon. But within this reading I also discovered some admirable souls and some true poets like my friend André Lafon, the fervent Robert Vallery-Radot, Eusèbe de Bremond d'Ars, etc.* [Mauriac's note]

21. Petit notes that the first draft makes it plain Mauriac was thinking of Gide here: it read, "His "Return of the Prodigal Son" remains the most seductive and dangerous alteration of the Gospel . . ." (Petit, 1347). Gide's 1907 multi-leveled fable is indeed an "alteration," as the prodigal returns home to find his father absent and his elder brother, who is obsessed with duty and restriction, in charge. Gide here, as elsewhere, takes a biblical text and rethinks it in order to get at the dominant theme of all his works, the pursuit of the true self and the obstacles the world puts between us and that pursuit. Mauriac had reviewed the book back in 1912, and Gide—who at that time he had not yet met—wrote him an impassioned letter criticizing Mauriac's use of the word "sacrilege" with regard to the book. "I wrote those pages," Gide objected, "with piety and respect." See Mauriac's essay, "Les Catholiques autour d'André Gide," in *Hommage à André Gide* (Paris: Nouvelle Revue Française, 1951), 103-107.

22. The word "sublimation" here should be understood not just in its Freudian, psychological sense, but also in the sense of "making sublime."

23. From Corneille's tragedy, *Sertorius* (1662), Act III: "Rome is no longer in Rome; she is wherever I am." The play concerns the conflict between Sertorius, a patriotic general, and the Roman senate, led by Pompey,

which is ranged against him. The allusion allows Mauriac subtly to align himself with the heroic Sertorius.

24. Edouard Estaunié's 1896 novel, *L'Empreinte* [Imprinting], is concerned with how religious education forms the sensibility of a young writer. The novel, little read today, was significant in its time as part of the controversy over the secularization of education in France.

25. Abbé Henri Perreyve (1831-1865) made an impression on the young Mauriac; he alludes to his work in his first novel, *L'Enfant chargé de chaînes* (1913, translated as *The Young Man in Chains*), where his characters read "the burning and sweet pages of" Perreyve and the great Dominican preacher Lacordaire.

26. Pascal, "Prayer Asking God for a Good Use of Sickness." Mauriac gives considerable emphasis to this prayer in his biographical study, *Blaise Pascal et sa soeur Jacqueline* [Blaise Pascal and his Sister Jacqueline], (Paris: Hachette, 1931, 65-69). Mauriac believes the prayer was written in 1646 or 1647 and that it is evidence that Pascal was converted long before the famous night in 1654 that most scholars say was the crucial moment; he says that Pascal's sickness stripped away his pride and opened his eyes to the mystery of Christ.

27. Daniel Halévy, *Jules Michelet* (Paris: Hachette, 1928), 68-69.

28. Matthew 27:40 and Mark 15:30.

29. While this passage is disturbing, the reader should recall that Mauriac was writing three decades before Vatican II significantly revised the Church's views on nonChristian faith traditions. And similar bigotry is rare—to my knowledge, nonexistent—elsewhere in Mauriac's writings.

30. Philippians 4:7, "The peace of God that surpasses all understanding."

31. These are Rimbaud's words as reported by his "angelic" sister Isabelle, in a letter of October 28, 1891.

32. Claudel wrote a preface to a 1912 edition of Rimbaud's works. Rimbaud was important to Claudel as a sort of spiritual father: in 1912, he went on a pilgrimage to several of the places Rimbaud had lived, and was greatly moved to see the table on which Rimbaud had written *Une Saison en enfer* [A Season in Hell] because on the table was "a radiating cross carved with the point of a knife" (Louis Chaigne, *Paul Claudel: The Man and The Mystic*, trans. Pierre de Fontnouvelle, New York: Appleton-Century Crofts, 1961, 140).

33. From Rimbaud's *A Season in Hell*, trans. Louise Varèse (New York: New Directions, 1961), 19-21. Both quotations are from the section titled "Mauvais Sang" ("Bad Blood").

34. Rimbaud, trans. Varèse, 39-41. This is from the section titled "Delirium."

35. As Petit notes (1351), the evidence of the chaplain's words comes from the letter of Isabelle Rimbaud to her mother, so Mauriac's Christian interpretation of Rimbaud's life and death is based on debatable evidence.

36. Mauriac here returns to the story of the Prodigal Son and, by implication, returns to a direct confrontation with Gide.

37. Charles Péguy, *Un nouveau théologien: M. Fernand Laudet* (1911). Péguy's essay, like *God and Mammon*, is a Catholic writer's response to Catholic critics of his recent work, specifically of his long poem, *Mystère de la charité de Jeanne d'Arc* (1910).

38. See Matthew 26: 69-75, Mark 14: 66-72, Luke 22: 56-60, and John 18: 25-27, for the different versions of Peter's denial of Christ.

39. Mauriac reflects on the failure of all Barrès' political hopes, and the emptiness left to him thereafter, in his 1938 *La Rencontre avec Barrès*.

40. *Nothing But The Earth (Rien que la terre)* is a novel by Paul Morand (1888-1976), and *Hunted Travellers (Voyageurs traqués)* is by Henry de Montherlant (1868-1971). Mauriac uses them as examples of writers with no spiritual allegiance, and their later lives would have given him further evidence for his attitude: Morand would be disgraced because of his involvement with the Vichy government, and Montherlant, also tainted by collaboration with the Nazi occupiers, would take his own life after a long career as novelist and playwright.

41. Julien Sorel and Fabrice del Dongo are the young heroes of Stendhal's great novels—respectively, *The Red and the Black* (1830) and *The Charterhouse of Parma* (1839). Both are often seen as pre-Nietzschean heroes exhibiting the "will to power," though Stendhal's humor and irony keep them from being only that.

42. The phrase echoes the opening line of Dante's *Inferno*, "Nel mezzo del camin de nostra vita . . .".

43. See note 27.

44. Henri Beyle (1783-1842) took the pen name of Stendhal in 1817.

45. Adapted from *A Poet's Journal* by Alfred de Vigny (1797-1863).

46. *The material in this chapter is taken from a conference I attended last year on the subject of "The Novelist's Responsibilities." I would not write about it in quite this same way today. Henceforth, for me the whole question comes down to this: purify the source.* [Mauriac's note.] The conference took place in June 1928; Mauriac's "conversion" took place in October-November of that year.

47. Gide, *Treatise on Narcissus* (1891-1892). The theme of this brief poetic essay concerns the artist's role as a causer of scandal, and his inevitable

treatment as a scapegoat as a result. Mauriac's quote implies that the essay argues for "art for art's sake," but Gide's point is subtler than that, and in fact he says the artist must serve truth above all else.

48. From a letter of May 1913, from Psichari to the Catholic novelist Paul Bourget (1852-1935).

49. *La Vie de Jean Racine* had appeared in the *Revue universelle* for December 1927 and January 1928. Mauriac's self-deprecatory tone here belies both the seriousness with which he took the task and the quality of the biography.

50. Pierre Nicole (1625-1695), the polemical theologian affiliated with the Jansenists at Port-Royal, wrote his sequence of letters known as *Les Imaginaires* from 1664 onward. Racine, having failed in his attempt to find a career in the church, had recently begun his literary work in Paris, and his first tragedy, *La Thébaide*, was performed in 1664. Racine responded to Nicole with his anonymous *Letter to the Author of 'Les Imaginaires'* in 1666. Nicole treated this letter scornfully in his 1667 edition of *Les Imaginaires*. Racine was infuriated, and wrote an even harsher reply; his friends prevailed on him not to publish it. Both letters are reprinted in Pierre Clarac's edition, *Racine: oeuvres complètes* (Paris: Éditions du Seuil, 1962), 307-314.

51. "Les Phares" ("Beacons") is poem VI in *Les Fleurs du mal*. Note that Mauriac returns to this poem in the novel *What Was Lost*.

52. Baudelaire, untitled poem XXXIX of *Les Fleurs du mal* ("Je te donne ces vers . . ."), translated by Richard Howard: *Les Fleurs du mal* (Boston: David R. Godine, 1982), 45.

53. Gide quoted Flaubert to this effect (cited in Petit, 1354). The role of "demoralizer" is close to the role of the artist as Gide described it in his *Treatise of Narcissus* (see note 46), and the idea of course is a descendant of Plato's image of the philosopher as gadfly.

54. Sophie Rostopchine, Countess de Ségur (1799-1874) was a highly successful children's writer—whose books, incidentally, are not as prudish as Mauriac seems to imply.

55. On the Abbé Bethléem and his list of forbidden novels, see the Introduction.

56. This passage may sound as if Mauriac dismissed Proust, but he in fact had a deep appreciation for his work, as revealed in his 1947 study, *Du côté de chez Proust*—parts of which had already been written in 1926.

57. Augustine, *Confessions*, Book III, Chapter II. In the J. G. Pilkington translation, the passage reads: "Stage-plays led me away, full as they were of my own miseries and of fuel to my fire. Why is it that man

wishes to be made sad in watching tragical sufferings which he would himself not wish to undergo? As an onlooker he wishes to experience from them a sense of grief, and this very grief is his pleasure. What is this but wretched insanity?" (London: Folio, 1993), 42.

58. Bossuet, *Maximes et réflexions sur la comédie* (Maxims and Reflections on the Theater), Chapter VIII (1694).

59. Gide wrote this aphorism in his 1923 essay, *Dostoevski* (637 of Pierre Masson, ed., *André Gide: Essais et critiques*: Paris: Gallimard, 1999).

60. From Jacques Maritain's 1920 study, *Art et scolastique*, an early example of Maritain's attempt to apply Thomas Aquinas' thinking to modern problems.

61. *Since these lines were written, Maritain responded to me in an issue of the* Roseau d'or *(#30) thus: "Do you think I mean that the novelist must be isolated from his characters, like a scientist conducting an experiment in a laboratory? Really, has there ever been a fictional character who did not live in his author, and his author in him? This is not the result of some metamorphosis, but rather it is through a profound analogy that the art of the novel is situated within the theological light of the mystery of creation itself." Further on, he says: "The novelist's role is not that of the scholar. The scholar only works with ideas, and is only concerned with truth. He writes only for a specialized audience.*

    "The novelist has a virtually unlimited sphere of influence. Only rarely are his readers the ones for whom he has designed his message (and they are a very small number). He knows this. He profits from it. And he continues. This unlimited public makes the problem more and more difficult . . .".

    Later, Maritain denounces what he sees as a Manichean tendency in me, saying: "The redemptive Blood of Christ, which can make a man into a friend of God, can also, if it touches them, exorcise art and the novel."

    Today, I realize how much I owe to the profound charity Maritain showed me in these pages of the Roseau d'or. [Mauriac's note.]

62. The novelist Emile Zola coined the term "naturalism" in the 1860s to denote a scientific approach to writing the novel: the novelist was to be a detached observer, reporting with a clinical objectivity. Zola's monumental work is the series of twenty Rougon-Macquart novels that tried to depict how environment and heredity together affected a single family. The naturalist school was long dead by the 1920s—killed off, in part, by writers like Gide and Proust who were deeply involved in, and even acted as characters in, their works.

63. On the Abbé Perreyve, see note 25.

64. Petit notes that Gide protested against this slight misquotation and greater misunderstanding of him (1354-1355). In the *Dostoevski* essay cited in note 59, he had said "One makes bad literature with fine sentiments." In fact, what Mauriac goes on to say in the following sentences is very nearly what Gide actually meant: Gide went on in his essay to add a note Mauriac essentially makes here, that "there are no artists among the saints; there are no saints among the artists" (638 of *Essais critiques*, cited above).

65. The references are to the English Catholic novelist, Robert Hugh Benson (1871-1914), the Italian Antonio Fogazzaro (1842-1911), and the French Émile Baumann (1868-1941) and Georges Bernanos (1888-1948). Bernanos' first novel, referred to in the next paragraph, was the 1926 *Sous le soleil de Satan* [translated as *The Star of Satan*] which involves the struggle between a young priest and the devil—a struggle that is the keynote of most of Bernanos' fiction.

66. The line occurs in Bossuet's letter of March 3, 1674 (Petit).

67. *In support of my opinion, I find a page on the "proofs of the spiritual life" in an admirable book by the Abbess de Sainte-Cécile of Solesmes, titled* Spiritual Life and Prayer: *"The soul is certain that it has committed no new fault; it knows that God has revealed His immense love innumerable times . . . but the new enlightenment reveals the soul's weakness so vividly that it can find no consolation or the least help in the memory of that love. The soul feels it has never done anything well or anything good, that it is the very embodiment of imperfection and of evil . . .".* [Mauriac's note.]

68. Petit notes that Bossuet's words, from one of his sermons, are not quite as Mauriac remembers them: "some follow nature, and others follow grace" (1355).

69. Petit notes (1357) that the exact phrase does not occur in Novalis, but that Mauriac frequently quoted it thus.

70. *My dear Mauriac,*

Permit me to protest in a friendly but forceful way against the interpretation you have given to my thought here. The lines you refer to were written following the conversion of Ghéon. We were speaking of repentance and contrition, and he opened up to me warmly, saying that his zeal and his love for Christ were so vivid that he could no longer feel anything but joy. He said it was sufficient for him to have a horror of sin and of anything that could henceforth turn him away from Christ, but that he felt almost incapable of contrition, and was finished with repentance and with gazing at a past that could no longer exist for him.

It was then, in thinking of him, who had been my most intimate friend for so long, that those words of Christ became clear to me. It seemed to me neither admissible nor possible that a complete adherence to the truths of the Gospel wouldn't entail, immediately, a profound contrition, and that the simple disavowal of one's sins, without repentance, would not suffice. And then, with the clarity of a new dawn, I saw the point of those words: "Whoever does not pick up his cross and follow me, is not worthy of me." Which is to say, "whoever pretends to follow me without first picking up his cross . . .". And this showed me the error in the way this passage is usually translated; I resolved to stick strictly to the Vulgate in the future. The idea of identifying oneself entirely with the cross, and of transforming this redemptive instrument of pain into a voluptuous pillow—such an idea had never before flowered for me.

André Gide [Mauriac's note.]

Mauriac had written an essay, "The Gospel According to André Gide," for a collection titled *Homage to André Gide* (Paris: Capitole, 1928). Gide's letter was printed as a response to this essay; only a part of the letter was reprinted in *God and Mammon*. In his article, Mauriac had disputed Gide's interpretation of Matthew 10:38, the verse in question here.

Henri Ghéon (1875-1944) was the pen name of Henri-Léon Vangéon. A critic and poet, he was a close friend of Gide since their first meeting in 1897. He was one of the founders of the *Nouvelle Revue Française*. He had abandoned Catholicism, but was reconverted while in military service in 1916. Thereafter, he wrote some fifty religious plays of uneven quality.

71. From Pascal's 1654 "Memorial," the written record of his conversion experience. Mauriac italicizes the last words, "et à mon directeur," in order to give even greater emphasis to the idea of submission.

72. Epictetus (50-120), the Stoic philosopher, was born a slave, and in his lectures (later written down by Arrian) he argued passionately that one's mind can never be enslaved.

73. Epistle to the Hebrews, 12:29.

74. The theme and even the imagery in this paragraph recall many of Mauriac's novels, from *Flesh and Blood* and *Genitrix* to *Thérèse Desqueyroux*.

75. The man Mauriac is describing now begins to sound a great deal like André Gide, especially the Gide of works like *Saül* and *Les Nourritures terrestres* [translated as *The Fruits of the Earth*], who calls on us to glory in our humanness, including our sensual orientation. The rest of the para-

graph is increasingly obvious in its reference to Gide, who was deeply admired by young readers.

76. The phrase "reasons of the heart" echoes Pascal's *Pensées*, "Le coeur a ses raisons que le raison ne connaît point." the heart has its reasons, which reason does not know (*Pensée* 277 in the Brunschvicg edition, and 423 in Lafuma).

77. "Seigneur je vous donne tout" appears toward the end of Pascal's document, "Le Mystère de Jésus." It was written in early 1655, shortly after Pascal's conversion experience, but it remained unknown and unpublished until 1844.

78. Among the well known conversions of French writers in this period were those of Paul Claudel, Francis Jammes, Henri Ghéon, and Charles Du Bos.

79. The man described here has not been identified, but Petit points out (1359) that in some respects he is similar to the main characters of Mauriac's short stories, "Coups de couteau" ("Knife Wounds," 1926) and "Insomnie" ("Insomnia," 1929).

80. This is the opening sentence of Mauriac's *Souffrances du chrétien* (and of course a major theme in the work of Bossuet). Thus the meditation in *God and Mammon* at last brings us out of the spiritual cul-de-sac in which Mauriac had been suffering.

What Was Lost

I

"I feel better already," said Irène de Blénauge. "We could have stayed a bit longer."

The car was dark, but although she could not see her husband's face, she knew very well its expression, that air of irritation he put on whenever he had had to cut short the slightest pleasure.

She said, "It was you, after all, who gave me the sign to leave."

"Had to be done, dearest. You were starting to look awful."

After six years of marriage, Irène was still enduring this same melange of tender words and insolent ones, just as she had on the first day.

"I regret it, anyway, all the more," she replied, "because you were in good form tonight. I've never seen you quite so brilliant." But now, she thought, she should say no more: what was the good of irritating him?

"I doubt I showed all that much brilliance with you there. When I know that you will gather up the slightest thing I say and pass it through a sieve, —what's the matter, Irène?"

The headlights of the car behind had lit them up for a moment, and he saw his young wife's shudder. "It'll pass. But it's high time I got in. It's time for my medicine."

Her tone softened, as if a moment of real sorrow had called her back to the order of things: "Listen, Hervé: I wish that, when you're out among people, you were more often on your guard. People push you to talk too much, and then afterwards they judge you."

He protested, though without much assurance, that for tonight he was sure of his innocence. Irène interrupted him.

"You know very well what I'm talking about, and you know very well what it was that you said tonight. Why must you pretend not to under-

stand me?" She said this heatedly, a very ill person no longer able to control herself. She had never gotten used to Hervé's lies, to that state of
constant untruth in which he lived almost without knowing it. "You were
very hard on your friend Marcel Revaux."

"Oh! *My* friend! You're the one he admires so, the one he praises to
the skies. Have you forgotten that he never even told me about his getting
married?"

"Yes," she said, "you detest him utterly. So much so that I sometimes
wonder if he isn't the only person who really counts for you. I know
you'll never forgive him for that phone call . . ."

Then, in that forced gay tone that, with her, always had a funereal
effect, she imitated Marcel Revaux's voice: "Oh, by the way, I forgot to
tell you that I got married today."

Hervé responded dryly that he had different reasons than hers for
finding that amusing. He added that he had not had any falling-out with
Marcel, but still tonight he couldn't help letting people know what he
thought of him.

"You certainly did that," she replied. "You made him sound loathsome."

"What did I say that was so bad? I said that his genius—and I did use
the word genius—was all back in his youth. And I said that if there are
people who are enriched by living, Marcel was the type who became
poorer every year. He hasn't written anything in ages, and his only interest nowadays is money. You're the only one who still denies that he's a
has-been. In 1918, young men could see themselves in even the slightest
of his pieces. He could do or write anything then without incurring any
criticism . . ."

"Yes," she answered with irritation, "and you've had the gall to speak
about him in front of everyone, to speak openly about his affair with
Marie Chavès. You even referred to some old gossip . . ." Her indignation
seethed within her, the indignation of a humiliated wife. She wished that
Hervé himself could be exposed for what he was in front of the people
who listened to him tonight.

He went on, protesting that Marcel's scandal was public knowledge,
that everyone had seen him ostentatiously spending Marie's money. It
couldn't have been his father, a simple shop employee in the Galeries,
who had filled his pockets for him. "Everything I said tonight, I would
repeat to his face."

"No!" she interrupted. "You know perfectly well that you wouldn't
dare. Anyway, do you know why it is that Marcel keeps you at a distance?"

Hervé denied it. "The other day, he invited me to come by and surprise him, like I used to do. I used to stand on the sidewalk and see whether there was a light on in his room. Then I'd just go up . . ."

Irène sighed. "My poor Hervé! You're forgetting that you told me this just last night, but then you gave it quite a different meaning. You told me that he said, 'Come up if you see the light. But nowadays, unfortunately, you won't be likely to see it. Tota likes to go out at night, and on the rare nights when we're home, we stay mostly in the other room, the one facing onto the courtyard.' Besides, he's never even introduced you to his Tota."

Her perpetual repetition of his words never failed to infuriate him. She would go to her grave loving nothing better than making him contradict himself.

"Once again, dearest, you've managed to misunderstand me. When I told you that, you were undoubtedly half asleep. Or your medicine had made you woozy. I assure you you're quite wrong."

She only gave out a short laugh and said, "We'll see, Hervé!" Which made him feel like a little boy caught in a lie.

"The truth is," he said, vexed, "that I plan, yet tonight, to walk over to the Rue Vaneau, and if there's a light on in Marcel's window—"

"There won't be."

"—Then I will come back home."

"No," she said sweetly, "you know very well you won't."

They drove through the dark Bois de Boulogne, and she could not read Hervé's expression, that aging rumpled face with its two clear eyes proclaiming youth and innocence. As they neared the Place de la Concorde, she suddenly said, "Stay home with me tonight, Hervé. I don't feel well."

She was breathing with difficulty. Furtively he glanced at her, her white face, her thin bird's neck where a little ribbon of muscle throbbed.

"You know," he said, "that when you've taken your pills you'll go to sleep, and I won't be any help to you then. As for me, I want to stretch a bit, go for a walk. I won't be able to sleep otherwise. And it isn't my fault. You put me in this state. But it's not your fault either; I know you're not feeling well. It's your nerves. Anyone else would be a lot more irritable, I'm sure."

He didn't see Irène's shoulders rise and fall in a sigh. She could only respond that he was right, and that she would be fine. He helped her out of the car and rang the bell.

"If I see Marcel, I promise you I'll repeat to him everything I said tonight."

She only just kept herself from replying, "You know, though, that you won't see him." She did say, "I'm sure that the next time you meet, you'll let him hear plenty of disagreeable things. But you'll package them quite differently than you did tonight. After all, you're so very wellbred." And she went in, closing the door behind her.

He watched her silhouette through the window. She was almost spectral as she moved with slow, short steps along the wall.

HERVÉ walked quickly, muttering insults: "Idiot. Horrible woman. Why doesn't she die ..." But he also knew that he had been afraid to let his invalid wife go in the house alone. It bothered him that she knew what he was going to do with his freedom tonight.

"But no!" he said half aloud. "I didn't lie. I'm going to go to the Rue Vaneau, and if I see a light in Marcel's window, I'll go up."

And yet he knew there would be no light. And he knew that he would hail the first taxi that passed, and he knew what address he would give the driver. Or no: he would get out, instead, at the Place de la Madeline; that would be more prudent.

The light rain and the gentle wind smelled fresh, smelled like rebirth; how sweet this February night was! Hervé thought of Marcel married, and of how he seemed lucky now, just when one would have thought him all washed up. Hervé had followed Marcel's decline with that bitter enjoyment that people like him find in the misfortune of someone they love. "What a liar he is," Hervé thought. "He used to brag that he'd come to detest writing and authorship and that he'd quite freely given it all up. He found a way to glory in his impotence, and compares himself to Rimbaud ..." Irène refused to see that Marcel had nothing more in him. The liar! And a worse one than I am, if the truth were known. Irène was shocked: was Marcel really living off Marie Chavès? The 100,000 francs he played on the American market obviously came from her: where else? And despite this, Irène continued to have respect for Marcel.

Marcel was just as culpable in his dealings with his father: ashamed of being his son, he disavowed him. Even there, Irène approved. She thought he owed it to his genius to break ties with the little people who couldn't understand him. She saw sublime motives behind his basest acts.

"It's because she admires his character: people don't judge us for our acts, but for our characters. And how he treated me!" Hervé again gnawed on this latest insult over the phone: in the middle of unimportant chatter, Marcel had simply added, "I forgot to tell you that I'm getting married today."

After crossing the Rue de Babylone, Hervé paced down the sidewalk of the Rue Vaneau, staring upward until he was sure there was no light in the familiar window. But then he realized he had been looking at the wrong floor: there was a single lighted window. So! Marcel was home after all, and in the study, just like before his marriage! What was going on? Maybe his new wife was forcing him to work again—or maybe he was in the room alone despite her. It didn't matter: it was significant that this lamp was lit tonight—not the lamp by the couch, either, but the oil lamp, the one Marcel used when he worked, the one Hervé recalled from their younger days. Taking a phrase from Barrès,[1] they had called it "the studious and romantic lamp." What if he went up anyway, as in those earlier days! The worst that could happen would be for Marcel to escort him politely out the door again. Yet after the insult he'd received tonight, Hervé could not bear anything further from Marcel. "If he puts me out tonight, I'll never see him again. The best plan is to take the initiative— I'll say right away that I'll only be there for a few minutes."

Just as he got in the elevator, the light went out. So he ascended in the darkness, his heart beating fast. And as he went up, the moon shone through the windows, illuminating the stairs. There was no response to his discreet knock. Then he could hear a door opening inside the apartment: he recognized the rapid, heavy steps of Marcel.

"I'm not bothering you, am I? I thought I'd knock and see if you were in."

"Come in. I'm alone."

"Alone? Why alone?"

Hervé was unaware of the mingled surprise and happiness in his own voice, which betrayed him more than he knew. He might have recognized the look on his friend's face—that amused disgust that he had often shown when Hervé appeared. But he was blinded by his own eager curiosity. He felt himself in the grip of a mad, vague hope.

"How could you possibly be alone at this hour?"

Marcel only smiled thinly, and showed him into the study. The lamp shone upon a photo album. Marcel had been pasting photos in it.

"Photos of our trip," he said.

Every picture showed the same young woman's form. Hervé sat on his usual spot on the couch, and saw there were bedclothes piled on it.

Why? Marcel was not sleeping with his wife? Pregnant, maybe, or sick? His innocent eyes glowed. He sat on the quilt carefully. Marcel stood above him; he seemed immense. How he had aged! Now you could safely describe him as old, old and getting fat . . .

"Yes, old friend. She's gone out."

"Alone? You let her go out alone?"

Hervé sensed that he was about to fall into a trap, but he gave in to his demon anyway; he was impotent to disguise his feelings, to hide his profound enjoyment of a crisis. His greedy desire crouched in the deepest part of his soul at all times; he could hide it only until a circumstance like this one revealed it. He knew himself very well, knew how to soften his heart and even make tears come to his eyes—a gift he had retained since childhood—tears that could dissemble his animal thirst for the misery of others. But he did not want to believe in this truth about himself; he preferred to believe those tears were really the overflow of his tender friendship.

But tonight, although his joy was so very strong, he felt an anxiety: a fear that perhaps after all there was nothing wrong with Marcel. He couldn't help feeling the shame of his desire; it contracted his throat, it illuminated him—an aged little child throbbing with a guilty desire. Marcel, standing before him, saw it and felt a wave of fear coming over him; he recovered the air of disgust he usually wore in the presence of his "friend." He felt he had stumbled into what might be a dangerous game. He went on: "Tota went out to look for someone."

There it was, a gift of hope for Hervé. But it had a greater effect than he intended—seeing Hervé's rapt face, he grew afraid again and hastened to add. "Don't worry. She's gone off to pick up her brother. He's coming in on the midnight train."

Hervé sighed and smiled, then said in a tone of forced tenderness with just the hint of a growl below it, "But I didn't know Tota had a brother. After all, what do I know of her, anyway, except that she's the ravishing girl you married?"

"She's not 'ravishing,'" Marcel interrupted, picking up again the tone of mockery he used with Hervé. "Haven't you seen her mouth? Look at these photos. It's a maw! I'm in love with a maw."

Hervé didn't react. "Undoubtedly," he remarked coolly, "but you've never loved the same one for four months in a row . . ."

"You're surprised? You who've gone around saying this wouldn't last three weeks. No, don't deny it, you know very well that everybody here says it—and you know that whatever gossip you spread, I hear about it within a day or two. Saying my marriage won't last, that's trivial. You were right to say it, my old friend, and everybody else is right to repeat it. It's not such an odd prediction. Maybe I should try to explain to you—here's a woman, finally, who doesn't stoop or cringe—she's in control of herself, she's her own person, she's . . ."

He saw the overgrown child's eyes fixed on him, and the face that was nothing but attention, nothing but avid curiosity. He interrupted himself. What need did he have, anyway, to speak about her? But it was in vain that he told himself it would be best to keep quiet, not to speak to this old hateful friend; he burst out: "I'm happy! What a shock—to be able to say I'm happy!"

And, like all the imprudent who dare to say such a thing, Marcel knew that he was lying. "Touch wood," he said. "You won't have a cigarette? Oh, of course—I don't have the right sort for you. I should have realized; it's been long enough . . ."

"Happiness . . ." Hervé repeated. Stupidly, he stared at this man who had just declared himself happy. He reached out and shook Marcel's hand, and he held onto it; Marcel did not remove it, feeling a warmth, a softness in himself because he wanted to express his feelings. And for this moment, Blénauge seemed a true friend; Marcel needed to believe it, to believe him worthy of his confidence. And in truth, for this moment Hervé was worthy. The pressure of his hand, his attentive and faithful expression, his body bent forward, everything about him provoked and welcomed the invincible desire to speak about the self, the desire deep within every human creature. We listen to others only so that they will listen to us. But this attention of Hervé's was no feint: people like him know their powers of listening are their unique gift, and that they would not be tolerated without it.

Hervé said it was a "fine thing" that they could spend a few minutes together like this, as they used to do. "But—why didn't you go with her to the station? Why did you let her go out alone in the middle of the night?" This time no hint of his foul curiosity betrayed him. Marcel, having raised the blind to look out, rested his forehead on the windowpane.

"It's raining, I think. Maybe they'll have trouble finding a taxi. Yes, I was wrong to let her go alone. But I'd promised."

"You promised?"

Marcel sat back down at his desk. Hervé, his head turned away slightly, strove earnestly to keep indifference in his voice. And he resented the effort to show nothing of what he suddenly felt, this instinct in him that was almost never wrong—as if, with an immense effort, he kept an invisible hound on its leash, barking and growling on the scent of some unknown calamity. He didn't have to open his mouth, though, because Marcel went on:

"I was an idiot. I promised Tota I'd keep out of the way while her brother was here."

"She didn't want you to come along to the station? Oh, I see: your brother-in-law and you don't get along."

"Him? Not at all; he likes me very much. He's the one who got Tota to agree to the marriage. I have no illusions about that: if he hadn't given his consent . . ."

He didn't see Blénauge smile. "That's amusing! Your brother-in-law is the one who accepted you? But what about their parents?"

Marcel replied that that was another story, a complicated one. Hervé would have to hear it eventually. Blénauge, in his most candid voice, said that he'd like to hear it. On the couch, in the shadows, he sat as still as the snake on a riverbank charming the birds: confidences were coming; they were already on their way. Out of the corner of his eye he watched Marcel roll a cigarette, hesitate, and say he didn't know where to begin.

"How about last August, in the hotel at Cauterets?" Hervé risked this sweetly, with the air of a child who already knew how the bedtime story began.

Marcel said that Tota and Alain looked so different from each other that he was surprised how easily he took them for brother and sister. The simplest way to get close to Tota was to become friends with her brother. Marcel was able to go in for the treatment at the same time as Alain, his best chance to be friendly to this country boy . . .

"It's only fair to say that you don't expect to please people," Hervé said; "every time it happens, you're surprised."

But Marcel protested that in this case it was a miracle. Could Hervé imagine the atmosphere on this estate, in this godforsaken country of the Gironde, the Entre-Deux-Mers, where Tota and Alain Forcas were born, where they had lived? This had given him an idea: their father had never consented to the idea of a season in Cauterets, even though the state of his throat demanded it. It finally took his paralysis, which made him dependent on his wife, for it to happen. This fortunate attack additionally allowed his two children to attend the University at Bordeaux; up to that time, the village schoolteacher had sufficed for their whole education: by good luck, he was a well-educated young man, having been relegated to teaching in this pit because of some communist mischief. Since the attack of paralysis, their mother, up till then a serf, had got her hands on the beast's leash . . .

"But I'm boring you, aren't I, with these country stories."

Hervé assured him that such stories put him to sleep when they appeared in novels, but not in real life.

"So, you were saying that your mother-in-law . . ."

Marcel had only spoken with her once; she had produced an extraordinary impression on him: she had a great resistive force, the kind one only finds among the women of these families. For years, she had had to learn both how to submit and how to stand up to her tyrant. He hated her only scarcely more than he hated his own children.

"Come on, Marcel—nobody hates his children!"

"Do you really believe that, that fathers always love their children? And the mothers themselves . . . I had a friend in my regiment whose mother hated him because he was scrawny: she was ashamed of him. She tried seducing me, I recall, never dreaming that I could actually feel any friendship for her son. She was convinced that I came to the house because of her."

"It's a simple fact, Marcel, that you've always had a sort of gift for attracting monsters. Why are you smiling?"

"It's comic, your saying that."

But Marcel quickly regretted what he'd said. He saw an expression quickly pass in Hervé's eyes, an expression he knew well, an expression that made him feel both pity and fear at the same time. He hurried to distract him.

"Anyway, in the Forcas household, this sort of emotion is easy to understand. The father is one of those men for whom the real family is their own blood: father, mother, brother, sister. Their own children are foreigners to them because they belong to foreigners, to the enemy. In the particular combat that pits spouses against each other, the children almost always take their mother's side. Thus the Forcas children, ever since they were old enough to understand, formed a bloc with the enemy. And the old man, he was in the opposite camp, with his sister . . ."

"She was married?"

"No, an old maid, but one who had had a child, fathered by nobody knows who. The child grew up to be all right, anyway—I think he's a doctor in the navy. Imagine the old, paralytic Forcas, lying in his big armchair, thinking about how to ensure that his fortune would go to the sister's son . . ."

"All this is very strange," cried Hervé. "I've never heard a story quite like this. What explains people like that? Don't they frighten you? They would certainly have frightened me."

Marcel, irritated, asked him what he would have been afraid of. "You come from these same sort of people, Hervé, these people who believe in the family. A man marries a woman, and for you, he's in a family. He enters into a family. Me, I'm only interested in these stories as a sort of documentary. Tota is my wife, and the others don't exist as far as I'm concerned."

He didn't hear Hervé murmur, "That's what you think."

"They don't exist. Just as with my own father, I can laugh at all these people I will never see again—except for Alain, of course. I owe a lot to Alain; Tota sees things with his eyes. Imagine these two children who lived, who suffered through their entire childhood, their entire adolescence, in that horrible pit . . . And when I call it a pit, I mean it. I remember the single meeting I had with the mother, before the marriage. It was understood that around her husband, she would pretend to know nothing. Officially, Tota was understood to have acted against her mother's will, and the mother was to act as if she shared the father's outrage. I mention this to show you how secret this meeting had to be. Alain had given me very exact directions for finding their house. But as it was, I couldn't have called for help from anyone anyway. The villages, in that autumn dusk, were as deserted as the roads. Like so many of these old places in the Entre-deux-Mers, La Hume is not located on a hillside but in a deep valley, out of the winds and close to the water. I drove along, waking up furious watchdogs, going all around the valley of La Hume without knowing it. Once in a while I would try to make out a name in the headlights, try to decipher some words on a post. Finally, at the opening of a roadway, I was hailed by Alain. From behind a ruined pillar, I saw a shadowy figure emerge. I scarcely had the time to make out that it was a woman wrapped in a shawl, her face hidden by one of those big gardening hats decorated with swallows, the kind you can still find in countryside armoires. But by the time I'd made this out, she was already back in the shadows. I took a few steps toward the phantom. She repeated several times that she was speaking to me in confidence, and she spoke of her husband. 'No doubt,' she said to me, 'we can defy him now, he's very sick, but just because he's so sick . . . Tota's letter announcing her engagement brought on a crisis for him, and for two days now he's been hanging between life and death.' When I assured her that she would be able to see Tota whenever she wished, she said: 'No, while he's still alive, which may not be long, I can't see her again. And you, I have never met you, do you understand?' She added that with an extraordinary intensity. 'You'll tell anyone who asks you that you've never met me? Even though we live a totally isolated life, my husband hears all sorts of things from his sister.' You can hardly imagine how strange this woman was, alternating back and forth between aggression and fear."

Marcel stopped, seeing Hervé sitting at the extreme edge of the couch so as not to rumple the bedclothes, and asked him what he thought of his story. "I thought you'd have a stronger reaction, you who are so easy to surprise."

"I'm less surprised by your story than by your manner of telling it. Yes," he added with his most innocent air, "in the past, you'd have found such a story comical enough. You wouldn't have taken people like that seriously. Excepting your wife and brother-in-law, of course! This Alain, I can see you like him very much, this fellow who in a sense has given you his sister, as you imply . . . But how has he managed to live to be twenty years old under a yoke like this?"

"Because of his mother and his sister, naturally. His sister especially."

He was nettled by Hervé's expression, and he said no more. Hervé nodded his head, saying as if to himself, "Yes! Good! Now I understand their joy at being reunited tonight. Yes, yes! You put it very well, old friend, families are very interesting! So, I see: your wife and Alain resemble their father; they imitate him."

Marcel stared at him inquisitively. Hervé added in a detached way that "if I understood correctly, the old man too had a sister who he preferred to everyone else." Marcel said dryly that he didn't see the connection, but then after thinking for a moment added that the old Forcas hated his wife and children above all things; his sister only served as somebody he could share his hatred with.

"Yes, of course, you're right. There's no connection to be made."

Marcel followed with a deepening sick feeling the roundabout paths and detours this fox made. He wanted to be rid of him, regretted that he had spoken in front of him, and wondered just what sort of prey he was dragging back to his den. He took a few steps toward the window, then quickly turned his head to see Hervé smiling with that childish expression he sometimes had. The smile was directed at no one, like that of a sleeping child who smiled at angels. Maybe it was the childlike facial expression that made this forty-year-old so repulsive. His lips moved back and forth, as if under pressure from the words in his mouth that he was holding back, that he dared not speak. Now his eyes were shining, and clearly he would not be able to keep himself quiet for much longer—like a hound who, once on the trail, could not be kept from baying by any force in the world. Whatever he had to say, he would be saying it soon now.

"What are you giggling about? Go ahead, spit it out."

"What should I say? I couldn't help thinking that they really do it up right in the provinces. I've always thought that Paris had stolen its reputation from them. We're only poor hands at it. All these nights when nothing at all happens, when we come together to wait till dawn for something that never happens . . . Whereas in the provinces! Ah, they're up to more than just cookery out there! What? Marcel, why are you looking at me that way? How you look!"

He rose from the couch, keeping his eyes on Marcel. Hervé feared nothing more in life than a man's anger, especially a cold anger. And at the same time that he felt fear, he had the sense that he was coming face to face with one of life's mysteries, forever unknown to him, one of the mysteries of love: the way a man in love mobilizes all his powers at the slightest word that seems to cast a taint on his beloved.

"What did you think I meant? I didn't mean to suggest . . ."

"Nothing. But leave now. They'll be coming back soon."

"Listen, Marcel, let me stay, let me meet them. I won't even sit back down. I'll only stay long enough to be introduced."

He felt shame at abasing himself this way. This all-devouring curiosity of his revealed itself like an open wound. But Marcel was leading him gently to the door. Hervé protested, smiling: "You can't tell somebody a story like that and then prevent him from meeting the main characters!" And then he burst out with, "And anyway, what's it to you if I get to see them, since you've already told me everything!"

Marcel reclosed the door, turned, and put his hands on Hervé's shoulders. Hervé's knees went weak.

"I told you everything? What did I tell you? Come on, speak up. Don't turn away from me."

Hervé got his shoulders free and whimpered, "Animal." Marcel got hold of himself again and asked if he had hurt Hervé. Then he added, "We'll part friends. But remember this: I don't know what you were going to amuse yourself with, what sort of construction you were about to put on things I'd said tonight, but remember that I will hold you responsible for the slightest piece of gossip . . ."

He stopped talking, seeing that Hervé wasn't listening to him, but was attentive to the sound of the elevator and of a key in the lock. "Too late! I'm going to see them!" he cried in triumph.

Marcel had scarcely the time to whisper to him, "Get out of here." He had to introduce him to Tota and to the young man who came in behind her. Pushed by Marcel toward the door, Hervé only had time to cast a look at them—but what a look! It was a look of almost unbearable avidity, a look as if from a being for whom vision was at once rapture and nourishment. At last he left, looking sated and replete.

"So that's your Hervé?" said the young woman. "But he seemed nice enough to me . . . Doesn't it seem funny to see Alain in Paris?"

Marcel observed the timid smiling boy, whose face nonetheless seemed sullen. The bridge of his nose sprinkled with freckles, his forehead low as a bison's, his was a face not made for smiling. A certain gravity seemed as natural to him as to animals. He seemed shorter than he in fact was, due to his overly long torso. As Tota took her cap off, Alain said, "What's this? You've cut your hair?" He drawled slightly, and his accent was often amusing, just like Tota's. Alike in their blue-gray eyes, they differed in the lower half of the face. Alain's narrow mouth and his chin with its pure line in no way recalled "this huge mouth that I love," as Marcel called it. This was a feature that made other women say she would age rapidly. Alain's suit with its too-short sleeves gave him the look of a schoolboy who was still growing. He kept his large, soiled hands hidden.

"I was able to come," he responded to a question of Marcel's, "because my father's health is even worse."

The surprise on her husband's face made Tota laugh loudly (she laughed too loudly, and made too many gestures).

"But just look at him, Alain! How is he supposed to understand! We must explain to him . . . No," she said suddenly to Marcel, "don't sit on the couch. It's not your couch any more; it's Alain's bed."

Had any woman ever spoken to him in that tone before?

"Go ahead, explain to him, Alain."

"My father can hardly move at all now. He never gets out of his armchair; his paralysis is getting worse. So there's no risk to Mama now; I felt safe leaving the two of them together." Alain pronounced his words in an indifferent tone, as if he were giving the most ordinary explanation.

"It wasn't long ago," said Tota, "when he got out of the chair every time Mama turned her back, whenever he found any scrap of paper he wanted to burn. Once, he fell and landed with his head in the fireplace. When Mama picked him up, he had nearly strangled her, that's how strong he is . . ."

"Strangled her?" interrupted Marcel. "Because he fell?"

Tota giggled and sought out Alain's eyes. He got up abruptly and said in a severe tone, "Come on, Tota. This is nothing to laugh about. It's not decent."

Brother and sister soon had nothing more to say, unsettled by Marcel's silence. Marcel thought of Hervé. He could imagine the sort of joy Hervé would be feeling if he had been there to hear all this. Where was he now? What was he doing? What ideas was he chewing over, out there in the silence of the night?

III

WHEN Hervé returned home that night, he was counting on Irène being asleep. But he could see her light under her door. He walked on tip-toes and held his breath. But in vain: she heard him and called him in a weak voice:

"Are you back already?"

She had dropped the book she had been reading. He picked it up: it was the second volume of Andler's study of Nietzsche.[2] She smiled, wondering if perhaps Hervé had come home early because of her. He had reason to be concerned about her; perhaps he really had been concerned. However, he didn't ask her how she was. Instead he paced around her room, knotting his fingers together, rubbing them against his palms.

What was going on? What was he thinking about? She only had to wait a bit. He would speak to her about it of his own free will, so long as there was nobody else to talk to. But Irène spoke first.

"Can you believe it—when I got back in tonight, I found your mother here waiting for me! Yes, she had been worried about our going out tonight, knowing that when I got home I wouldn't wake up the maid. She had warmed the bedclothes, filled my hot-water bottle. Then she wouldn't leave, under the pretext of watching over me. I had to pretend to be asleep. Even though the Rue Las-Cases isn't far, it annoys me to think of her out alone in the streets late at night."

"You were nice to her, at least?"

"Not nice enough," Irène sighed. "She irritates me so! I can't help it. Look, these candy mints she brought me . . ." Hervé saw the bag, picked it up, and voraciously stuffed several of the candies in his mouth. "She wouldn't even taste one of them for anything in the world, because it's the first Friday of the month!"

She repeated the phrase, "the first Friday of the month," and broke into a nervous laugh.

"What does that matter to you? Laughing at her isn't worthy of you, Irène."

"I know; I'm ashamed of myself. And I couldn't keep myself from asking her if she thought that the Supreme Being actually got any pleasure out of her denying herself a piece of candy. I pained her, poor woman; I just can't help myself; it's so irritating! And you, Hervé—why are you home so early?"

"Well, I did just what I told you I was going to do. I went and had a talk with Marcel for a few minutes."

He turned away from her as he spoke because he didn't like to look at Irène, but she thought it was because he was embarrassed at lying, and that the lie would be obvious if he looked her in the face.

"No, Hervé, no," she said gently. "It isn't worth it. You know I won't believe you. Anyway, I won't ask you any further."

But then he turned and looked at her with that triumphant expression that she knew so well: the expression of the schoolboy who has found his parents in the wrong.

"Telephone him yourself. Phone him tomorrow. He introduced me to his wife and his brother-in-law. Did you know he had a brother-in-law?"

"My dear, I beg your pardon."

She was both embarrassed and happy to have suspected him wrongly. It only took one time like this, one time when the suspicions were unjustified, for her to say to herself, "Could it be that my mind is going? This is the simplest man imaginable, after all! I've created a monster that doesn't exist. Maybe he still is fond of me."

She wanted him to reproach her. But instead he spoke of the notorious Tota, of "her very pleasant brother," of their impossible family, of the countryside in which they had lived.

"Yes," she said sleepily, "Marcel has told me . . ."

"What? And you haven't told me about it?"

She excused herself on the grounds that she had promised Marcel.

"Well, now I know more about it than you do."

He paced back and forth in the room, his overcoat unbuttoned, his face shining. Her eyes followed him with anxiety, with fatigue. "But look, Hervé, there isn't anything so strange in this story of theirs; I don't understand you. And I beg you, please stop pacing around my bed like that."

He sat down, but continued to manifest a deep joy. Irène detested him as he looked then—the man she knew well and who, despite all her tenderness, she could not help but find repulsive. If only he would leave! If only she could think of him again as a poor boy, mistreated and sick! If only he were gone so that she could alter her image of him, the image she could form in her half-sleep when the drugs worked on her. He was speaking . . . What was he saying? She was in pain now and could no longer make the effort to follow him. And anyway, to follow him when he was in a state like this would only lead to some rottenness. There, where his thoughts were turning about, just as at a place where crows circled in the air, you would be sure to find some carcass. But the crows never made a mistake, whereas he often created the very corruption for which he so hungered.

Hervé saw her suddenly prop herself up on her pillows, and sweep the hair off her forehead, the forehead making her look almost bald. She asked, "What did you say to Marcel? I want to know."

He forced himself to fix his eyes candidly upon the sick woman. "Nothing at all, Irène. You were quite right! I kept my thoughts to myself. Thank you. It would have really been something . . ."

"Are you sure?" Now she fixed a challenging gaze on him. How could anybody tell? Even when he wasn't lying, he had a lying air about him.

"Can you imagine me going to say this horrible thing to Marcel?"

She asked him, 'What horrible thing?"

He shrugged his shoulders, and said, "Don't play the innocent. You understand me very well without my saying it."

But she was not listening any more. It was as if the weight of her head were pulling her down from behind. The pillow rose up around her half-buried face. Hervé could only see her sharp, pinched-looking nose. He asked her if she needed anything.

"To sleep," she said in a sigh. "Let me sleep."

IV

THAT same night, Marcel put out his bedlamp and lay stretched out on his back in the huge bed, his eyes open. Even though the bedroom door was closed, and the living room was separated from the bedroom by the entryway, he heard the alternating voices of the brother and the sister, but without being able to make sense of their words. Tota had told him to go to bed, promising to join him soon, so as to be able to have some time to talk with Alain. He had obeyed. She found it natural that he should obey. How could she have known that never before had any woman had the nerve to order him to get up or to go to bed?

What were they talking about? He got up, opened the door, and listened. But it was no good. Even straining to hear, he could only make out a confused murmur, sometimes broken by the sharp laughter of Tota. Perhaps by trying a bit harder he could have made out a few words, but an anxiety obsessed him and kept him from being fully attentive: Hervé the fox—what had he succeeded in taking back to his den? What was the stinking animal's prize? What did he know? What had he understood?

"No, I gave him no idea at all about what's been tormenting me," he thought. No, he had not admitted to Hervé that this unexpected visit of the brother-in-law had shaken him. Hervé did not know that for several weeks now, Tota had been restless and hostile, had uttered obscure threats, and that Alain had clearly only come because his sister had made an appeal to him. An appeal regarding what? Marcel could not have said exactly at what moment their relationship had changed. Perhaps he had not handled her tactfully enough. He had not taken sufficient account of the difference in their ages: practically eighteen years! "She thinks of me as old." The more women a man has known, the more he makes of woman a rudimentary idea. Not all are slaves to pleasure. That modesty in a woman that a man believes he has killed off has sometimes strange reappearances and avenges itself.

And then, the day after their wedding there was this incident: the two letters from Marie Chavès, addressed from the institution where she had gone for her drug treatment. The first was a piece of insanity, and Tota gave it scarcely any weight; but the second one was a letter full of excuses, in which the poor woman asked forgiveness for all the things she had insinuated about Marcel. And though Marie had not intended it that way, it appeared much more precise and thus more disturbing. "No, no— it's not that. Tota is not so madly in love with me that she's jealous about an old mistress of mine. She's too young, too inexperienced, to understand anything of these money issues. Anyway, I did explain to her that Marie had once brought me a hundred thousand francs, and that I returned it to her in due course. If the money grew while it was in my hands, it's my business. I recall that Tota scarcely listened to my explanations; all that didn't interest her. Did my little primitive know the world's views on all this kind of thing? There must be something else: what?"

Now Alain's voice dominated. He sounded angry, protesting. What would Hervé think if he were here? "I didn't tell Hervé anything. Still, he left here gloating with joy, carrying off something with him to dirty me with, to dirty all of us. If I tried, perhaps I could reconstruct the ugly little scenario that he's improvised in his head, by going back over everything I said . . . Don't think about it."

Strange Tota! The other women he had known had certainly been around, as they say, but their love for Marcel had always delivered them from the weight of their past. In loving him they had made a revolution in their own lives, and had thrown their old lives into this new flame, everything that they had been before. As if they were mad, they had thrown everything into this new passion without keeping open any route for a retreat. But Tota—Tota had remained free; this adolescent who had hardly lived at all walked into Marcel's life, but she also walked out of it whenever and however she wanted to. And wherever she went, he could not follow. Tota did not depend on him; but a woman always depends on someone: upon whom did Tota depend? Marcel felt he could see Hervé's shape gleaming in the shadows. He felt he could hear him sigh, "Idiot! You don't understand, do you?"

He turned on his lamp, got up, and opened the door to the entryway all the way, then got back into bed and hid himself under the covers, holding his breath. The two alternating voices resonated more loudly, but the words remained indistinct. Then he thought he could hear, "—able Tota."

Then nothing. He repeated it to himself: "—able Tota." A thousand words ended like that. He imagined them all. And he suffered.

"It's unbelievable, Tota," Alain was saying, "that you've forgotten how all this came about. Remember that oppressive month of July. Father, who was then at his full strength, was just on the eve of his first attack. His fits of rage frightened us to the point where we thought Mama's life was in danger, and I went to Bordeaux one day to buy a revolver. You were at the end of your courage. I can still see you after lunch—remember that heat!—I can still see you pacing along the paths. You wanted to run away. I hardly dare remind you of what you said to me, about how you planned to make a living. I had to work at not believing you; it was too horrible to me."

She turned toward Alain, her small face full of rage, and in a tone of defiance told him it would have been better if he had let her go and take whatever chances she might, rather than deliver her up to the first bidder who came along. "It couldn't have been worse; and it might have been a lot more amusing . . ."

"Tota!"

His scandalized manner both softened her and irritated her. She told him that, for a man, he had a ridiculous modesty. He really should rub up a bit against some of the people in Paris!

"Do you think," he sighed, "that the peasants where we lived . . ."

"And so what? They're right."

This hurt Alain, but he didn't know what to say to her. So much force in him, so much blood. But where did this sadness come from—as if things didn't concern him, as if he, and he alone, were outside the game? The young woman took advantage of his silence.

"You're playing innocent, but back at Cauterets you were much more knowing. You advised me, remember, and you ended by convincing me that Marcel—this old wreck of thirty-seven years—would actually please me. You can congratulate yourself on having thrown me into his arms."

She suddenly saw that grimace on her brother's face that she recognized, the same one that he made when he was a little boy and about to cry. Taking his head in both her hands, she kissed his forehead and growled, "Little fool!"

"There's no doubt," he stammered, "that I was wrong. But your meeting him seemed like such a chance for you. I have to tell you . . ." He hesitated. "But no, you're too malicious, you'll only mock me."

"We'll see. Go ahead."

294

But he refused to tell his secret. And Tota, to avenge herself, used the threat she had always used as a girl, and used it in her little girl's voice: "Very well then. Me neither. I'll never tell you anything again."

He said nothing, thinking of this one thing in the world that he dared not admit to Tota. It was one night in that terrible July; their father, whom he had been able to master, actually made him less afraid than this furious young woman, this young animal who was all desire and all instinct. That night, in the moonlight, he saw her. Tota, in her white dress, had gone to the end of the road, and he heard her laughing there with the children of the sharecroppers. He looked out at the circle of hills that closed off the horizon: no way out. He walked a few steps through the dry grass, as far as the large shade pine, and there, without having planned it at all—no, no, Tota must never know it—he suddenly fell sobbing to his knees, and words came stammering out of him . . .

A few days later, their father now having been reduced to powerlessness, he made the trip into Cauterets and met this Marcel Revaux whose wartime poems he had greatly admired. The events that followed seemed to him like an answer to those stammered words, though he would not say it to himself. Tota was right: he had been foolishly credulous, and he had nothing to say against her accusations.

"You didn't find out anything about him. We barely knew that there was a father somewhere, with whom he had quarreled—an employee at some big department store! This marriage without any family . . . I felt like I was marrying an abandoned child. You knew Marcel by name, and you thought that was enough; you were only too happy to get me off your hands."

"Yes," thought Alain, "I thought, I believed . . ."

"If you had made the slightest inquiries in Paris, you would have learned plenty about the lover of Marie Chavès. She had talent when he met her; people talk about her paintings. He's the one who organized their sale—for his own profit, as anyone here will tell you. They will also tell you that if he is rich now since the fall of the franc,[3] it's because he played on the stock market with Marie's money. And that's not all: when everyone started to see that his talent was gone, that he was burnt out as a writer, Marcel the neurotic began using drugs. He dragged Marie into it—Marie who at first was horrified. But everybody knows that drugs cost money, and the woman paid the costs. Marcel loathed this situation inwardly, and he soon got himself cleaned up. Meanwhile the other one is in the process of dying, people say."

"This is revolting. How can you put up with people saying horrible things like this about your husband?"

"Because it's common knowledge. Anyway, stories like that aren't so unusual here. You're still the village boy, aren't you!"

"Tota, aren't you coming to bed? It's after one."

Marcel had pushed open the door noiselessly and was glaring angrily at the brother and sister. The whites of his eyes were darkened by fatigue. His feet were bare beneath his old red pajama pants, and the unbuttoned top revealed a hirsute chest. A thick lock of hair draped over his furrowed forehead. Unshaven, his beard was growing upward and devouring his cheeks. Two deep creases came down from the sides of his nose and flanked his half-open mouth.

Tota innocently asked him for just a few more minutes; they had so much to say to each other! And she wasn't sleepy at all.

"A few more minutes, then? I can't stay up any longer."

When Marcel had left the room, Alain was disturbed: if only he hadn't heard them!

"So what?" asked Tota. "Don't you think he knows what I think of him?" She looked down at the floor.

"You aren't thinking of leaving him? And then what? Go back to La Hume?"

"No, you wouldn't want that!"

She stood up and paced around the room. "I've thought of it sometimes. From far enough away, our life there seems almost pleasant. There is peace in you, Alain. But—how can I say it? It's comical to feel embarrassed touching on certain subjects in front of a man your age. Well—I have certain tastes—you understand?—at the moment. Pleasure, love—I don't know!"

Alain, who had remained seated, lowered his head. "Love," he said.

She said, her voice lowered and mischievous, "Yes. Have you heard of it?"

He raised his head and looked at her seriously, attentively.

"Have you? Yes or no," she insisted with her nervous laugh.

He continued to look at her, saying nothing in response. Tota blushed. After a long silence, she said abruptly, "Well, I'm going to join him tonight again. Do you have everything you need? A couch like this is good for sleeping."

He got up and took her hand. Since she had assured him that all these ugly stories about her husband were commonplace events here—then why, if he was indeed guilty, must she nurture this grudge against him? "Why not forgive him," he said, "and use your influence to make him a better man?"

She seemed to consider this, and then shrugged her shoulders: "What a child you are! Do you really believe that, if I truly loved him, all these things would be enough to turn me away from him? Maybe even, if I loved him, all these things would even please me instead of horrifying me. But I don't love him; there it is. Look, I need to tell you: there's a young man you'll meet while you're here, William Turner. He's twenty-five, and he's wild about me. I like him well enough; and sometimes I like him a lot. This isn't any grand passion yet, but it's closer to one for him. A totally different type than Marcel. It's funny: one dare not call these things by their real names in front of you. Anyway, whatever William has done or does now, I'll have fun with it; I find him amusing. It's enough that I like him."

Alain did not respond. After a silence, she suddenly said in another tone, with another voice: "I horrify you. Admit it."

"No, Tota."

"You won't love me anymore?"

He took both her hands in his. She put her head on her brother's shoulder, as if to hide herself.

Marcel lay on the right side of the bed, and she stretched out beside him and pretended to sleep. He prevented himself from making the slightest movement until her breathing evened out and she was evidently asleep. He lacked the courage to speak to her. Better to wait until morning; the nightmare would disappear with the night. How wrong he was to have fallen into the suggestions Hervé had made! He had thought it better to face them, to give them form in order to vanquish them more easily. It had been a horrible game—but a game still—to let himself entertain what Hervé must think. But now he was unable to exit the game. His imagination, which he had exercised powerfully ever since his childhood, now composed terribly vivid tableaux. He possessed the art of creating hideous images, but not that of managing and escaping from them.

How impatient he was now to find traces of the approaching dawn between the curtains! Tomorrow, no matter what, he would seek out Hervé. Not that he wished him any harm; he only wanted to converse calmly with him, to assure himself that Hervé perhaps did not really believe in these things, that he was pretending, that he was playing the game too, in his own way. With Hervé, Marcel would be able to prowl around this enigma, without speaking openly about it. But how many hours must pass first! And now he regretted having let Tota go to sleep. She had taught him never to wake her: "the first one who gets in my way . . ."

So what! He wouldn't fight against this obsession any more; why not abandon himself to it, since he was sure to be delivered from it in the morning? It was as if he sat down at his desk to begin work. At first he groped. He strained to evoke the image of La Hume, which he had only seen once as it slept in the moonlight, in its crevasse in the terrain. There was the entryway, the living room darkened by the closed blinds, closed due to the ghastly heat . . . Why did there have to be heat? He could also imagine the family in the dead of winter, their chairs huddled around the sole fire. He could also imagine hearing the continuous rain pouring on the dead vines, on the muddy pathways, during the times when one would have to light the lamps before four o'clock because the trees surrounded the house so closely and shadowed it; and the water pouring from the gutters partly obstructed by dead leaves . . . But no, this drama could only be set in the inferno of the long summer vacations, only in this vast numbing of human and vegetable life, when neither body nor soul could fight against the fire, when the ancient lust grew and strengthened itself amid the universal devastation.

Marcel groaned suddenly, like a child who has just done something very wrong: "What a fool I am! Because it's not true. I know perfectly well that it's not true. Does Hervé believe it? No—he wants it to be true; he loves disasters; only a universe full of disasters would satisfy him. And in any case he doesn't have any real evidence. The only things he knows of La Hume and its residents, he knows through what I've told him." How impatient Marcel was to phone him, to talk with him!

He pulled himself up, sitting and leaning against the pillow. "Why did Alain come? Why did she make him come? That's the only question. I'm getting wrapped up in a fantasy and ignoring the reality: this trip of Alain's . . ."

Tota would be angry, but what of it, he had to question her, right now, without waiting another moment.

"Tota!"

She was going to get angry, but he would tell her that she had awakened on her own, that she had only heard him calling her in a dream. The young body turned over, then remained immobile. He felt at the same time both thwarted and comforted almost, so courageous a thing had it been to brave Tota's anger, and to violate her sleep.

V

IN the morning, as Hervé entered into his wife's bedroom, he was struck by the waxy, almost gray figure that lay motionless among the pillows. The only sign she saw him was a smile that revealed her gums. He asked her if she was feeling worse.

"Not worse. I'll go back to bed after my bath: Romieu is coming to look me over at eleven o'clock."

But Hervé replied with irritation that he could see perfectly well she felt worse. Why did she have to pretend?

"You know you never fool anyone. I fear there's a little of the show-off in your stoicism, my dear."

She looked at him without responding, with a poor smile. How young he seemed this morning! Terribly young.

"Your overcoat is lovely. But not too light? It isn't spring yet." Her thin fingers played with the fabric. He assured her he wasn't cold, and he planned to walk this beautiful morning. It would be superb—what a fine sun today! He would go to his mother's, and from there he would go to Fouquet's, where he would meet Marcel for lunch.

"Yes, it was he who just phoned me. He absolutely insisted on having lunch with me. We'll be inseparable from now on," he added with an air of extreme contentment. "He wants to speak to me again about our conversation last night."

"And after lunch, Hervé?"

Shouldn't he come back home, to find out what Romieu had said? He replied that he would telephone the doctor tonight. He was engaged for the whole afternoon. Irène knew this tone of his, this accent of false indifference, which always betrayed him. Even with her eyes closed, with nothing but the sound of his voice, she would have understood that he was devoting this entire day to pleasure, to his own kind of pleasure.

"Anyway—Romieu! I have much more confidence in Terral. We should have followed his advice, and sent you to spend a year at Leysin." Romieu had not thought this displacement necessary. But it would have been most agreeable, to know Irène was in good hands in a sanatorium, while he remained alone in Paris.

"Romieu assures me that I am not tubercular," Irène said vigorously.

He reproached her for being afraid of a mere word. Terral affirmed that she was tubercular; so much the better, anyway, for the tuberculosis was healing itself.

"So you mean to say that Romieu's diagnosis was the better?"

He denied it strongly. Romieu didn't know what she had; he belonged to that sect of doctors who affected not to believe in medical science.

"Well, I know what he thinks in my case."

Hervé should have pretended not to understand her; but he was unusually maladroit today. "You know as well as I," he said, "that the x-rays showed nothing."

She nodded her head, and said quietly, "That hardly means anything, if it's a matter of a malignant tumor. But let's let this go; it's not important."

He didn't know what to say. She remained on the bed, immobile, her eyes fixed. He went to the window. He could hear a pigeon's cooing, though he couldn't see where it was; it must be perched up on the bedroom's chimney.

"Tell your mother that I would be happy to see her today."

He turned toward her with some unease. For her to say such a thing, she must be feeling much worse, as normally nothing annoyed her more than a visit from her mother-in-law. He felt fear—the fear that he might not be able to go out today. This had been his chance! She was going to keep him until the last moment; she would make him lose out on everything. Irène thought she read his feelings, but she was wrong about the cause of his anxiety, and she smiled tenderly at him: all the same, he did care about her, a little.

"Don't be worried, my dear: I have something I want to ask of your mother. No, I can't tell you what it is."

He did not insist. This morbid curiosity that was like an addiction for him, this compulsion to pursue, to track down the secrets of other people, lost all its virulence when it was a matter of his wife. Nothing about her held any interest for him.

"Now that I think of it, no," she said. "No, don't have your mother come today. I'd rather stay alone."

Irène was worrying about some poor people whom she had lost sight of after having seen to their care at the health clinic. In the fear of not being able to go out herself anymore, she had thought of consigning them to the care of her mother-in-law. But now she rejected the idea; the old woman might think that Irène wanted to gain her admiration and her praises. "And am I absolutely certain that there isn't an obscure desire in me to prove to her that charity is not the privilege of any one sect?"

And now, seeing that Hervé had left the room, she cried after him, "Remember, don't let your mother trouble herself!"

Hervé walked along quickly, putting his delight into each step that carried him farther from the house and Irène. Happy as he was to be lunching with Marcel, he knew this lunch invitation was solely related to Marcel's confidences from last night. That would not be terribly interesting. And then the image that Hervé conjured up of his afternoon obscured, effaced everything else. Nothing else counted except for that which made up his happiness—only that made life worth living: that one thing.

Just as it did every time he closed the doors on the elevator, in the apartment building on the Rue Las-Cases where his mother lived, he recalled one evening in June when he came home from school, when he saw the elevator soiled with brown stains that turned out to be blood, the doorway open, the entryway invaded, and the body of his father stretched out on the wooden desk. The concierge and the domestics had just picked him up in the courtyard. A policeman was writing down notes. His mother still had on that straw hat decorated with primroses. Far from fearing this vision, Hervé continued to feed on it. As a criminal who, in order to deter suspicions, invokes an alibi and implicates his accomplices, Hervé threw the entire weight of everything that was worst in him on his father's suicide. He found comfort in the thought that the polluted stream running through him did not have its origin in his own heart. That source had welled up and begun to seep out well before he was even in the world. He was only the living stream-bed over which this mud made its way. And at any rate, it would not flow on after him; he had given life to no one: in him alone the corrupted water of several generations would well up and die off.

Once Hervé entered into his mother's room, he changed his expression and his voice; he changed his soul. He became again a little boy in order to enter into this kingdom. This day, as on each of his visits, she rose up off the prie-Dieu, excusing herself for not having quite finished her prayers. But then, had they ever been finished? She worried whether he was cold; she was always too warm: how can a person live with this central heating?

"Yes! You're cold. I'll go get some firewood."

"But mother, ring for it. You have servants."

She was always afraid of bothering them. She came back with the wood, saying to Hervé: "Sit there," pointing to the easy chair by the fire. And then, "Tell me something good that you two have done." He described their outings, the people they had seen, the plays, and all that in the eyes of the old woman would be seen as filling up a pointless but innocent life. And he nestled himself into this recollected narrative. From a great distance he could see, as in a flare of lightning, the things he had planned for this afternoon, the secret gestures and unnamed acts. And all this future ugliness, so soon to be accomplished, appeared unreal to him, as if it did not concern him at all.

But this recreated world of childhood, in Mama's room, all collapsed at the name of Irène.

"How was she this morning? What did Romieu say? What? You didn't stay for his visit? My child! But surely he would have things to say which must be hidden from Irène."

Again he became the guilty one who invents reasons, defends himself, conceals himself, covers up his tracks. The lie got back on its feet within his head, and his mother suddenly· remembered that even this pointless life of his had its strange and imperious exigencies. What office, what business affairs, what consuming work had ever so monopolized a man's life so entirely as Hervé's was monopolized—this man who did no work, who was consumed by who knew what?

"You'll be going back home after lunch?

He hoped so—he would try to—he wasn't sure.

The old woman continued to knit without looking at him, and suddenly said, "Then I'll go."

He assured her that Irène would far rather sleep than make conversation. "Just yesterday she said to me: 'Turn me toward the wall to sleep.'"

"She said that? You're sure? But that's frightening!"

Madame de Blénauge pressed her creased hands, with their big veins, to her eyes. "I have to handle her with kid gloves so as not to irritate her," she replied. "She must be watched—do you understand what I'm saying? Don't pretend you don't understand me, my child."

Hervé shot her a guilty look. She had not raised her voice; her eyes never left the knitting she had taken up, and her head bobbed gently in time to the rhythm of the needles. A Chantilly shawl covered her almost bald scalp, only allowing two locks of yellowish white hair to show. A gold cross was attached to her corsage, buttoned on below.

"You'll make your lunch a quick one, my dear, and then you'll go back to Irène."

"Yes, Mama."

"Is that 'yes—yes' or 'yes—no'?" she asked him, as if he were ten years old.

He promised to do his best, and she understood that he would not go back home until the evening. He had turned his face from her: nothing in the world would prevent him from doing, this afternoon, what he planned to do; to give himself up to this sad intoxication—to thrust himself into a world that this old woman could not even imagine. He could see the streets that the taxi would take, the boulevard, the square, the house set back, the courtyard, the ground—floor door whose lock one had to fumble with in the dark, the inner stairway, the room on the next floor.

His mother fixed her eyes on him, eyes that remained so pure, so childlike in that shriveled face—eyes of that blue he had inherited. Hervé was dreaming of all that he would soon see, all that he would devour with those eyes that were the eyes of his mother.

He repeated, "I'll do whatever it takes," knowing that his mother did not believe him. She followed him out onto the landing: after he had gone down a flight of steps, he raised his head and saw her leaning over the railing. She watched him descend, sink, disappear.

VI

THAT morning, the old woman again irritated the servants by eating hardly anything of the abundant lunch they had brought her. Before three o'clock, she rang at her daughter-in-law's; and although she was assured that after her morning's crisis, the sick woman had finally been able to get to sleep, she insisted on going into her room: "Just to see how Madame looks." The cook couldn't get over the rudeness of it: how could a person just force her way into people's homes like that?

The curtains, tied by the window, let a ray of light in which fell on the cluttered table. But the patient, lying on her left side, was in half-light. The old woman made no more noise than a mouse. She waited a moment until her eyes were adjusted to the shadowy light; then she bent forward over the poor body. Irène was breathing quickly, and there was some color in her cheeks. A sign of fever, perhaps? Terral would say it was a sign of tuberculosis. Cancer doesn't cause fever—and then, a cancer at thirty-four years of age! But Romieu maintained that these sorts of tumors impaired the liver's functioning, and thereby initiated febrile states. She slept; her mother-in-law could contemplate her at her leisure, and join her hands to pray over this martyred body. Next to a half-emptied glass of water there was an open bottle of tranquilizers. The old woman examined it: only two were gone; she slipped it into her purse. Only then did she see the half-opened drawer in the bedtable, and saw that it was full of similar bottles, not yet opened. She did not resist, and took them all one by one, with a deft thief's hand. The sound of her purse snapping shut made Irène turn over and speak some confused words.

Madame de Blénauge, petrified, held her breath. Nothing moved in this empty room. She thought of the sound of children's footsteps in the corridors, of their laughter—what a shame! What could she expect now out of life! How could she turn away for one instant from her suffering and her love? She did not have to detach herself: blessed is the old age where nothing interposes itself anymore between the soul and God! The world moves away; solitude and silence precede death. Old age is already an entombment. She considered that she did not suffer enough, that she suffered hardly at all: her husband, Hervé, Irène, all these souls to carry . . . And she managed nothing more than ridiculous gestures like stealing the poisons out of a drawer.

If Irène woke up, perceived it . . . The old woman left the room, slipped through the entryway, and only took a breath when she was on the landing, and she had to hold on to the railing to descend.

In the street, she dragged herself along, not daring to stop a taxi, because her sight was bad and she could not make out the posted price, or gave too small a tip and ended up having to take abuse for it. She too, just like Hervé at that moment, saw in her mind's eye a street, a courtyard, a house set back, a door on the ground floor . . . She trailed along the Rue Babylone, feeling fortunate that the distance was not long: "I won't get on my knees; I'll remain seated." She passed under a carriage entrance, crossed the sleeping courtyard, and struggled up a few steps. It was time: she collapsed at the feet of her Love and felt herself weak no more: she held out to Him this son and this daughter-in-law—this leper son and this blind daughter. Then her busy spirit, in an instant, abandoned them and descended among the dead, bent itself over this man whom the servants had picked up out of the courtyard and who groaned (and the envelope with his last wishes was still pinned to his pajamas). The eye, already invaded by the shadows, was fixed and did not see her; his bleeding head rested for the last time on her faithful shoulder.

Bit by bit, her "intentions" escaped from her without her being able to retrieve them. And now there was not a person in the world, or out of it, who occupied her mind except the One who watched her in the darkness.

VII

MARCEL insisted that Hervé have a drink after they ate; he was in no mood to leave this tepid restaurant where his anguish was somewhat dulled. But Hervé had things to do; he was in a hurry; people were waiting for him.

"Before you leave, explain to me what you meant, just now, when you said that Alain had the look of someone obsessed?"

"Only that! Nothing more than that! How funny he is, poor little Marcel!"

"You swear to me?"

"Swear what? It's nothing more than a very vague impression. There's nothing more to say about it. How changed you are since your marriage! Listen, I'm very sorry, but people are waiting for me."

Marcel held onto his arm. "Come and join us tonight at the Boeuf. Yes, Alain will be there. Tota finds some pleasure in taking him there, without telling him in advance, just to see his reaction. Try to chat a little with him; I'd love to hear what you think of him. I don't know why I'm asking this."

He had scarcely formulated this request when he felt a bitter regret. But Hervé did not manifest the same joy he had the night before. He was no longer there, he was already living and breathing within the four walls that would contain, within minutes, his happiness. He could put Marcel away the way a dog buries a bone; he knew where it would be when he wanted it. Yes, it would be amusing, tonight, to speak a bit with this young Alain. But he would lose no time now with thoughts of tonight. An eternity of pleasure separated now and then. He didn't like to think of the hours that followed his satisfaction—hours of a sadness and a horror impossible to imagine before the glutting. For the moment, he had no

more than an abstract awareness; he knew that this disgust would find
him, but first it would have to cross over a universe of joy.

While the host helped him with his overcoat, he observed Marcel in a
mirror; he chewed his nails, bit off little bits of skin from around the nails,
and sucked away the blood.

Marcel had missed a meeting at the Chamber; he had not given the
order to sell his shares of Puerto Belgrano. He didn't have any taste for
doing anything. Tota and Alain were visiting museums. What to do until
they get back? Go to St. Cloud, and pass the afternoon with Marie
Chavès? That would occupy him, and above all it would be a "good thing
to do." But it would be to re-enter the pre-Tota world, a dead and
bleached-out life that filled him with horror. If only he could speak with
someone about Tota! There was always Irène; but Hervé had assured him
that she was in a health crisis and could not receive him. And then she
would bore him stiff with Nietzsche! He was within life, he; he was not
ill; he did not talk a lot of hot air. She would insist that he return to the
novel he had interrupted for years now. She didn't understand that it was
over, that he was a finished man; that nothing remained for him now
except to live; what is called living. He searched in vain for the name of
an available friend. The waiters were removing the last tablecloths. He
would leave, and wander around Paris. And the old instinct led him back
to that half-opened door, which he pushed open into the furtive corridor.

VIII

HERVÉ turned the key in the lock with the least possible noise. But there was light visible under Irène's door. As he had presumed she would be, she was sitting up in bed, supported by her pillows.

"I'm sorry . . ."

"Why? I don't want to condemn you to never being able to go out. Am I really so demanding?" Her voice had a singular sweetness about it. Her hands were hidden beneath the blanket.

"Sit down next to me for a moment."

He obeyed and kissed her forehead: had Romieu come? Had he found anything new?

"Only a bit of fever which surprised him a great deal . . . You don't look so good yourself. As usual, your tie is crooked."

She straightened it with a gesture that reminded Hervé of the first year of their marriage. And then point-blank, without raising her voice:

"I have to tell you something I've learned about you, my dear."

He shot her a worried look, a hunted look, even though her tone was the tone of long ago—a slightly rude but indulgent and tender tone. She shook her finger at him: "You know perfectly well what I've got to say."

He signaled that he did not understand.

"You are a thief, sir."

He breathed. He didn't know what this accusation meant. He only saw that Irène appeared relaxed.

"Rest assured, I'm not asking for it back. Anyway, tomorrow morning I'll buy more again."

"You'll buy what?"

"Don't act innocent. But this time, I won't keep it in the drawer; it will be kept safe, and locked. Don't look so sheepish. I wouldn't have thought you were so anxious about my health. What you have done is both clumsy and generous: an act that doesn't suit you at all. I mean, it isn't like your usual personality."

She interrupted herself. How alarmed he looked! He couldn't feign surprise this well.

"Where have you put my tranquilizers?"

"Your tranquilizers?"

"Wasn't it you this afternoon who took the bottles out of this drawer?"

He protested that he had not returned home this afternoon. He had dined out in the same suit he put on this morning.

She looked him up and down; then, after a silence, she thought "What's wrong with my mind?"

And she smiled. "I really am an idiot. Pardon me."

"But I made Mama promise that she would come by this afternoon. She must have been here while you were sleeping."

"But of course," she said and laughed again; "it was your dear mother. I accused an innocent."

Her intolerable laugh redoubled. "Imagine me! I accused him of having come while I was sleeping, poor thing! And he didn't even come home to change his clothes. Maybe he did change his collar, though: I don't recognize that soft collar from this morning."

"I borrowed this one from Marcel."

"He must not wear it much, at least if he doesn't want to strangle himself. —I'm in good form tonight, don't you think? Where are you going?"

He said he was going to change his clothes: Marcel was waiting for him at the Boeuf along with Tota and the young brother-in-law.

When she was alone, Irène's mood blackened. All she needed, she thought, was the slightest straw and she would cling to it. When would she fall into the despair with no possible exit? "He did not return for Romieu's visit . . . He didn't even telephone . . ." She said softly to herself, "If, when one is dead, one could know one was dead . . ." And then: "It was the old woman who came and fumbled through my drawer, the old idiot, the only one who keeps any watch over me, and that's because she doesn't want to have a daughter-in-law in hell . . . No, poor woman, you love me in your way, you believe I have a soul, you believe that someone watches us suffer, and you live happy in that delusion . . ."

In the next room, Hervé was dressing. "*Always deny,*" he thought, "what an absurdity! One should never deny before one knows the accusation." To say that he passed for a liar! There was nobody in the world less capable than he was of dissimulation. "If I had known what the game was, Irène would have become indulgent, and the atmosphere between us more breathable . . ." Too early to leave. He stretched out on his bed, his lips curled bitterly; and he fantasized dreams of tenderness and calm, of resting against a shoulder—signs that he was sated and exhausted.

IX

ALAIN abruptly got up from the table, and roughly forcing a path for himself among the dancers packed together like sardines, got to the bar and asked for his coat. There was no other reason except the blood that was burning in his cheeks, making his ears buzz. Accustomed to going bare-headed in fog, wind, and rain, he had been unable to breathe and he feared he was dying. Tota, seeing his flight, broke away from William and rejoined her brother: "What's making you run away?"

Only that he was suffocating. "How can you survive for hours in this furnace?"

"I can see that your face is red as a poppy."

And with a maternal gesture, she put her two hands on her brother's face. From a distance Marcel saw the gesture. He drank his third whiskey at a gulp, and in his turn threaded a path through the sardines.

"Are you mad?"

"Why mad?"

Tota whispered in her brother's ear not to attach much importance to Marcel's words: after three whiskeys, he was not in control of himself. Above all, one should not contradict him.

"We're leaving too," growled Marcel.

When they were outside, Alain refused to get into the car. He would get back on foot, he needed to breathe some fresh air, to cool himself off in the night air. Tota reminded him that the key would be under the doormat. He looked at his sister: fatigue and rouge—which she had kept adding to in the course of the evening—had aged her. Her hands with their red nails looked dirty to him, as if dipped in the blood of cattle—just like those of all women, or at least all those who had this same sickness about their fingernails. And Alain recalled the tanned, scratched-up hands that Tota would hold out to him across the hedges.

He walked alone and quickly. The fog, in this street near the Place de la Concorde, had a smell familiar to this country child. One of the largest cities in the world could do nothing against this eternal freshness, nor against the forest—like perfume of the night—no more than it could rearrange the order of the stars. He was breathing well, his chest widening, his lungs dilating. Someone was running behind him: "Oh, sir!" It was Hervé de Blénauge.

"You walk terribly fast. I wanted to tell you that I have my car. If you like, I could drop you off . . ."

Alain thanked him; he preferred going on foot. Hervé was approving: "After getting out of a smoky place like that!" Unfortunately, he had his old car with him. But if Alain would permit it, he would willingly walk along with him for a while . . . Undoubtedly the young man's face expressed his feelings clearly enough, as Hervé just as quickly decided that he shouldn't leave his car behind. Alain bolted off. Standing fixed on the edge of the sidewalk, Hervé watched as he moved away. Another one of those trivial incidents that filled his heart with an atrocious bitterness; he saw himself alone, despised and rejected, lost. And the horror he felt at himself went beyond any he could inspire in anyone else.

Alain had crossed the deserted Champs-Elysées, and he was now wandering along the allées, passing near a bandstand surrounded by a metal railing. Suddenly he felt how tired he was. Despite the moist wind that agitated the branches in the halo of the streetlights, he sat down on a bench. He forced himself to think of Tota, and of the difficulty of her situation: "She's right," he thought, "I alone am responsible." But he also felt shame at his own strange indifference; he could not bring himself to take his sister's complaints as tragic. No, it was not really indifference, but rather a startling sense of security: "I was mistaken," he repeated to himself. "I've acted like a superstitious person, as if I believed that all these events had been willed . . ." But he continued to feel deep within himself that same confidence, that same sense of abandon: "All this is horrible," he repeated to himself, and he smiled at the sight of two stars visible through a gap in the fog. "To die of sorrow . . ." he said aloud. And at the same instant, he felt his heart warming within him from some unknown joy. "It's my youth, maybe it's my youth . . . What's this?"

A man sat down beside him on the bench, quite near him. It was not a thief, but a "gentleman," as was said, middle-aged, wearing a prince-nez.

"Aren't you afraid of catching cold?"

He addressed Alain without turning his head toward him. The young man got up and walked away rapidly. Under the trees, the solitude was not quite what it had appeared to be. He left the dangers of the shadows, but suddenly stopped. Yes, that had been a sob, coming from behind the bushes. He wanted to flee, then blushed at this first feeling, and walked around the line of bushes. On an iron chair resting against a streetlight sat a woman, her posture straight, her head thrown back, her white throat like an offering to the knife. She thought she was alone. Her attitude, her sighs exhaled at long intervals, suggested a hunted-down creature, one who no longer felt any need to save face or even to cope—a creature without any touchings—up, in short, and such as sorrow had fashioned her, molded her.

Her neck rose up out of a fur stole that Alain did not know was chinchilla but that he could tell was very expensive. "It's a lady," he said naively. He hesitated, took a couple of steps. She turned a face toward him which the tilted felt hat shadowed, letting one see only a mouth almost without lips, marked by two deep wrinkles at the corners. Her too-short nose made her face look as if it had been gnawed away. He asked her if she was ill.

"No. Leave me alone. I don't need anything."

He had drawn closer to her, and she looked at him with surprise, distracted for a moment from her fearful grief.

"With a face like that . . . What a pity!" She sighed. "You are no more than twenty?"

"Nineteen, madame."

"Poor boy!"

With this woman, curiosity overtook every other feeling. It was she who asked the questions, but he did not understand what she asked. Could she have been drinking?

"Can I help you at all, madame?"

"Well, yes: go find me a taxi."

He asked her where the closest taxi stand was, and when she said at Maxim's, he asked again where he would find Maxim's. She thought he was making fun of her, but having looked him over for a moment, she saw it all clearly at once:

"You don't live in Paris?"

No, he was here for the first time, and was about to look for a taxi himself as he did not know his way home. She seemed embarrassed and murmured "Pardon me . . ." but he did not know why she was apologizing.

"I should have remembered that faces never fool me," she said. "I should have been able to judge you by yours. Besides you have a Midi accent—Girondin? I could have sworn . . . I know it very well! I have paid dearly for knowing it . . ."

She got up. "I'll try taking a few steps. Would you accompany me as far as the Rue Royale?"

They walked together in silence. Alain searched for words and could only ask her what she was suffering from. She responded, "Someone," with a certain emphasis. He turned his still juvenile face toward her.

"That's not a turn of phrase. One suffers from someone; one has someone the way one has cancer, a tumor inside. It's the most physical of all illnesses. You have not yet felt it?"

He shook his head. She looked at him: "You are a child." She stopped at the edge of the sidewalk, where the trees ended.

"You see that bench? We sat there together last July, one night. It's over." She said no more; she waited to be questioned. But when Alain could find nothing to say:

"I don't know why I reveal myself this way. It's not in my nature . . . You've been good for me," she added; and after staring at him: "May I give you my card?" She groped in her purse, but could not find what she wanted.

"I'll tell you my name and address, anyway: Thérèse Desqueyroux, 11 bis, Quai d'Orléans.[4] Will you forget it?"

"Oh!" he said: "That's a name from my part of the country!"

In the taxi that was bringing him home, Alain pictured to himself the face of this woman without lips, with the short nose, the used-up, gnawed face, polished as a pebble: always their madness, the same madness, always the exhausting pursuit, always these beings who hunted themselves: "And me? Why not me?" It was frightening not to be like all the others. Why did he feel himself set apart, different, as if put on one side? What was this destiny? What was it that demanded he should be an observer at this melee, instead of plunging into it headlong? "It's horrible," he repeated to himself without conviction. This strange sensation of fullness and happiness! He pressed his hands over his eyes and repeated to himself, "What's wrong with me?" and shook his head like a young bull who felt the goad, fighting against a new and unknown yoke. La Hume, his father, his mother, Tota, Marcel—he climbed back up to find the source of his anguish: his eyes were wet, life was too atrocious . . . But why didn't this horrible life change that living peace in his heart, nor that confidence of the child who holds a hand in the dark?

X

ALAIN bent down to get the key under the mat. But before he had the time to pick it up, the door opened and he saw Tota. She must have taken off her rouge, and he saw she looked like she did before she began to use makeup—the round eyes, the cloudy complexion. She spoke at once:

"A telegram from Mama: nothing serious. Read it, she says herself: *'Nothing serious.'* But she begs you to return. Most likely it's a matter of an offer to buy the latest harvest."

They stood in the entryway which smelled of the cold food in the kitchen. Alain had not had time to remove his overcoat, and as he reread the telegram, Tota watched him.

"What is it?" he asked.

A rhythmic moaning, rising and falling, reached them. "It's him, naturally," she said quietly with hatred in her voice. "It's always like this, especially when he's been drinking. He's like an animal."

When Alain asked her for the train timetable, she protested vigorously: "You're not going to leave? No, no: you promised to stay a week. I'll write her and tell her to send an explanation. Whenever she says 'nothing serious,' you can take her at her word."

Alain preceded his sister into the studio where a fire was still burning. Her coat had been thrown on the couch. He looked for the timetable, and she knew that she had failed.

"I won't go to bed," he said.

His heart was far from this house, this city: "nothing serious" might mean in fact that things were going very badly.

"Remember the night when we went into Mama's room; she kept repeating, 'It's nothing, it's nothing.' And she had bruises around her neck . . . I want to be going, I want to get there."

Tota reminded him that the old man was disarmed now, that a child could master him with no difficulty. But Alain thought he had seen signs of his strength returning. And then all it takes is a single motion: a weapon is dangerous even in the hands of a very ill man.

His voice weakened; he said no more out of the sense that she disagreed with everything he said. No, it was not this issue that was driving him to depart. He wanted to go, and leaped at the offered pretext.

"And me, Alain?"

"You?"

"What's going to become of me?"

He smiled, and shrugged his shoulders.

"You won't believe me," she cried spitefully, "when I assure you that it's very serious, that I'm at the end of my rope."

No, he could not believe that this was all that serious:

"You know yourself that your husband is no worse than any other. Make an effort: put up with him. You don't need me. You're not very happy? But who is very happy?"

"I've already told you there's someone in my life. I told you his name. You saw me, tonight, dancing with him all night."

He made an effort to conjure up the image of a tanned young man, good-looking but with a face that was emaciated, one might say almost spiritualized by debauchery, who returned to the table, after each dance, to empty his glass. Tota spoke of him without Alain being able to follow her. Did she really love him? But what was love for Tota? And suddenly it came to him irresistibly that none of all this mattered to him, that his spirit could not become attached to these shoddy games. Games played by shadows, debates among phantoms—he could not believe in them; he did not believe in them. Tota's voice, somewhat harsh and cracked, moved him no more than the furious cats on the rooftops of La Hume in June. He watched her sniffle and dry her eyes. He heard her say:

"Yes, I know, I'm aware of his cowardice, his vices, I know he uses drugs . . . But what do you want from me! Maybe that's the only sort of person I find attractive: the desire to protect him, to defend him against himself, to save him."

She lied with sincerity. But Alain smiled at these pretexts that were just as arbitrary as the ones she had given herself for hating Marcel. In truth, William, this young man, inspired less of pity in Tota than Marcel did of indignation. She was scarcely more softened by the weaknesses of the one than shocked by the self-interested love affairs of the other. She was coloring things the way she wanted them—this attraction and antipathy equally born out of the most animal instincts. No, this was nothing! This was nothing! He only heard what Tota was saying in snatches:

"Is William capable of loving? His friends say no. But I know that I could give him the taste for happiness. The day he finally becomes happy, he won't keep trying to evade it. I say this to reassure myself. But finally, could there be the slightest chance of happiness with him?"

What was this happiness she was talking about? They talked about happiness and they didn't know what it was. And all at once, Alain's lucidity was coupled with a sorrowful sense of his own solitude—as if he had been the only one in the world to recognize the nothingness that was agitating this young woman, and millions of other human beings at the same time. Before Alain had really begun to live, what people called life subsided into a strange insipidity in his eyes, an immense depreciation.

"You aren't listening to me," said his sister. "You're thinking of Mama and La Hume . . ."

Then he enumerated again for her all the reasons why he had to respond to his mother's appeal. But as he spoke, he saw more clearly yet that if he had not been called away, he would have come to be avoided by the people in this milieu, like an odd piece of furniture whose use was uncertain.

Tota cried a bit . . . She was in pain. Their pain, at least, is a reality . . . But after all, within a few months, maybe within a few weeks, the insignificant drugged-up young man would have become for Tota just an insignificant drugged-up young man. Alain felt ashamed at his lack of feeling, the absence of any pity for her. Did he not cherish Tota? Yes, more than all the world! But this was not the real drama. He sensed confusedly that the real drama was being played out elsewhere.

"Listen, my dear one: I'm going to go; for Mama of course, but also in order to be able to think of you, to reflect; I'll write you. And if you call for me in the meantime, I'll come back."

Thus he cradled her with vague promises. And in turn, he obtained her assurance that she would make no serious decision without telling him.

"Don't leave without kissing me goodbye."

"Shall I wake you up, if you're sleeping?"

They had moved into the tiny kitchen. "There are some apples and bananas still," said Tota. "Do you remember how, at La Hume, we used to get up in the middle of the night to 'have dinner'?"

Yes, he remembered: they would tiptoe down the stairs; their arrival in the glacial dining room would always startle a fat rat. The children would light a candle from the candelabra. Shivering in their nightgowns, they would search out the biscuits, lap up what was left of the milk . . .

Alain looked at this same little girl, delivered from her pain by these memories, who was saying with her mouth full:

"You really must eat apples with the skin on: that's where all the vitamins are . . ."

He asked her what vitamins were, exactly, and she could only respond by bursting out laughing.

"I'm laughing even though I don't feel at all like laughing."

But Alain was reassured by her laughter. They went back into the studio. The couch was prepared for the night. Tota made sure he had plenty of covers. He didn't want to go to bed: it would be enough just to stretch out. He embraced her, and she repeated to him what it had long been her custom to say, in other times, when he had made her cry:

"Not on the forehead, not on the cheeks, but on my poor eyes."

She smiled at him, and hesitated.

"Whatever I do, Alain, you won't abandon me?"

He shrugged his shoulders: how could he abandon her? He added, with a tone of authority, that she would not accomplish this act she was contemplating.

But when he had said these words, she was already out of the room. Alain looked at the pictures glued on the wall, some fixed with tacks, reproductions of sports photos: soccer matches, boxers. Instead of a table, there were some planks supported on two trestles. False simplicity, false economy. He sat, and bent down to remove his shoes: "I am not good," he said to himself; "I'm becoming indifferent and dried up." And suddenly his throat contracted, his heart beat violently, and a swift stream of emotion flooded him. Maybe these gestures of Tota's, her words didn't move him because they didn't correspond with what they pretended to be expressing? "Love is not love; life is not life. Why repeat that? What does that mean? I am an idiot," he added almost aloud. Outside, a bell chimed. He didn't know that it was Benedictine church nearby. He knew nothing of this blood that was beginning to well up in the sleeping Paris. "I must close my eyes," he thought; "I can't stay awake any longer." He could not imagine that the great wave of Paris, of which he had seen only the froth, could be a holy city, and that in this sad dawn, in the suburban parishes, there were frail Atlases, men and women, who were rising and, their arms extended, were holding up the city and the world.[5]

3 18

He repeated, "I can't stay awake . . ." As if he were denying this state of waking and watching in which he found himself, in body and spirit. No tumult rose up to disturb this strange silence into which he had fallen. Could it be the alcohol? No, he had scarcely drunk anything. Anyway, wasn't this joy familiar to him? It would come on without his asking for it, and it would not return when he called it. But suddenly, at the instant when he was not waiting for it, it would be there. Stretched out in the darkness, he saw already a thin stream of daylight creep between the curtains, but even this dismal dawn could do nothing against his happiness. This was it, this was the joy that rendered all the others insipid, all the ones everyone else intoxicated themselves in, died for. I must search this side of things, he thought, advance in this direction, mount upward toward the source of it. But suddenly he lost his footing, and lost his way. As he had done beneath the chestnut trees on the Champs-Elysées, he repeated aloud: "It's my youth . . ." And this word seemed a derisive one. Instinctively, in a gesture of protest, he pressed his crossed arms against his chest, clasping tightly this happiness whose name he did not know.

XI

MARCEL, still half asleep, knew that Tota had got out of bed: he heard the door slam. She made some angry exclamation, and the chambermaid responded in confused words. Marcel didn't want to know anything about this debate, only wishing to stay in a state of unconsciousness as long as possible: he could already tell he would have a headache, that he was about to be sick, and that he would be paying for all last night's drinking and smoking by a long day of vomiting. He could feel himself retreating bit by bit from sleep, despite keeping his eyes shut and staying absolutely immobile.

Tota came back into the bedroom; she tore open the curtains, growling, "It's too much! To leave without even kissing me goodbye!" Now it was impossible for Marcel to delay his return to life. Between his just-open eyelids he could see Tota, thin and jaundiced-looking, in her worn bathrobe, her hard small face bilious with its morning-after look. Her hair was misshapen from the pillow. Marcel, yawning, asked, "What's too much?"

"He left, this morning, without kissing me goodbye. I made him promise he wouldn't go without it; I had it all arranged so he wouldn't miss his train. But he must have doubted me. No, he was only thinking of La Hume and of Mama. He doesn't care about me!"

While she spoke, life reentered Marcel in waves, just as the drab day had entered the bedroom. His physical illness put aside, for the moment, all his other sufferings. But he knew the other suffering that was lying in wait for him—but first he must decide whether or not to take some aspirin. Aspirin carried the risk of bringing on the vomiting. But maybe that would be the best thing. Oh, that vague odor of café au lait—Tota had, then, already had breakfast. She was sitting now on the edge of the bed, leaning forward. He asked her if she felt ill.

"Me, I'm not doing so well."

"But I didn't do any drinking," she replied grumpily. "I do have a slight migraine, from lack of sleep. But I slept too much, because I didn't hear Alain leave."

"Look, what's it to you if he's left?"

He straightened himself painfully, searching out a fresh spot on the pillow for his aching head, and observing Tota, who said nothing. How ugly she was this morning, this woman, his wife, this stranger established in his house! But still, how young she seemed! A little girl, really. And as for him—all it would take would be for him to raise himself up a bit and catch a view of himself in the mirror. He imagined how his head would feel this morning. But Tota was not looking at him; her eyes were distant; she saw no one, or rather no one except the one who was no longer there.

"Look, Tota, he would have been leaving one of these days very soon anyway. What does it matter to you? I do agree that he left a little rudely."

She heaved her shoulders: as if that were the issue! As if there could exist between brother and sister any matters of etiquette!

But Marcel thought she was not so much suffering as feeling disappointed. Her eyes were red. He asked her if she had been crying. Irritated, she snapped that she had had enough of this perpetual inquisition. She was going to cry; she was crying.

Women's tears had always upset Marcel; but when he was the one that caused the tears to flow, he couldn't help but find some pleasure in them. But now he felt the horror of an experience that he had never imagined, one that now, thanks to Tota, he knew: tears shed for someone else, a hidden wound that he had no share in, a sorrow that he did not cause and could not cure.

"Dear," he said, "is it Alain's leaving?"

She nodded without turning toward him. And as she got up and left the room, he called out, "Where are you going?"

Where was he afraid that she was going? She was simply going to take her bath and get dressed. She would go out; but Marcel was scarcely worried at all about what she could do in the Paris into which she plunged every day. Another worry obsessed him: Why did Alain leave? Why this sudden flight? Last night, at the Boeuf, he seemed hurt. He suffered physically, unable to endure the close air of the place. One of these country boys couldn't breathe that sort of air . . . Yes, he had only felt a physical reaction . . . At least . . . But no, his mother had called him to return home; he left in response to his mother's request. Foolish to search for any other reason. There was no other reason. Just don't move, fight against the nausea, be absolutely still: play dead.

But he didn't count on the telephone. He could simply not answer it, but he had to, no matter what the cost, stop that hideous ringing:

"I didn't wake you? It's me, Hervé. Hangover? Not me, I didn't drink or even smoke. Listen . . . You're there? I wanted to ask you . . . I'd like it to be thought that you and I were going away together, Saturday, for the weekend. You could tell this little white lie, couldn't you? So if Irène phones you, you could tell her that, confirm the story."

"Oh no—I'm not getting mixed up in your stories."

Hervé responded with irritation in his voice: "How many times have I done the same for you? How many lies have you made me tell poor Marie Chavès . . ."

"That's not the same thing: it wasn't a question of lying to my wife, and it certainly wasn't a matter of lying to Irène . . . (Hervé, raging inwardly, thought, "What's so extraordinary about Irène? How is she any different from any other woman?") "Anyway, I remember that I promised to go see her tomorrow or the day after. She'll be expecting me. Even if I put off the visit, she'll phone me and ask questions. This is not the sort of woman one lies to . . . It's ridiculous for you to be talking about this on the telephone!"

He heard Hervé's voice: "Yes, you're right; it's idiotic. But I'm speaking to you from my study . . . No danger at all. Anyway, I'll arrange it some other way. And I may not even go."

The movements Marcel had just made were enough to bring on the nausea. It wasn't true that he wanted a meeting with Irène. But he resolved to call on her. He would confide in her. If anybody in the world could release him from this awful fantasy, it would be Irène. She possessed all the virtues of men—the virtues he had never discovered, however, in any of his men friends. Discreet to the point of seeming to forget the confidences she had received. The only being he knew in whom paying attention was accompanied by the desire to help out. "Marie Chavès too, maybe, but she was in love with me, and even the most generous love is also terribly self-interested. She would deduce from what I said what I really felt, and from that how she ought to behave. Irène will try to help, to do good; it's like a vocation with her. She suffers and people forget to care about her. Everybody talks about the miseries of this miserable woman married to Hervé, this woman who may be about to die. Speak to her about Marie. Perhaps she could go see her, take care of her a little, bring her some books . . . Books! What a barbarian I am, uncultivated compared to her! To think of finding help in Nietzsche! She looks vainly for some salvation in certain books, and as for me, I know that nothing can console me for not possessing what I really want."

His thoughts strayed, found their way back to their habitual track. He said half aloud, "No, not that, above all not that! There's no evidence at all, nothing to base it on! Why wouldn't Tota feel desolated and sad when he left? My anguish has no foundation at all. What's it really based on, after all?" He pressed his hand against his eyelids: "Yes," he said to himself, "in talking with Irène, it will all become clearer."

What did Irène think of Tota? She had only seen her once: a mute and intimidated Tota: "I have a horror of disease and sick people," the young woman had said, the door barely closed behind her. For her part, during the conversation, Irène had seemed as if turned into ice by this adolescent so full of life.

XII

UNID that morning, Irène had not perceived that by picking up the phone in her bedroom, she could listen to her husband telephoning on the floor above her. She should have hung up immediately, should not have listened to this conversation between Hervé and Marcel: it was the first time she had done such a thing. Hervé was so sure of her discretion that he would leave letters lying about: he knew she would never even glance at them.

Irène rose, took a few steps, stopped before the mirror, and interrogated the phantom she saw there. She could not even say to herself that she was surprised, nor that her curiosity was awakened, because for a long time now Hervé had not even bothered to give his lies the slightest tinge of believability, and she had learned nothing new by listening. It was even rather touching that, this time, he had sought out the complicity of Marcel in order to avoid upsetting Irène. But since she had inadvertently heard the conversation, she had to admit it to him. Her character was such that it was not a matter for discussion or doubt: she had to admit it as quickly as possible. But she still hesitated. Not that she felt any shame or fear about doing it: they were both skilled masters of the veiled allusion. (And for situations like this, she thought, it was a good thing to have a well-bred husband.)

Still, as she got ready to join him, her heart was beating violently. After the first steps on the stairs, she stopped to catch her breath. An idea took shape for her, an idea she had long brooded over and caressed. Had she ever done anything better for herself than this idea? Could she have ever done better than by imagining it, by diverting herself with the thought of it? And now she knew the time was come for her to act. She knew the rules of the game she was about to initiate. She held on very loosely to her miserable life, staring at her hand on the banister, breathing the dusty air of the entryway. The carpet was worn at the edge of the stairsteps. She stood still, listening attentively to the rumbling from the street, the cars' horns, the squeal of brakes, to everything that the ear could apprehend, to all the things that dead people did not apprehend.

"Let's go!" she said. But she seemed to change her mind. After a moment of thinking, she went back down the stairs, went into her bathroom, and began putting on her makeup in front of the mirror. She made up her cheeks and lips with more care than usual—she who was known for her indifference to the world's view of her, for her lack of taste. She was known as the worst-dressed woman in her circle. Above all, this prim chignon at the back of her neck was ridiculous, and when she married into the Blénauge family, where there was a love of nicknames, she was called the "austere muse."

When her face was finished, she contemplated it a long while, without indulgence. The skin on her forehead seemed waxier, and her ears whiter (it had never even occurred to her that one could apply rouge to the ears). She smiled, but only with her mouth, and her painted lips took on a ghastly contrast to her exposed gums and teeth. "And all this for nobody!" This time, her smile was genuine, and suddenly, taking a sponge, she destroyed at one stroke all the work she had done.

She felt less fear now, her ravaged face somehow strengthening her appearance. Like a woman who is suffering from the cold, she wrapped her bathrobe around her and, one more time, ascended the stairs and, gathering herself for an instant before the door, knocked.

Hervé was writing a letter when she appeared in his doorway. He looked at her with surprise, because she never came to this room except when he was out, to look for books. And that was his first word:

"You want a book?"

She shook her head and sat down, her eyes closed. She was so pale that Hervé felt fear, and he took her hand.

"It's nothing. I just came up the stairs too quickly."

He waited, trying to divine what had made her come here; she dared not raise her eyes upon this pretty, wrinkled man whose air of combined challenge and fear she knew only too well.

"It's a matter about the telephone," she said, "that we have to discuss. It needs to be fixed."

When Hervé assured her that it was working, that he had just made a call, she replied in the most neutral tone that it was not right, because she should not have been able to listen in on a conversation on the downstairs phone. She could make out Hervé's anxious and hunted expression, even though she still lacked the resolve to look him in the face.

"Oh, but with you," he essayed in a light tone, "that's not a problem. I know you, Irène: as soon as you would have heard my voice, you would have immediately hung up. Am I right?"

She shook her head. "I don't know what came over me. I listened to the end. And I came up to apologize for doing something so base."

Doubtless he imagined the atrocious scene that any other woman would have been making right now. He said softly, "Irène!" in a tone marked with veneration and shame. He was sincere, for the space of a few seconds; then, very quickly, he only thought of how he could turn this attitude to his benefit. He assumed that Irène would leave without saying anything more, and was nonplussed to see her continue to sit there, immobile. She surely was not going to have the bad taste to demand explanations from him?

He watched her furtively: she was breathing quickly and she looked flushed and feverish. (He thought, "Terral says that cancer does not lead to fevers. Romieu, though, is sure she has a tumor.") Even when she was a young girl and Hervé was hesitating as to whether to marry her, he said to his friends that Irène Verley had the look of a death's head. But now! The bones of her face were visible underneath her parchment-like skin. One day, maybe very soon now, he would be free . . . Hervé, full of fear for himself, closed his eyes, shook his head imperceptibly, and took Irène's hand:

"My dear one . . ."

He dared not squeeze her hand, that small packet of tepid remains. She did not remove her hand. She said:

"I want . . ."

He did not recognize this humble, almost supplicating tone.

"This Saturday, Hervé, this Sunday—I want—remember that I never ask you for anything"—how long it had been since she had spoken to him with the familiar "tu"! "This is perhaps the first time—maybe the last time: I want those days from you, so that I can forget what I just overheard. If I'm strong enough, we'll go to a concert. No, I can see that would bore you. But, for example, you could read to me: you like to read aloud."

He was seized by panic at the idea that this thing he had waited for and desired so much that he was counting the days, the hours, would be frustrated and snatched away by her. He responded quickly:

"But tonight, Irène, tomorrow, every day, we can pick out a book that you like, a really long novel so that the reading will take us weeks: *War and Peace*, do you think? Or *The Mill on the Floss*?[6]

"Not tonight," she said, but without perfect assurance. "We'll start Saturday night—all right?"

He couldn't face up to her bright, feverish stare, and he stammered that he would love to, but that he had a party arranged with his friends, and it was too late to break it off, and finally that it really didn't depend on him. He wished he could change things. But she couldn't demand the impossible.

"I'm begging you, Hervé."

The gravity of her tone shocked Hervé. Usually, when she had tried out absurd schemes like this on him (though she had never tried one so absurd as this), Irène quickly saw her mistake, took the idea back, and smoothly covered her retreat. But today, she insisted.

"You must."

Hervé was afraid. He knew well enough that there was no one in the world who could prevent him from having the fun he had planned for the weekend, no one who could make him sacrifice this pleasure. But he saw Irène, and he had the confused sensation that this was the person who could do it; that he would have to walk out over her dead body. Ardently, he defended his menaced weekend: every night this week, if she wished, every one of next week, except Saturday and Sunday, except those two days.

"All right. Let's drop it."

She got up. So thin, so grand; and this time, she looked at Hervé for a long time. This sign was necessary in order for her to take the path she had been meditating for months. She had obeyed, she thought, some old religious instinct: she had drawn the lot, consulted the oracle, questioned this miserable sphinx, this weak and despicable man. And now . . .

She raised her eyes, and she was struck by the delicate pink of three chimneys against the misty blue sky—chimneys that reminded her of the teats of a young animal—and everything that the human ear could hear in a city, on a morning in winter, she heard.

"I'm sorry . . ." she said.

She had already closed the door. Hervé reopened it:

"Irène!" he called. "Listen." She knew, then, that he had understood. He said to her, "I'll arrange it, I'll do whatever's necessary. Don't worry."

He didn't see her face in the shadowy corridor, only her long, thin body leaning against the wall. She asked in a breathless voice, "You'll stay?"

"Yes."

"Saturday night? Sunday?"

He repeated yes, firmly. He heard Irène breathing with effort and watched her move away, her hand feeling the wall, like a blind woman.

XIII

TOWARD the end of that same day, Marcel was waiting for Tota, who should have been back long before. He was not worried about what she might be doing, but imagined there had been an accident: this little provincial still didn't know how to cross streets in Paris. He sighed with relief when he heard the door.

"I was beginning to worry."

"I'm exhausted . . ."

She chattered on at length about trying on clothes, about an exposition at Bernheim's. He watched her with concern, and she assumed he suspected her. Had he had her followed? What did he know about what she had done today? Had somebody already told him that she had driven around for more than two hours in William's car? William had counted on either her fatigue or the cold eventually bringing her around, making her agree to come to his place, or to the studio of an absent friend. But she had stayed calm and confident of resisting him. Marcel wouldn't believe her if she told him the truth, that she was in no peril from this young man, his face spoiled and drawn by fatigue—as he was this afternoon in the car, with the stub of his Maryland cigarette hanging from the corner of his mouth, with that pimple on his temple, with the breath of someone who has been smoking and drinking all night and going without sleep. Each time, she had gone out feeling the excitement of the risk she was running with him, the prey of both her fear and her desire for adventure, and each time, from the moment she saw him, she knew that nothing would happen. Tota could hardly have said whether she felt more comforted or deceived. All she had to do was toy with his desire, and frustrate his pathetic ruses:

"No, I'm not hungry," she said to William. "No, I'm not tired. I'm not cold. If I could eat anything, it would maybe be a bit of cake, in a patisserie. I'm still dazzled by the memory of when I was a child and we went to Bordeaux and ate at a patisserie."

"How much does he know?" Tota asked herself, observing Marcel. Then she said out loud:

"Are we eating in?"

They almost never did.

"Have you arranged anything for tonight?"

He shook his head and watched her.

"So much the better," she said. "I want to go to bed right after supper. I'll read in bed."

She found it strange that he consented to staying in. They sat down to some cold cuts; Maria had forgotten to get them wine. Every time Tota raised her eyes, she surprised Marcel looking at her. "He knows. What does he know? Someone may have seen us kissing in the car."

"There's hardly anything to eat, and I'm really very hungry now. You too?"

No, he was not hungry. He lit a cigarette, got up from the table. She followed him, and suddenly decided:

"I did something today—I have to confess to you. I acted without thinking."

He still said nothing, and she went on. "Picture it—the Boulevard Haussmann, and somebody calls my name. It was William in his Talbot. I had packages, so he had pity on me and had me get in. I never thought that this could be a little compromising. We went by the Bois, St. Cloud and Meudon. Then, I realized, and I got mad at myself . . ."

"People saw you?"

"Not that I know of."

He made a gesture that signified, "Well, then, what does it matter?"

She observed him uncomfortably, fearing some sort of trap.

"You aren't angry with me?"

He shrugged. She said, smiling:

"I thought you'd be jealous!"

"Of that child William? You wouldn't want him."

She was deceived into believing he didn't care about William; but his air gave the lie to his words. Maybe it wasn't her who was bothering him? The thought made her feel disappointed.

"Did you get some bad news today, from the rest home? Is *she* doing poorly?"

"No, no; don't worry about Marie."

"Her cure isn't working? Poor woman! You know, you can talk about her to me."

He got up, and took her by her wrists:

"Don't be a hypocrite. Don't pretend to be jealous."

He went over to the far side of the room, away from the lamp, and he hid his face behind one of his hands. She didn't know what was bothering him, but it was her, it was due to her. Liberated from her worry, she only felt her customary irritation with Marcel, and she asked him with bitterness what she had done wrong.

"Nothing," he said, "nothing at all."

And after a short silence, without looking at her:

"Have you got over Alain's leaving?"

"Yes, because he'll come back."

"He promised you?"

"No, but I want him to. And he always does what I want him to. What's funny is that he says the same thing about me. I'm not worried; I won't have to insist much at all."

They were quiet for a moment, and then Marcel spoke again:

"When Alain gets married . . ."

"Are you crazy? He's only nineteen. And then—no, my future sister-in-law isn't born yet."

"I'd guess," Marcel said with a smile, "that you'd scratch her eyes out!"

She replied, sulkily, that she couldn't scratch the eyes out of a woman who didn't exist.

Marcel was surprised to find in these words, meant to shock her, so much comfort. And suddenly he was able to judge and measure his madness. It appeared so plainly to him that he couldn't imagine how he had been possessed by it. His body sunk in a deep armchair, he lit a cigar. This weight had been lifted off him as if by a miracle. This young woman who came and went at loose ends, from one room to another—she was his wife. She loved no one, not even him. All that had yet to develop. But now that he was free . . . he called her; she replied that she was busy putting things away; but after a few seconds he saw her trailing slowly across the room. She put a record on, began vaguely dancing, then sat down, but at a distance from him. His anguish dissipated, Marcel could find nothing else in him that had anything to do with her. They didn't know what to say to each other. The needle screeched on the record. When would he decide to buy a better record player?

She yawned and sighed:

"I'm bored . . . I think I'm hungry," she added.

"It's true that there isn't enough to eat here."

She looked at him.

"What if we went to the Plantation? There's time enough for us to dress . . ."

The name of the place dissipated the discomfort of their time alone together. Marcel felt humiliated that he couldn't spend one single night alone with Tota. But already he thought that he wanted to go out and drink.

"But you were tired, you said?"

She protested that she wasn't tired anymore, that she was hungry, and that she felt like dancing.

"It's too early," he said weakly.

"We can stop first at the Boeuf." William had told her he would be at the bar till midnight.

"Okay. I'm not going to dress," Marcel said.

She went to change her dress. It was as if they were fleeing from a fire, so impatient were they to stop being a couple imprisoned by four walls, already lost in spirit, lost in the light, in the din, in the odor of other couples.

. She called out from her makeup table:

"By the time you get a taxi, I'll be down!"

While he straightened the knot in his tie, Marcel saw, in the mirror, Tota elongating her eyelashes with a single stroke of the brush. She brushed her nails and was gazing at them with an expression utterly empty of thought.

XIV

EVEN though it was still day, Irène interrupted Hervé's reading and asked him to draw the curtains and light the lamp. When he had done so, he went back to his place and began again to read aloud. Since he had to lean toward the lamp, the lower half of his face, his hands, and the book were brightly lit. But if he raised his eyes, he could scarcely make out Irène enfolded among her pillows. Sometimes he would stop, and she would say weakly:

"I'm listening . . ."

Then he would take up the reading again, in the tone of a docile schoolboy—exactly like a schoolboy whose parents have deprived him of his day out, who has resigned himself to his tasks because he has no other choice, but who can think only of the circus, of his friends, of his forfeited fun.

Never before had Irène been so struck by her husband's childish air, that hideously childish air. She had hoped to be able to go out with him, this Saturday that he had consented to sacrifice for her. But in order to be sure of sleeping so as to be strong enough, the night before she had imprudently overdone the dose of her sleeping medicine. And now she had to battle against a crushing somnolence. Hervé did what he had to, and never imagined that his bitter regret was visible.

"Does he know that he's given me a reprieve," she wondered, "that my life depended on this poor sacrifice—what remains of my life? Or am I only playacting?" No, she knew only how much she wanted to sleep. No one could begin to comprehend the force of this desire. She was consumed with it, and at the end of her strength. She had counted on Hervé's refusal; she had solicited from him this little push toward the abyss, toward the blackness. And, contrary to all expectation, there he is, with his air of an unhappy, locked-in puppy. How wrong she was to double the dose of the Phenobarbital! Impossible to follow the reading. And it was that beautiful life of Nietzsche by Halévy. She concentrated her thoughts, made an immense effort of attention:

> "I hunt men, as a Corsair does, but not in order to sell them into sla-
> very, but to carry them off with me into liberty." This savage liberty
> that he offered them did not seduce young men. One of his students,
> M. Scheffler, recounts his memories: "I took Nietzsche's course,
> though I didn't know much about him. One day, chance threw us
> together, and we walked off together after the class session. Thin
> clouds passed through the sky. 'Beautiful clouds!' he said to me;
> 'how rapid they are!' They look like the clouds of Paul Véronèse, I
> responded. Suddenly his hand seized my arm: 'Listen,' he said to
> me, 'the vacation is here, I'm leaving soon—come with me, and
> we'll go see the clouds in Venice!' I was surprised, and I stammered
> out a few hesitant words. And then I saw Nietzsche turn away from
> me, his face glacial, closed, as if dead. He moved off without saying
> a word, leaving me alone."[7]

Irène could barely follow to the end of the anecdote. "Nietzsche brought us an answer, a rule for living," she thought. "He had found something; and he no longer looked like those who don't want to find it. But you cannot find it; you dare not even want to find it. How much trouble I've taken to find it! Despite myself, I search, as if there were an answer somewhere. It's because I'm not free, not free in spirit," she added, unaware that she was speaking out loud.

"What did you say?" asked Hervé.

She excused herself; she had simply been saying some words at random.

"You're not listening—you're falling asleep," he said dryly. "Do you want me to stop?"

But she dreaded more than anything the effort of sustaining a conversation. He took up the book again, with his docile schoolboy's tone:

> Actions are never what they seem to us to be. It has taken us so long
> to learn that external things are not what they appear to be! But there
> is still the inner world. Acts are in reality "something other." Perhaps
> we can go further and say: all acts are essentially unknown.[8]

Hervé stopped reading and cried, "Now that's beautiful, that is!" She understood that he was applying the words to himself and was moved. "Yes, our acts are unknown," she thought. She would no longer judge Hervé; anyway, she had never condemned him. In her deep weakness, she no longer tried to fight against this torpor, or to follow the monotone. Memories of other readings came back to her: "Human reason is mobile, and must reinvent solutions for every new particular case: the case of Hervé. Do not judge him against a stable, unmoving reason."

The bell from the door downstairs made her jump.
"You told them downstairs that I'm not at home to anyone?"
"Perhaps it's Mother."
"Above all, not her: tell her I'm sleeping."
Hervé left the room, took a few steps in the shadows of the corridor, and recognized his mother's voice.
"Ah! You're there, my child?"
Her somber clothes and her old furs smelled of vinegar, of pepper. She didn't leave him time enough to lie: as long as he was there, she didn't need to come in.
She seemed contented. She was glad he was there, at his wife's bedside. How was she?
"Calm, but a little weak. She's not eating."
"I'll leave you together."
The old woman pronounced the words with an air of happiness.
"I'm reading to her," Hervé said with satisfaction.
"That's good!" And she embraced him. "Say, I brought some violets . . ."
He re-entered the bedroom.
"It was Mother; she's gone. She brought you some violets."
"Cut the stems and put them in the little vase. Yes, continue reading."
For the very ill, fighting off sleep is the hardest thing. But the few words she did hear when he began reading again resonated within her deeply:

Where do we want to go? Do we want to cross the sea? Where are we dragging this powerful passion of ours? Of us also it may some-day be said that, in bearing steadily to the West, we have arrived at the unknown India, but it was our destiny to run aground finally in the infinite. Or else, my brothers. Or else . . .?

Irène's thoughts clutched tightly to this "or else." Or else we will, maybe, not land after all? Absurd obstinacy: she wanted to find an answer, but she was not free in spirit. She thought of the ocean that she would never see again; and confusedly she thought that there was something even more beautiful than the sea that extended along the shadows of disease, of solitary suffering and of death. She was surprised to feel this sudden joy in the depths of her being whose origin she did not know,

which did not come from the presence of Hervé, because she was no
longer thinking of Hervé: a few words still remained just perceptible to
her:

> "Lux mea crux," Nietzsche wrote in his notes, "crux mea lux." The
> light is my cross, the cross is my light! His agitation, which time did
> not ease at all, remained extreme. He was afraid, because he did not
> know the threat hovering over his life: "Thoughts are rising on my
> horizon, and such thoughts . . ."

Hervé could see that his wife was sleeping, and he closed the book.
He listened to her as she scarcely breathed. The lamp illuminated her
skeletal arm on the coverlet. She always slept like this when she had taken
too much Phenobarbital. He looked at his watch: only five o'clock. He
would have thought it was much later. But Irène had told him to close the
curtains when it was still daylight . . .

"At this time, I would have been . . ."

But they had not gone off for the weekend; everything had been put
off until the next month. If Hervé had been free to leave, he knew just
where he would go. And from the moment when she fell asleep, nothing
prevented him from going out. No, he had promised. But one can go out
for a walk, stretch one's legs, buy some cigarettes. He would be back by
eight. But no—he knew very well that if he went out, nothing would make
him return. It would be dinner, an evening out, the night, perhaps all of
tomorrow—as it always was.

The maid came in to close the outside shutters. Hervé suggested she
do it very quietly. The sound did not wake Irène. How she slept! If he
could be sure he was strong enough to come back right after dining, he
could leave without worry: surely she wouldn't wake up before he got
back. Ah, how wrong he was to let his thoughts light on this idea! Didn't
he know he could never resist a temptation like this?

"Now, I can't not go out," he said to himself.

And really, where was the risk? It wasn't a matter of deceiving Irène.
Even if he didn't come back tonight, that would be just like any other
night. She wouldn't want him to change; she didn't want him to. She
knew that a sick woman had to be indulgent, to close her eyes to some
things. It's true, too, that even if she were not sick, he would not act any
differently.

"So, if I go out tonight, and if I'm late in getting back, it won't be
anything new."

Why did he have this sense that he had to persuade himself it
wouldn't be anything new? Certainly, he had often disappeared for days at
a time; but then, he hadn't been violating any particular promise, whereas

tonight . . . "I gave in to a whim of hers. Maybe she herself attaches no importance to it." No, no: not a whim! What woman was less capricious than Irène? He had given in to a hidden threat, to a solemn warning, even if it had been expressed in the most ordinary terms.

But hadn't he stayed at her bedside for several hours? The day was done. It was night time, and she was sleeping. Anyway, he never promised anything specific. And how deeply she was sleeping!

He moved toward her, bent over her, attentive to her slightly too rapid breathing. He said to himself, "At six o'clock, if she hasn't awakened . . ." And now he was calm and easy, as if he had given the matter over to a higher power, as if the decision no longer depended on him. He frequently looked at his watch with some anxiety, not knowing any more what he really wanted—or rather, he knew what he wanted, but he feared it. He was afraid. "Whatever happens," he thought, "I'll be both happy and miserable."

If she woke up, it would put an end to the anguish, but also to the hope—that ugly hope in which the heart counts for nothing, that hope of the flesh, that hope that infects every fiber of the obsessed, possessed being. He pretended to think that he hoped Irène would awaken; but still he kept himself from so much as turning a page of a book, or lighting a cigarette; he held his breath and felt anxious when a truck drove by, making the windows rattle.

To make time seem shorter, he diverted himself by imagining the pleasures he was going to be tasting—that he was perhaps going to be tasting, so long as that woman there on the bed continued to sleep. And at the point where he now was, there was nothing in the world that could have kept him from running out after this happiness. Even if Irène were to wake up right now and hold out her thin arms to him, he knew perfectly well that he would invent an excuse for fleeing. He said: "I can't help it any more; free me from my promise."

From time to time a sort of sigh would escape from Irène's lips. Her hand sketched a confused gesture as if, even in her sleep, she had to defend herself against someone. Hervé paid no particular attention to it; he paid attention solely to his delicious imaginings—to this vision that so utterly and so terribly reflected itself in him that even his mother herself, at this moment, would not dare embrace him.

When six o'clock struck, Hervé immediately got up. He did not bend over the still body in the bed, nor did he even turn his gaze toward her.

XV

THE sound of the door closing woke Irène—just as, when she was a child, at eleven o'clock at night, when the servants had retired to their upper floor, the departure of her father, announced by the same sound of a door closing, tore her out of her first sleep, and reminded her of her solitude and her abandonment. Though she had no doubt that it was Hervé who had left, she wanted the maid to tell her so in order to be sure. She told the maid she had not taken anything, that she was going to sleep; she told the maid that she should be quiet around the house and, tomorrow, wait for her to call her. Then she felt calm and easy.

Hervé had done well to leave. What could he do for a sleeping sick woman? If Irène had wanted to give herself this signal, if she had solicited fate to give her this little push toward the abyss, Hervé was in no way guilty of anything. Anyway, she asked herself, who really is guilty, and what does that word even mean? Even if he had understood that he held Irène's destiny in his hands, what value could such a life have in his eyes, a life already half ruined? Did he really believe in this benign, latent tuberculosis, as he pretended to? Didn't he realize that she was dying slowly of something else? That she was being consumed, or rather gnawed away? All the more reason, then, to have some pity on her and make this sacrifice for her . . . But no—he had no reason to have any pity, and there was no real weight to put on this one word: sacrifice.

In this state in which she found herself, he could no longer love her. He could only remember having loved her, and spare her in favor of that memory. But he had never loved her, not even for a single minute, never. Nothing outside her existed for Irène, nothing but these feelings that were smothering her: nothing corresponded to this love, to this desire to give herself and to be deserving ... Deserving of what? Deserving. Worth. Dignity. Baudelaire:

This, O Lord, is the best evidence
That we can offer of our dignity,
This sob that swells from age to age and dies
Out on the shore of Your eternity![9]

Did Baudelaire really believe that? A poet has the right to give a name to his disquiet, to his anxiety: God. Perhaps the desire actually creates its object? An excess of grief brings the consoler to life.

How all this disgusted Irène! She did not want to be consoled, she asked for no consolation. These poverty-stricken people who make their requests in order to persuade themselves that they are not alone! She had no fear of annihilation, but neither did she fear physical suffering: she did not want anyone to believe that it was because she suffered so much that she ... But what does it matter what anybody else thinks!

This need in her could have been satisfied by a child. That's it, naturally! Who wouldn't have thought of it! She was happy to give a name to this desire suffocating her: frustrated maternal instinct. It's not that children were especially attractive to her ... How she was suffering now! If she could only walk a little around the room—but she was too weak.

A glass of water stood there, half full: she swallowed one, two, three, six tablets. If she hadn't been an invalid, she could have helped certain other people. Marcel would miss her; she could have helped him with Marie, in that nursing home ... "Even as an invalid, I could have been of some help to them." Marcel had told her once that everything she said took on a singular kind of authority. When she had described a life of effort and beauty to Marie Chavès—work at your own perfecting, familiarize yourself with great and beautiful works of art, steal from Nietzsche the secret of going beyond yourself—did she really hope to be understood? Marie had listened to her with fervor, but that same night she sought out her own oblivion. For those who have known love, nothing can console them for having lost it: "A hypocrite, I pretend to believe that we're in this world in order to understand, but we are made for love ...."

Words, only words! What did Marcel and Marie matter to her? Hervé. She had already been in love with him during the dancing lessons, when he always came in late, wearing that boutonniere that everybody laughed at. One day, he had given it to her. "It was for my money. In his world, it was almost always for money. He went to all the concerts, in order to see me; he even took that course from Pierre Janet and, at the Sorbonne, that one from Henri Delacroix; he sat next to me, he took notes. I pretended to be duped by it all; I was playing at being loved, although I had been told that he had already made inquiries about my fortune through the banks. The marriage almost didn't come off because, that year, my father had lost two million at Deauville, and if he hadn't died suddenly when he returned, the negotiations would have been broken off. I remember that during our engagement Hervé said to me one day, speaking of his friends, that they were becoming jealous. I was the best thing he could find, since his mother had turned down both the Jew and the American; as an orphan, I had no close family, and the Verley business seemed to be an honest one. He couldn't get involved with a shady fortune; in that matter, at least, he refused any compromise. And me—I loved him. And the devout old lady, my mother-in-law, already knew what I've learned since . . . No, no— don't think of all that."

Her conscious delirium showed her, like so many objects, her love and the object of her love: an immense sea, sparkling under the sky, whose millions of waves rocked and battered against this tiny indifferent being, this minute stone: Hervé. She could see his wrinkled, sneaking face clearly. She was lucid. She knew that nobody in the world could love her, cherish her. She had believed that you could live while loving without being loved; and that a patient love would end by shaping and modeling, into the form in which it saw the beloved, the being to which it was attached. She conjured up the long train of Hervé's lies, and set herself to straightening everything up without any anger. Poor idiot! She had never had any power over him except that of disgusting: the power to repulse. He would rather be anywhere she was not.

How strange it is, she thought, this powerful force of a love without object, this immense surging of a heart toward nothing! Since—since always—since her childhood, when it was her doll that she pressed to her- self so tightly at night in the little bed, pressed it to her with an unimagin- able power of adoration . . . The apartment on the Rue Vézelay. She had often sensed it again, in other apartments, the odor of the entryway. The Chinese lamps on the chimney in the small salon, lit by gas; once she broke one of the lamps' sleeves. And that was the only fight she could recall between her parents before their separation, the only quarrel. (She was then just eight years old.) On the contrary, she always thought they were too polite with each other. She had only stayed with her father on the Rue Vézelay for a few months before entering the Duruy lycée. But it seemed like a very long period—perhaps because of her solitude at night, when her father's closing the door behind him woke her up suddenly. None of the domestics slept on her floor. She had been shown the speak- ing trumpet that linked the apartment with the servants, in case she ever needed help. She did not reproach her mother: everyone has the right to reshape her life. But there was no place for Irène in her mother's second life: another husband, in another country, with other children. Don't pretend to have suffered much over it. The lycée, and Mademoiselle Fermeil: "Spinoza, Nietzsche when you're a little bigger . . . Intelligence above all. The cult of ideas. Whoever sincerely loves beauty will never commit a base act." How did one do good? "The poor." Irène came to feel that her visits, her alms sanctioned her place in society, legitimated it. Their hypocrisy: they chose to see her as devout, speaking of "this little one's First Communion . . ." Tiptoeing around in order to say what they wanted her to say. In the infirmary, at least, she could care for their bodies without speaking. Never did she manifest her pity, her love for them; and never did she betray them. They found her dry, distant. She could avow with truth that she loved, above all, all the bodies in pain. Disease: our normal, habitual state. Thousands of maladies . . . And the healthy ones poison themselves deliberately, as if they wanted to join the order. One should be able to occupy oneself solely with suffering bodies. Futile love. Fire burning for no one, for nothing. This need to give oneself, and no one in the world to receive the gift. No one.

There was no water left in the glass, but the carafe was half full. Conquer this thirst; fill the glass; swallow at once as many tablets as possible, because in a few minutes you may be unable to do anything at all. Hervé, at this moment—where was he? With what creatures? Doing what? Why is it so horrible? Evil. She had always been obsessed by this mystery: an order of values, a hierarchy among actions . . . Too late to think anymore. These ties that Nietzsche speaks of, that he himself said were impossible to break: *"This tenderness toward that which is always venerated . . ."* *The Moral Problem*, by Dominique Parodi—how weak it was![10] She was unable to finish reading it. All these roads led nowhere. Toward nothing. She seemed to be drifting off, but did not lose consciousness.

"Who's there?" Did she speak these words, or did she only think them? "Who's there?" It's that woman, that concierge with her children swarming around her, on the Rue de la Gaîté, the one to whom Irène went twice a week to help her with her injections. "It's me"—but the voice was not hers. There were other poor wracked bodies lying on the ground, leaning against the wall; Irène could make them out despite the darkness. Maybe her bedside lamp is still on . . . But no—it's their flesh, so white between the bandages that it illuminates the shadows. These bodies and their flesh held no secrets for her, for she had made the dressings, she knew the shape of the wounds, she was used to the smell. They all repeated: "It's me . . ." as if they were already parts of one body. Marcel and Hervé himself bent over her, heaped among these sick and wounded, they the sickest. She suffered, but not in the flesh anymore. She had the sense that there was perhaps another form of renunciation, another night, another death besides the death that she had sought out, that she had willed. Half engulfed now, she could no longer get back to the surface; she tried to claw; her nails broke, her elbows were bloody. She could no longer make the discovery, not fall to her knees, weep with joy. She could no longer give witness. She had to cross all the way to the end of these shadows into which she had insanely thrown herself. But slipping and losing her footing in the abyss, she knew, she saw, she called finally that love by its name, which is above every name.

XVI

THE maid showed Marcel into the dining room, where he found the Countess de Blénauge, the cook and the chauffeur.

"Where is Hervé? Do you know?"

The old woman asked him this at once, without replying to the condolences he tried to stammer out. She had kept her hood on, and a few stray scraps of yellowish white hair escaped from beneath it. Her beat-up old black purse lay on the table, next to an umbrella and a pair of much-used gloves.

The maid began her story again: Madame had told her strictly that she was not to enter the bedroom until she had been rung for. Often Madame slept late and did not get up until nearly noon. She had gone in once, but had retired at once believing that Madame was in a deep sleep. The girl, who had only held the job for about two weeks, hadn't had the slightest suspicion. It was the cook who, returning from the market, became worried. She opened the curtains, and understood everything at once; the sheets were soiled by her vomiting. The carafe had been knocked over. Some tablets remained on the bedtable. Poor Madame wanted them there for her convenience. But Monsieur had told her to pay attention to them. Pharmacists should not be allowed to sell things like that if they're poison.

"No," Madame de Blénauge responded to a question from Marcel, "you can't see her yet. Two nuns are with her, making her ready. Monsieur," she added, without looking at him and as if embarrassed, "you must know where Hervé is?"

Marcel shook his head and turned his eyes to the chauffeur. He was an old man, a man from the country, with an air of integrity about him. He understood that no one dared to question him, but that everyone was waiting for him to speak. He said that Monsieur never used the car during the day: "He preferred taxis."

Marcel did not know the address of Irène's mother. He knew only that she lived in London, that her husband wrote plays, or at least that he was a director in the theatre. But he could not recall his name.

"Hervé can tell you. He'll be coming back any minute, I'm sure."

"One never knows when Monsieur will return. It could be tonight, or tomorrow, or the day after tomorrow."

No one said anything to the maid's observation. The sunny and cold daylight entered through a large bay window. Everyone looked out on the rooftops of apartment buildings bristling with chimneys. A roofer, standing upright, looked larger than life. Madame de Blénauge said quietly, "My poor legs . . ." She sat in the chair Marcel pushed toward her and didn't budge. One of the nuns came in and spoke to her in a low voice. The old woman shook her head:

"There isn't a crucifix in the house."

She opened her purse, took out some keys, and pulled out a rosary which the sister took with her. Marcel said that they would have to wait for Hervé before they began the necessary steps.

"If he's not back tomorrow morning, we'll discuss it then."

The maid, who had been listening carefully, called out almost joyfully: "The elevator!" Everyone waited in a great silence. They heard the outer door open, then the sound of the key in the lock.

So there would be better light in the dining room, its doors had been removed and replaced by a curtain which, except when they were dining, remained open. Thus Hervé could see, as soon as he stepped in, all these people brought together. He understood. In a single movement, the domestics disappeared into the butlery, but stayed just behind the door. They only heard these words, pronounced dryly by the old woman:

"Go into her room—go!"

She had repulsed him when he stooped down to embrace her. His collar was crumpled and dirty; he had not been able to shave. His look passed from his mother to his friend; he stammered:

"The Phenobarbital?"

Marcel nodded.

"But there is hope?"

He asked it anyway, even though he knew already that it was over.

He took Marcel's arm, but Madame de Blénauge intervened:

"No," she said sternly. "Don't go with him. Let him go into her room alone."

343

Hervé, stupefied, stared at her. This wouldn't last; it wasn't possible. He removed himself, disappeared. Irène dead caused him less fear than this mother he didn't recognize, this mother who seemed not to love him any longer. A door was opened and closed from deep within the apartment. Marcel hesitated and almost followed him, but dared not disobey this little old woman sitting motionless in her chair, her eyes closed. Thus a few minutes slowly passed until she said to him:

"You can go join him now."

Left alone, she maintained the same posture. Her head trembled in the manner of old people: she seemed to be saying no continually to some one. She opened up her old worn purse and sought her rosary, then remembered that the sister had taken it. Then she began reciting the rosary on her fingers, but soon interrupted herself: the only thing she felt capable of at the moment was to try to keep herself from thinking.

She could see a plate with some bananas and mandarin oranges; she had to prevent herself from eating, even though she was hungry. She hadn't felt such a desire for food in a long time. She got up finally, took her purse and umbrella, and made her way into the corridor. In front of the bedroom door, she waited and listened a moment: no sound; you would have thought the room was empty. She couldn't make up her mind to go in, as if she expected to encounter again the irritated frown of her daughter-in-law. What good would it do now, to walk toward that bed again? How many times had she been stationed here, not daring to cross the threshold, certain that she would only exasperate this afflicted child! It had been necessary; at least she had believed that it had been necessary; as if Irène had had the slightest difficulty in overcoming her watchfulness! She would have had to be there always. But she had come last night; she would have stayed on unknown to Irène, if only Hervé had not been there. To think that she could have trusted in Hervé! Useless to try to overcome the repugnance she felt at opening this door. It was Irène's soul that she had loved, and not this dried out little face, with its hard and impenetrable forehead. This shell didn't need her anymore; she had nothing more to do here; now there was nothing left to do but to go and hide herself at home and await her own turn. The Master would do whatever He wished with this old heap of rags, whose every plan He had foiled . . . She cast an almost hateful glance at the door; let them arrange things together, Hervé and his victim!

Perhaps she would not have gone away, if she hadn't known that her son had a friend with him.

XVII

BUT the two friends, in the funereal bedroom, were not sitting next to each other; instead, the dead woman separated them, and their incommunicable thoughts separated them more widely still. Marcel contemplated Irène's face—magnificent in its peace. What imprints the vanished spirit had made on this flesh! From these lips no more much-anticipated words would issue—those lips and words that had so often reassured Marcel. He felt as if his doubts were now fully liberated; only Irène would have had power to exorcise them. And that she died on the very day when he was coming to beg help from her—the superstitious Marcel took this as a uniquely malignant sign.

Was this sleep, this motionlessness, Irène's true response? He who had thought he loved life, how vividly he understood this counsel of hers of silence, repose, annihilation! He suddenly knew what, earlier, would have surprised him: that, just as fire leaps from tree to tree in the forest, so the desire to die communicates itself from one being to another, and that a suicide never kills only himself. And then Marcel thought that he must keep the news of the death from Marie Chavès. He had so much hoped that Irène could save Marie! She had promised Marie that as soon as she was well enough to go out, her first visit would be to the home at Saint-Cloud. But the example she had just given risked being more potent than any of her words. "Look how easy it is," the dead woman seemed to say to those who had known her, "see: the heart stretched thin no longer asks to beat." Arrange it so that nothing is said to Marie. He would tell the servants, and he would phone the rest home tonight.

But Marcel knew how this act of Irène's was the easiest thing in the world to accomplish, and that every day it was done by even the weakest of women without any ostentation, without any fine phrases. If only he

could hide her death from himself! He would think of it all night long—
for how many nights?—while he lay next to Tota, hostile to him even in
her sleep—next to that body on the defensive, as if contracted and tight-
ened to defend the secret that she nourished every day with delight and
with terror. And even if he were to find that this thing he so feared was not
real, into what other anguish would he tumble? Thirty-seven years old,
already. And the judgment that had been handed down was well known:
no talent. Before he had even begun, here he was, finished. Why live, if
he was not loved?

In the apartment's silence, suddenly angry voices were raised. The
maid came to tell them that representatives from the neighbors were arguing in the entryway. Hervé begged Marcel to see them and to decide on
everything as he saw best. "Make it as easy and simple as it can be, without fuss . . . And please see to sending the necessary telegrams . . ." He
gave him the addresses in a low voice.

Hervé, alone now in the bedroom, sat down and closed his eyes. He
tried to work up some remorse within himself that he didn't feel. Or rather
the remorse had been covered over and smothered by some worries he
was ashamed of, by a vague hope that horrified him. He could not rid his
spirit of the thought that the funeral and the mourning would make him
lose an entire week: the meeting he had so looked forward to, and the
dance this Tuesday at the young American painter's . . . No doubt, one
could get back into normalcy quickly. The best thing would be to travel
for the first six months: nothing would get in his way now; nothing would
hold him back. An end to having to invent things, an end to lying. She had
made a will; he frowned; no, no; don't think about that. He forced himself
to smother this hideous joy he felt. He had so often imagined this death
that it seemed to be his doing, and not because he had abandoned Irène
that night. Rather, because everything he had so ardently desired was
coming to pass. Everything that he wanted to happen, necessarily had
happened.

"The only being in the whole world who loved me, perhaps; and here
I am the one who . . . But no, she was already lost. Whether it was tuberculosis or a tumor, all the doctors had sentenced her to death. What an
existence she had had to drag herself through! She preferred dying to living like that. If she had been healthy, she never would have dreamed of
killing herself. Anyway, it isn't really a suicide. An abuse of tranquilizers
in order to calm her unhappiness. I did nothing. If I had not gone out that
night . . . let's assume that she would have lived on for a few more weeks.
And even while I was reading to her, she was under the influence of her

drugs: the poisoning had already begun. If I had stayed home and gone off to bed, she would have died while I slept."

He looked at the corpse and reassured himself: "She can no longer know what I feel. She always saw my lowest thoughts; she revealed them to me. Now she can't know what I feel. Anyway, I'm not all that free to simply feel this or that. I may have suffered more in my life than I'm aware of. I don't know yet what it is that I've lost; it's often shown to be that way in books. Just like the soldier who doesn't realize he's been wounded: it's a well-known phenomenon. Keep away from Mama, with that intolerable gaze of hers. It must be said that I've gone to ground, that I don't want to see anyone. Am I such a horrible person? No, not at all: I'm simply lucid, simply sincere . . . But yes—I am horrible." Suddenly he could see himself as he really was, and he sought within himself some trace of a truly noble feeling, as he might have sought out a branch to cover his nakedness. He forced himself to look at the corpse so that the grief might rise in him. Finally an emotion began to be born within him, and he softened. He was consoled by a sweet sadness; he no longer seemed so horrible to himself; he felt himself judged as Irène would have judged him, with indulgence, but purified from all her disdain. A strange impression came to him, lasting only an instant: she was there, she was speaking to him: "I see you, miserable one, as, left to your own powers, you cannot help being . . ." His immense affliction appeared clearly to him, but as if it were bathed in a light of mercy and of pardon. It was only a brief flash. Marcel came back in and said, "It'll be tomorrow, at eleven." Hervé thought, "The day after tomorrow—by then, it will all be over."

In his imagination he could see the Lyon station at night, then dawn among the olive trees; breakfast in the dining-car; the inn, in an unfrequented region, where he was well known; all the pleasures of the future now so very close at hand. Then, having turned his eyes away from the corpse, he wept for himself, like a leper who has glimpsed his own hands.

XVIII

THE old woman made her way into the chapel, which was empty at that hour: it was nearly noon, but she knew she would find the one she was looking for. She knew he was there even before she saw him, and, making some noise to get his attention, she moved a chair next to the confessional.

"Understand me, Father: if there was ever anyone in the world who knew she had caused a soul to be lost, it's the miserable person speaking to you now. You have often heard me weeping in shame because this poor young woman judged religion by me; for her, I was the image of religion. I didn't even have to open my mouth—my mere approach irritated her, the way I carried myself. Irène had read everything, she knew everything, she understood it all. And I, I scarcely even knew the names of the authors she saw as her masters. Remember, I told you how she once said, "Catholicism is my mother-in-law . . ." Hervé told me, as he thought it was funny. Father, you who save so many souls, you who possess this immense happiness, can you conceive of it, of what is so horrifying to admit: by my presence alone, I slander, I ridicule, I mock the One that I love? I make Him despicable. I've distanced Him from a poor child who, without me perhaps, He would have drawn to Himself. I am like a caricature of all that is most holy in the world. And despite my stupidity, I could see what she felt about me. Hate seems to me to be less fearful than that disdain. She felt the same disgust for this poor old woman and for the Truth. I know: you will tell me that I am not responsible; that I should turn to prayer and penitence. I tried to be of some value for her; I thought I was doing what I could. I considered it a great instance of grace that I was allowed to divine Irène's attraction to suicide, her temptation to die; I kept watch over her. It seemed to me there wasn't the slightest danger as long as I was on the watch. For some time now, I haven't even minded that I exasperated her, so long as I kept up my surveillance. And I told myself that these things don't happen twice. It was enough with my husband (not to mention my little Nadine, who would have been thirty-seven today). My husband was enough, I believed; as if I had not seen the four children of my older sister disappear, one after the other . . . But what we accept in others' lives, we believe will never happen to us. Father, please listen and understand what it is I am confessing to you. I've always feared that you didn't really grasp the full extent of my sins. At first, I rebelled; no, that's not the right word: I felt something like indignation. After so many tears, so many prayers, so many communions . . . It seemed to me that some-body was mocking me. I held it against my victim: can you believe that I refused to get down on my knees beside that corpse? Yes, I fled from that despoiled soul, whose eternal destiny I dare not even imagine. Back at my home, I closed myself in and gave myself up to blasphemy, demanding enlightenment . . . Oh Father, the light has come, but not the light I wanted. A terrible light. I suddenly saw, I understood just how deeply I was involved in this disaster. I had thought that I was only guilty in hav-ing diminished and weakened the Truth in the eyes of this child. But now it suddenly appeared plainly to me: I had delivered her up to my son; I moved heaven and earth to get them married, to get her married to my son. Not once did I ever question myself; not once did I doubt that he was worthy of her. But still I knew—I knew . . . What did I know? What does a mother know of her son? I suddenly saw—I say it to God and to you. Oh, Father! As if anything were permitted when our own child is con-cerned! I wanted for him to be married, no matter what the cost. This stranger I delivered to him, whose earthly happiness I was toying with, perhaps even her eternal happiness . . . This thought never occurred to me. She was very rich, and I rejoiced in that, only wanting to make sure of the origins of her money (because I was always scrupulous, and I remem-ber asking you once whether one should fear that the inventors of Verley Kina had not contributed to the spread of alcoholism). You invited me, after my husband's death, to detach myself, to empty myself as much as possible. I did so, I thought I was doing so in giving my son practically everything I owned—as if emptying oneself were giving everything to a son who was one's entire earthly hope and desire! After I had made Hervé happy, at least in the eyes of the world, I became ferocious. I had to find a young woman for him, one who was isolated and defenseless. You know that Irène's mother is remarried and lives in London. The girl lived in Paris with an aunt who was anxious to get rid of her. She was the target for every family who had a son to marry off. We only hesitated because of her father, the businessman who "saw too clearly," as Hervé put it. I never confessed to having felt joy when I heard the news of his sudden death. (It is true, though, that I have had masses said for him, the only ones the poor man had.) Oh, I acted like a saint; I got up every day at five; it cost me no effort. I channeled all my lust into my son. I gave him counsel about being prudent, about being tenacious, I whispered to him all the things he wanted to hear; I told him the things he must not say. All that seemed natural to me; I lied for a long time, passionately. I denied that my husband was a suicide. I repeated many times the fiction about a hunting accident. Without the slightest shadow of any remorse. Am I confessing that it was just for myself? No—it was for my son. And you could begin to see his father in him. I don't want to go any farther; I don't want to know what I know, but I delivered an innocent girl up to him. With my own hands, I plunged her into despair. And I imposed my odious solicitude upon her. She saw this pitiless old woman every morning at her bedside, as if after having ruined her earthly life, I had taken on a mission of separating her from God, making Him disgusting to her. I am at the edge of despair—nothing remains for me but this crime, and I'm desperate already. How could the grace have been given me to get there in time? But I came there, that night. But it had to be Hervé who opened the door. I put my trust in Hervé, one more time! I had never felt so calm, so tranquil. All during that interminable night, until she died at dawn, that poor girl, she was alone; I was not there . . ."

She repeated, "I was not there," mechanically. The confessional's grill darkened her aged face. Her questioning eyes sought out, through the darkness, the priest's face, his head with its thick white hair, but all that could be seen was the tip of his nose and one lowered eye. Her heart had been emptying itself to the dregs without receiving any help from him, without a single interrupting word of pity or encouragement. The holy man, she thought, can't find anything to say to me. What would he say? She waited for his condemnation.

"My daughter," he finally pronounced.

And the word itself was filled with sweetness. The voice in the darkness repeated, "My dear daughter . . ." She could see that his face was bent down, never turned toward her, his two hands joined together at the level of his lips.

"Rejoice, my daughter."

The invitation to joy struck the bent and stooped creature like a thunderbolt.

"It seems to me—perhaps I'm getting ahead of myself—but no: there was no need for you to help the dying woman."

Though his voice was muffled, each syllable seemed utterly detached. "Father, have you understood me?"

In her stupor, the poor woman forgot to speak quietly; but she was interrupted:

"I can only repeat to you, and I tremble as I do, that the Lord has inspired me to say to you: 'She was absent. But I, I was there.'"

This was said almost breathlessly. Already the old woman was only hearing the customary words: " . . .And in order to obtain all the graces necessary for you, you will recite the Magnificat each day of the following week."

She had no awareness of the absolution, and she only arose at the sound of the grate closing. As she always did after confessing, she went to kneel as close as she could to the holy altar, thinking of nothing but her penance.

"My soul glorifies the Lord. And my spirit trembles with the lightness of God my Savior." She could not go beyond these opening verses, and she did not move.

XIX

MARCEL, returning from the rainy burial, was surprised to hear Tota asking him in an almost sweet voice whether he was tired, and whether he had had the time to get something to eat. Surely his feet were wet? She went off to look for his slippers. Marcel watched her with shock because when they had separated that morning they had been in the midst of a quarrel: she had refused to take part in the funeral ceremony: "I didn't know her," she repeated stubbornly; "I only saw her once." "It ought to be enough for you that Irène was my friend," he protested.

She pretended to be a stranger to everything connected to Marcel. "As soon as I care about someone, you turn away," he said to her. "You look for any reason to create distance between us, to oppose me."

Far from defending herself, Tota felt herself glorified by these words best calculated to wound him. But now he found her relaxed and more attentive to him than she had ever been since they had begun to live together. He felt moved, and he pressed her against his chest. She let herself be embraced with docility, even indulgence. "Not angry anymore?" he asked. He noted that she was wearing a dark dress with a folded-down collar and white cuffs. Only then, on the bed, he saw the suitcase open. Tota saw him look at it, and prevented his questions: she was going off to rest for a few days and hoped Marcel would approve. Only a few days to reflect on things.

"To think about me, about us . . . I'll leave tonight, or if you'd rather, tomorrow morning."

"Not for La Hume, Tota?"

It was not the protest she had expected. She had thought he would find the very idea of her trip offensive. Why should he care where she went?

"Wherever you like—to Rambouillet, to Fontainebleau, or maybe, better to Trianon, to Versailles."

Then she said that Versailles would be too close, that he would come to see her, would telephone her. Marcel seemed not to feel the blow, as if her desire to escape from him were nothing compared to the other torment within him, whose presence she could sense but which she could not make out.

"All right, then, go into the Midi—to Villefranche, or wherever you like . . ."

But she didn't want him to spend that much money on her alone. He thanked her, acidly, for her concern about his finances.

"But look, Marcel, why not La Hume? I haven't seen my mother for six months . . . My father never leaves his room, and he won't even know I'm there. I'll have Alain . . ."

"Alain's only been gone for less than a week."

She said nothing, surprised and disconcerted by the turn he had given the conversation. Marcel, standing, leaned against the radiator. He was making a great effort to remain calm.

"Remember, you can't live anymore at La Hume. The atmosphere at that house will stifle you. And now, everything there is worse than it was when you left; your mother is more than ever the prisoner of a sick man, who is crazier every day. You've often told me what winter is like there in that valley: the mud that gets stuck on your shoes, the humidity in that old cracked, fumigated house, the station six kilometers away with no decent car . . . I have no illusions, or at least I don't anymore: I know that the only reason you consented to marrying me was to get away from La Hume."

She saw well enough that she should have protested against that, but all she could do was make a vague gesture of denigration.

"I'll find the money," he was saying. "Don't worry about it. Anyway, I know some places in the Midi where the living is very cheap. Since the time when I was there . . ."

"No, no—you can't see me all alone in some little hotel?"

He said quietly, in a deliberately indifferent tone:

"If Alain could accompany you . . ."

"Oh! That would be too wonderful . . . Do you really think so? But no, he wouldn't want to leave Mama so soon after his trip here. And then he'll have even less money."

Marcel remarked in the same detached tone that, in any case, if all she wanted was to see Alain, she might as well go to La Hume.

"Yes, you're right," she exclaimed happily. "I didn't dare tell you because you seem to fear that he has a bad influence on me . . . But if you could only have heard the advice he's given me!"

And when Marcel asked her if they had often spoken together of him, she replied that they had hardly spoken of anything else: "but always in a manner you would have approved of, I'm sure."

Marcel did not reply. He looked out the window at the sad facades of the apartment buildings across the street. Tota thought that he seemed to have calmed down and that she could go ahead and make her preparations. But she was aware that there was something deeply troubling him. What ideas was he dreaming up in his head? Maybe he was afraid she was leaving for good? She wanted to reassure him and promised him she would be gone no longer than three weeks. But he only shrugged his shoulders. No, that wasn't what was bothering him. He would have consented to an even longer separation if only she weren't going to La Hume.

"At this time of the year," he said, "Alain must not have much to do: you'll have a lot of time . . ."

She assured him that on the contrary, in February, Alain would often be working among the vines.

"But there are the evenings," she added.

"Ah!" he said.

And she heard him swallow as if his throat were swollen shut.

"The evenings . . . when you're both free and you have your little private dinners together, after your mother has gone up to bed . . ."

"We won't be having any little private dinners," Tota replied with a smile.

But Marcel's look put an end to the smile.

"Why do you look so gloomy? I've told you I'll only be gone a couple of weeks."

She turned on the light, but he turned away brusquely and faced the wall, begging her to turn it off as his eyes were tired. She obeyed, surprised.

"I like dusk the best for conversation," he added. "There are some things one can say better when one can't see."

She protested that she hated the dark, but she dared not turn the light back on. She could make nothing out of that bland, unmoving face full of contradictions. She felt afraid of him: the acts he might commit? The words he might speak? She didn't know, but she sought some way out of this.

"Let's pull ourselves together a bit. When I get back, it seems to me that everything will be simpler. It has to be. And look, you have your mail to deal with: an urgent letter, a telegram. That's all you occupy yourself with anyway. What are you thinking about?"

"Stay a minute. I was thinking of Alain," he added with his indifferent, deliberately calm voice. "It's strange, isn't it, that a boy of twenty is so little involved with girls, don't you think?"

"What do you know about it? What do either of us know?" she replied with irritation.

He interrupted her to affirm that she would certainly be the first to be told about the slightest affair . . .

"Why would I be?"

He noticed the alteration in her voice. She said:

"A man like you can't understand Alain. I gather that you are supposing . . ."

"What do you think I'm imagining?" he asked with anguish.

"Apparently that he's a pervert? One of these people you talk about endlessly."

"Ah!" he sighed, somewhat comforted. "I see what you mean. No, no, I've no doubt that Alain wouldn't be capable . . ."

"All the same!" she said, reassured. "He's not twenty yet, just a boy. He's still too candid and open, true, but in other ways he has a great deal of maturity, of seriousness. There's something reserved, or maybe preserved . . ."

"Preserved from what? Reserved for whom?"

Tota didn't know how to reply. She sensed her husband was laughing, and she could barely see him. She had the sense of an impending threat. With an impulse that came to her intuitively, she switched on the light in a sudden movement. Marcel hid his eyes, crying out, "Turn it off! I can't stand it!" But while he stood there with his hands spread out before his face, Tota looked at his convulsing face. She had never really seen it, this face that Marie Chavès and so many other women knew well and often saw again in their dreams. He was murmuring some words whose sense escaped her; he was saying that Alain had no more need of women than she had need of men.

"Of a husband, that's something else. You were only too lucky to find me . . ."

She didn't understand him, but tried to get near the door, as if this man crouched before her had been armed with some immense power. She did not believe, though, that he wanted to strike her; but she had the sense that he was searching her heart, and that he was a threat to her heart. She thought of her brother, and couldn't keep from speaking his name half-aloud.

"You're calling him!" he groaned. "You see! But am I frightening you? You're not afraid of me, Tota, are you, my dear one?"

His face expressed nothing more than enormous pain. He forced himself to speak gently:

"I don't want to frighten you, it's not your fault; it's not your fault. I could picture so clearly your childhood, your adolescence in that deep valley, in that hollow of dust or mud, depending on the season. I know them, these houses more isolated in the countryside than some rock of an island in the Pacific; and your mother enslaved by that old evil god that you two always had to defend yourself from. He alone would have been enough for you two to be united against him, even if there hadn't been all the rest: the big fire in the kitchen in winter; and the seasons of great heat, when there was that worn-out sofa in the billiards room, the one you both spoke about so often at Cauterets . . ."

"Yes," said Tota, reassured, "it was on that sofa that we played together as children; and later, it was there that Alain read to me . . ."

She stopped. The way Marcel was looking at her frightened her. Where was he going? She protested to him that she didn't understand what he was getting at. But he cried:

"You understand me, because while I was speaking, you were shaking your head no. It could be that you haven't had any awareness of what I'm revealing to you today. Nothing has actually happened, I believe that . . . I'm almost sure . . . But . . ."

He was interrupted by Tota's laughter. She said:

"This time, I think I understand. How could it have taken me so long? What a creature you are," she said to him with contempt. "This is the sort of thing you occupy your mind with!"

She went and sat on the divan, her elbows on her knees, her head in her hands. Marcel wasn't sure if she was still laughing or if she was crying now. He approached her and tried to put his arm around her, but she pushed him away.

Far from being pained, he felt a deep joy in her revolt and in the repulsion that his words had caused in her. No, this time he could no longer doubt: he had created his absurd monster all by himself. The young woman's shock was not play-acting. She had to absorb all these hypotheses in order to get a glimpse of the suspicions with which he had tainted her. She had laughed, laughed at these things that seemed to her nonexistent, unreal. He could breathe at last: "She is going to loathe me; too bad! My spirit is at rest. I don't have to worry about this or try to conquer it any more. The ground is cleared now for rebuilding." His obsession dissipated and already the old concerns, which she had masked over, were reappearing. Could he throw himself into a novel—maybe on jealousy? "They'll see that I'm not finished yet."

Tota fixed her hair in front of the mirror. She took up a book and left the room without his daring to follow her. He could hear her, behind the door, turning pages. It didn't matter to him, now, not being with her. The profound calm within him was all the happiness he needed. Every jealous person has savored this feeling of peace, of inner silence, which sometimes interrupts the torture. But it was not true! It was not even believable! How could he have believed in this horror? When had he begun to believe it? The night when she had gone to the station to meet Alain, and he had entertained Hervé . . . Hervé's insinuations—were they really all it took to set off this madness within him? "No, I was already prepared for it. Hervé only made me reveal to myself what had been building up in me for a long time. But it's over now. The end of the suffering. Everything must be rebuilt. But where to start?"

Marcel considered that he had never troubled very much to make himself loved. He was not used to being the one of the couple who suffered, having been born the executioner the way others were born victims. Since Tota had entered his life, he had the feeling of playing a role he was not made for. All that would change. Without waiting another minute, he willed it, he demanded that this would change. The separation, to start with. A few weeks at La Hume: the cold, the mud, the glue-like surface of the roads, the mildewed papers, the saltpetered walls, the night soon arrived, the interminable evenings, the smell of illness, the howlings of the old man in the early hours . . . "She'll soon miss our bed, her dresses, dancing, alcohol . . ."

Marcel pushed the door half-open. A dim lamp was lit near the divan where he could just make out that she was stretched out, half turned toward the wall, her face hidden. When his embrace surprised her, she shuddered and, without looking at him, pushed away his hand. He did not get angry, but instead said:

"Can't we both be reasonable, both at the same time? It's your turn to be moody, and as for me, I no longer understand at all the insanity that possessed me just now; it's gone altogether, forever. I swear I'll never speak of it again. Let me kiss you."

But she struggled away.

"Tota! Can't you even look at me?"

As her face was pressed against the cushion, he could not hear what she was saying, but recognized the word "horror." He withdrew a bit, and he looked at her body which, from time to time, trembled. Her right shoulder, a little too pointed, had raised itself up. How he loved this slender neck, this child's nape! One of her legs was bent, the other extended— a leg that was a little too muscular, which didn't quite seem to belong to this body—what some people would call an ugly leg; but Marcel loved this hidden robustness, attaching aesthetic importance only to the ankles and the knees. Now he felt pain at the idea of her parting, of this separation; but it was almost nothing to be suffering for a real reason and not over some fantasy. He would have to spend several weeks without Tota. Well! Above all, don't let your unhappiness about it show. He offered to get her a seat on the Southern Express for the next day.

"The Southern leaves at a manageable hour. It's a good idea you've come up with. See, I can be reasonable."

As she said nothing in reply, her face always turned away from him, he asked if she wanted him to get the trunk down, or if she would make do with the smaller suitcases. Then, without turning, she said:

"I'm not going."

"But I've already told you, dear, that now I think it's a good idea for you to go."

She repeated that she was staying. He said to her, laughing, that she was nothing but a sulky and headstrong little girl, a real little beast; and taking her by the shoulders, he tried to turn her toward him. But she resisted, and he recoiled when he saw her face, furiously angry, shining with tears.

"I think," she moaned, "that I'll never be able to go back to La Hume, never!" Sitting up now, erect and straight, she looked ahead with a lost expression. "How horrible!" she said.

"But darling, since it's not true . . ."

When she didn't reply, he thought that perhaps she had not understood, and he repeated:

"But since it's not true!"

This time, she turned her petrified face toward him, and he couldn't doubt that she had understood.

"You know very well that it's not true!"

His anguish started to surge up in him again. It mounted, invaded him, overwhelmed him: it wasn't possible—Tota would surely find some word, make some gesture, smile. Yes, Tota's laugh would have been all it would have taken for him to find his calm again.

But she neither laughed nor spoke—overcome as she was by this new vision of her life turned upside down—this life that, just last night, she thought she understood; this life whose key *maybe* she held in her hand; was it the real key? She was innocent in both her thoughts and in her actions, of that she had no doubt . . . But beyond thoughts and actions, there was this confused sensation that she had never defined—had it been called by its right name tonight, for the first time? It only existed because it had been given a name. If she had died yesterday, if it had been her and not Irène who was buried today, this sensation would have had no reality at all. But two syllables, which she repeated continually without moving her lips, were enough to raise up before her this passion that men feared, this shame, this love. But the power of shadows, whose joy it is to taint and pollute all the sources of our hearts' springs, went much further this time and overshot the mark. Tota shook her head, holding her hands out in front of her as if for protection:

"What insanity!" she cried. "It is absolutely not true!"

She smiled finally, but it was not the smile Marcel had wanted; her voice had a begging tone; she was asking to be reassured. Now it was up to Marcel to prove to her that he had conjured this chimera up himself out of nothing, to prove to her that they were now both trembling in front of the monster like two savages who, having carved a hideous image of their god out of a tree trunk, now shrank before the obscene image.

"I've been going back over my memories," she said, "and I can't find a single scene, not a single instance, not a word, not a gesture that could . . . I swear it to you," she added, weeping.

"There, you see? Why do you search for it? What bothers me, Tota, is that you have to search . . ."

He sat beside her and took her hand. She did not withdraw it, being entirely elsewhere in her thoughts: Alain? He has a modesty, a chastity almost ridiculous in a young man. These are things that I would never dare tell anyone, and that people here would never understand. He never came into my room; he didn't like to see me in his. When I went swimming, that whole side of the river became a forbidden region. "What? What were you going to say?"

"Nothing . . ."

Marcel just kept himself from asking the question that was burning on his lips: "Exactly what was Alain afraid of?" She understood him, and was silent. They stayed that way, side by side, lost in their thoughts.

Marcel lit a cigarette and smoked uninterrupted. He thought about the rest that Irène had found. There, there was the only answer she could give him! When you can do no more, go to bed and sleep. But Irène had not been, like him, attached to life by precise tastes. She had never known real pleasure.

"It's not true," Tota repeated. "I know that it's not true. There's no need for me to prove that it isn't true."

They could hear the sounds of dishes being laid out in the kitchen. Marcel was worried:

"We won't be eating in, I hope?"

Tota got up without responding, and called out to the maid that there was no need to set the table.

"You won't leave tomorrow, Tota?"

No, she would send a telegram.

He asked if Alain was expecting her; she admitted that she had telegraphed him this afternoon.

"I'm going to get dressed; and you?"

He too; though not, tonight, the usual dinner jacket. They would be going to quite a few clubs tonight.

Tota thought about William. If only he would be free tonight! She would phone him to tell him to get free at all costs. They would dance till they couldn't stand up anymore. She went to put on the red dress that was always lucky, even if it was a little the worse for wear right now, and not low enough in the back. Really, she was glad not to be leaving; she would have died of boredom at La Hume. She came back in the room where Marcel was stretched out, smoking:

"You see, I'm happy not to be going. I'd have been so bored there."

He breathed out: this was the statement he had been waiting for; these were the kind of words that made him feel better. He had no real hope that this respite would last for long, but for tonight, at least, he knew where help lay: none of their dirty champagne, no cocktails: just whiskey.

After a minute of silence, he called Tota:

"But dear, do you think, on the very night of Irène's burial . . ."

She looked at him with astonishment.

"All the more reason," she said.

"Yes, you're right—all the more reason."

XX

AFTER the last shovelful of earth, after the last handshake, Hervé, seated in the car next to his old mother invisible beneath her veil, knew that the worst trial was yet to come: he would have to face his mother, as she had appeared to him on the day of Irène's death. He would have to look into that implacable face, so terrible to him that the sight of Irène dead had been less frightening to contemplate. Since then, she had hardly spoken a word to him, except to ask him to spend the night tonight at the Rue Las-Cases. A whole night to live through under that gaze!

He tried in vain to observe her behind her crepe. He saw nothing there but a profound insensibility, the same one that had horrified him the evening he returned: no tears, no sighs, not the slightest quiver or tremble. Thus, in this car, even more than Irène's death, his lost mother occupied Hervé's thoughts. So much the worse: nothing remained for him, and that only meant he would be all the more free. The little that, until now, he had been unable to accomplish due to his mother, all that was now open to him. He would turn this curse into a blessing. The ground was cleared, the old woman was distancing herself, and she no longer barred his route. Why had she asked him to spend the night at the Rue Las-Cases? "Maybe she's afraid that this very evening I'll start in again . . ." He giggled, walking alone up the stairs (he had left his mother in the elevator). No, she could rest easy: he would behave himself tonight. Now there was no pressure, no hurry; he had all the time in the world.

She waited for him on the landing, and with her trembling hand tried to open the door, unable to find the lock. He followed her in. One window had been left partly open, and, after the rain, a bird was singing as if it were Easter time, here at the end of February. Hervé regarded the sad inte-

362

rior of the apartment with complete indifference and lack of feeling; he was resolved to be indifferent.

"Hervé!"

He turned. She had thrown off her veil and, standing before him, still breathing a little heavily, she smiled at him. She smiled at him—no, this was no longer a judge, but neither was it his mother, exactly. Her face looked like that of a heart-attack victim, and Hervé looked at her pinched nose, her bluish lips, thinking that perhaps she was going to die herself, that perhaps it was a question of days, perhaps of hours. He took one of her old deformed hands in his, a hand with a spattering of brown spots, and with oversized bones. She called him again by his name. She was not crying, and she didn't seem to be in any pain. But what was worse was this deathlike face seeming to shine so visibly that Hervé's first thought was that she must have gone insane.

"My dear one," she said.

Ah! This was enough to reassure him. And suddenly, what neither shame, nor the horror expressed on his return, nor the wake with Irène, nor her funeral could get from him, this simple phrase did: his heart was at last opened, cracked and split open, and the heavy head of the grown man found again the place from childhood; and he hid his eyes against the shoulder and neck of his mother. No one can be upset by moistening his mother's neck with tears, nor by doing any harm to her dress; one even need feel no shame at grimacing and sniffling like a ten-year-old. And now he was ten years old again, and he had done no evil. His mother's gaze crossed over the thick bed of all his unknown acts, and she saw him again today just as he was then. Some purity remains in the least of men, so long as his mother is not dead! "Cry," she repeated to him. But she herself did not cry. With her hand, she cradled his head against her shoulder, while her eyes turned toward the window, searching out, above the court-yard, the dingy sky where a little blue sky flowered; and she thought that it must be later than she had believed, because the days were getting longer. Thus passed a few minutes; then she felt the head of her son escape her. Hervé rose, remained standing, and using both hands wiped at his face with his handkerchief. She called him again, and since he did not move, she went to him; she tried to force him to be held once more, but he resisted:

"Mama, you don't understand me."

"What a fool you are, dear!"

Using the same tone she had used to subdue him when he was a child, she added, as she would have then:

"Come on, Hervé: look me in the eyes."

But he turned away, stammering: she did not know that he had promised Irène he would stay in that night, that he had betrayed his promise, that if he had stayed . . . As his mother said nothing, he assumed that she had understood him. He hoped that she would repeat, "Look at me, my little one." But no. She dared do nothing more; she could do nothing more. He shot a rapid glance at her and was surprised to see her smiling and shaking her head. Had she finally understood him? And again he feared that she had lost her mind, because of what she then said: "What does that have to do with anything? It's unimportant. Everything is fine. Everything is for the best." And suddenly a burst of joy overwhelmed her, rendering her for a moment almost young again (as she was when she appeared so big, so majestic to the young Hervé):

"Oh my dear, if you only knew how we are loved!"

This time, he understood. His mother's favorite hobbyhorse would stand up against all the denials of it that the world could make. He should have said nothing, but all the same, this time it was just too much. He removed her arm from his shoulder and said with open irritation:

"Ah no, mama: don't say that to me." And then, with his voice lowered: "You can't know. I want to tell you that I could not . . . (Oh well—so much the worse: tonight, he would speak.) It's only your innocence that lets you believe that all is for the best. It would already be too much if there were only the ugliness, the isolation, poverty, all the world's diseases, and finally death; but there are other things beyond those. You pray, you go on repeating your prayers; and you're completely unaware of the existence of the gulf into which those closest to you are hurled. It isn't their fault; they didn't ask for it; they're horrified of it, once they've come to know it; it was all decided in advance, long before they were even born. They were already howling from the bottom of the abyss, they already had mud up to their mouths, and they still didn't even know where it was that they were, nor what this mud was . . . But what am I saying to you, mama—forget it. Don't even try to understand. What I've just said doesn't mean anything."

She appeared in no way moved. She observed, in the dusk, the form of her son bent over the low chair, his chin practically on his knees. And he could hear his mother breathing, and he expected no reply. Thus he was surprised when her peaceful voice rose up. She said, as if it were the most obvious thing: "Despite yourself, my son Hervé, you have received among others one very great grace."

"Me?"

"Yes, the greatest of all; you see it, you know it. You call the mud mud. You know that mud is mud."

"Yes," he said softly and as if despite himself, "I know it."

He felt no more anger. It had done him good to speak out even though, as he thought, his mother did not understand what he was saying. She asked him to come and sit near her, and he obeyed, putting his face again up between her shoulder and neck. His mother spoke about Irène, swearing that "the poor little one is sleeping in the Lord," that she herself had received assurance of it. Dreams, he thought, but he did not reject the comfort that came from the words, from the voice. A patch of sky was reflected in the glass front of the armoire. Mother's room, invaded by the shadows, had drifted back in time. He could recognize, leaning against this black dress, the scent of his childhood tears. If Irène had heard what the old woman was saying, perhaps she would have felt less disdain. What was mama saying? He forced himself to listen: "When the leper sees his ulcer, how can he help but wish to be cured? And if just one single time the promise of healing rang out in the world; and if millions of times this promise had been kept . . ." Hervé allowed himself to be cradled, abandoning himself as he did when he was very young, when his mother used to carry him almost asleep into his bedroom, undressing him in the glow of the nightlight, warming his feet by rubbing them with her hands.

And now she was speaking of Irène. She assured him that now Irène knew everything:

"She sees what I will see soon, my child. Before this year is out . . ."

When Hervé protested, she repeated again that her hour was near and that she knew it. And he was so struck by her tone of peaceful certitude that he could find nothing to say. He simply got up, turned on the lights, and gazed, as if it were for the first time, or for the last time, on the suffering face of his mother, who was still living.

XXI

THE afternoon maintained itself in that peace; and during the quick dinner they had by the fireplace and continuing until about eleven o'clock, Hervé could have believed he had become a different person. He had already kissed his mother and was thinking of nothing but going to sleep when one of the servants came in to tell him a woman wanted him on the telephone; he went, and recognized the voice of Marie Chavès.

"Pardon me, Hervé—your wife? Is there any news?"

He responded "no," gently. He heard her breathe out.

"Ah! You've taken a weight off me!"

She said that she was speaking to him from a café she'd been able to get out to, thanks to one of the workers in the rest home who helped her: there was definitely a conspiracy to prevent her from using the telephone. She had first asked for Marcel's number; the maid there had given her so ambiguous an answer that she would have been thrown into a panic if the maid hadn't added that Marcel and his wife were out at a restaurant and wouldn't be back until late.

Hervé could not help feeling an inner movement of joy: Marcel then was capable of that, of going out on the night of a good friend's burial; nothing could prevent him, for even an instant, from continuing his shabby nocturnal life. "He looks down on me, and he's just as low as I am."

Marie Chavès apologized for phoning Hervé's house, at the risk of waking up his sick wife. There too, the maid's tone had seemed to be embarrassed. She knew nothing at all about her mistress:

"She told me to call you, that you were dining at your mother's. I was imagining all sorts of horrible things, and I panicked—all for nothing, I'm sure."

Hervé knew, she was sure, the love and admiration she felt for his wife. Could he please reassure her that everything was all right?

He saw clearly, at this instant, that he must not hesitate. It would be enough to say, "Rest assured, everything is fine." But Hervé did not do it; he could not do it. He, the liar at so many junctures in his life, could no longer lie. The truth was oozing out of his pores, since it was a matter of a mortal truth.

"Pardon me for insisting: but you seem to hesitate. You seem troubled. No, nothing could happen this suddenly, could it? At least . . . She's a strong woman, incapable of . . . Say something! Are you there?"

"Poor Marie," he sighed.

And the cry escaped from her:

"We are so cursed!"

He heard her exclaim:

"No! It isn't possible. Her first visit, she promised me, would be to me at the rest home. She promised me: within the week . . ."

If there had been an accident, why would one have hidden it from her? Undoubtedly, she dared not speak the suspicion that haunted her. And at that moment, Hervé felt that jealousy that he had felt before, when people praised his wife instead of him. This sordid jealousy, then, has even survived Irène! And when Marie Chavès repeated:

"The only really strong woman I've ever known . . ."

"We are all weak, my poor Marie," he said flatly.

He heard her brief, stifled cry, her sharp intake of breath.

"But no, Marie, you've misunderstood me," he said. "There was nothing premeditated; it was only an accident; she was in too much pain, and she took her pills; she was only a little imprudent, taking too large a dose without thinking . . . Marie? Are you there?"

There was no one. Hervé hung up the receiver. He stood still a moment, in the middle of the dusty antechamber, in the sleeping apartment. What had he done? This evil force that emanated from him almost without his knowing it, that struck like lightning, left him in a state of stupor and lethargy. Tell Marcel about it, at all costs. But where to find him, at this hour? He looked in the phone book for the bars' numbers. Over the phone, he heard murmured laughter and the hiccup of a saxophone while a customer opened the lavatory door. The waiter confirmed for him that Marcel had just arrived.

Hervé did not hesitate to put the blame on his domestics. He heard Marcel curse, and then thank him for having thought of telling him—and above all on this night, when Hervé could be excused for not thinking of others. He added that he would phone Saint-Cloud immediately, but Hervé said:

"No, Marcel, don't you have your car? You need to go there without losing a minute: it may be a question of minutes."

Marcel was astonished at Hervé's solicitude—he seemed so impassioned! He did have his good side, after all. Yes, Hervé was right: it would be wisest to go immediately. He had not yet ordered a drink. What it was costing him to go back to the clubs, after this day, and after that scene with Tota! Marie Chavès . . . What a blow! It doesn't matter; he must leave; Irène would have thought it best for him to leave; Irène mustn't be the cause, even the involuntary one, of another disaster. He slipped between couples. No one paid any attention to how ravaged he looked from all he had been through that day.

"No!" Tota cried furiously. "We just got here. You go if you want."

He asked her to speak more softly, and she said:

"Go: William will take me home. Is that all right with you?"

Yes, William would be glad to. He blushed, and shot a glance at the husband who seemed indifferent about the proposition. Marcel, he thought, didn't take him seriously; he thought of him as quite harmless; he was wrong: tonight was the night. The boy repeated to himself that he'd have had her before dawn. Never had he felt himself in better form. He had forced himself, these last few days, to be more reasonable. He had reduced his dosages. But tonight was the night. Most often, his desires never coincided with the opportunity to satisfy them. And then Tota seemed, tonight, so defenseless . . .

Once Marcel was no longer there, they all felt irritable. William, between dances, did not sit next to Tota on the bench, but across from her, and he observed her with a somber and troubled eye. Waiting gave his young, worn face a serious, almost grave expression. If he had spoken freely, he would have said that what he was going to do that night had no importance, but secretly his whole being was reacting as if he were on the verge of a solemn event. He couldn't drink any more, and he no longer felt like dancing. He held the wine list, and was ashamed of his alcoholic hands, which shook.

Tota, her head leaned against the wall, stared into space and smoked. He saw the young woman's lips moving, and he tried to tease out what it was she was saying.

"What's not true, Tota? Oh yes, I could hear you: you kept saying, 'It's not true, I know it's not true . . .' What isn't true?"

She leaned forward on her elbows, and looked at him fixedly.

"Tell me what isn't true?"

She asked him to bend down: nobody else should hear it. Each saw the other's face very close. Tota noticed his beard was coming out a bit already, his heavy red eyelids over his burning, circled eyes, his large mouth half opened. And he saw her teeth, white but badly shaped, her forehead a little too yellow, her cheeks with their makeup slightly lined, her thin shoulders and her child's eyes full of tears.

"What's true," she said quietly, "what's true, is that I love you."

He shook his head; he didn't believe her. She asked why.

"Because you said it right away; because it isn't true."

As she said nothing in reply, he begged her to leave with him.

"I'll go out first, and you can join me in the car."

Sitting next to William as he drove, she said to him:

"It's strange, but I don't know anything about you, your parents, your childhood. Me, I talk all the time about La Hume and Alain. You could be the son of a—I don't know—of a convict!"

He laughed; he said he didn't like talking about his parents, and gave her only some dry facts: English origins, a house in Le Havre, coffee and cocoa; horrible people . . . His childhood? A lycée, vacations in Dinard—she interrupted sulkily:

"I know, I know—you've already told me all that . . . Essentially, you haven't got anything to tell me. That's not a true childhood."

She felt contempt for people who had no country roots.

"Where are we?" she asked. "You're not going toward the Seine?"

"It's the Boulevard Haussmann. We're here."

"But we're not going to your place, William?"

"We have to," he said quietly. "I want to; you want to as well."

He wrapped his left arm around her shoulders.

"You're shivering, Tota! Why are you trembling?"

He wanted to kiss her, but she turned her head away, and his lips only made contact with a moist and soiled cheek.

"No," she pleaded, "no! No."

"But sweetheart, I'm not some brute . . . Well—it won't be for tonight, then."

Then she felt more comfortable with him close to her. Until they reached the Rue Vaneau, she rode with her head on his shoulder. At times he felt her shudder slightly, like a child who was calming down.

"Here you are, Tota."

She got out, and looked at him.

"This is idiotic," she said to herself. "I don't know what came over me. What was wrong with me?"

Nothing remained of the little hunted-looking girl except the red eyelids and the damp cheeks. William looked with surprise at this disillusioned woman:

"Ah!" he growled. "Next time . . ."

XXII

SHE had just gone to bed when Marcel got in.

"It's a good thing I went to Saint-Cloud," he said. "There was a terrible scene, and I was the only one who could have settled her down. But at what a price! The doctor wants to send her to the country; and she wouldn't consent to go to the Midi unless I promised to go with her and spend a couple of weeks near her. What could I do? I promised . . . This is going to be hard."

He saw Tota stretched out on the bed; she also observed him narrowly.

"Really," she said in a mocking tone, "who could believe it? I think you're becoming a good person."

He shrugged: it wasn't a matter of goodness, he said, that made him do it, but the fear of having done anything he could be blamed for in case of a disaster. He didn't quite dare tell her that he wanted above all to do what Irène would have wanted him to do, if she had been still alive. He hesitated a minute:

"No need to add that nothing will happen between us, that nothing could happen between that poor old sick woman and me . . ."

"Old? How old is she?" asked Tota insolently. "I wouldn't have believed it. But if this is a part of her treatment, and if you so badly want to do it, don't deprive yourself over me."

He ground his teeth and tried to contain himself:

"This is a little too much, you know! Really, I never thought I'd see you jealous."

"And you either, I don't think? Anyway, you're going to leave me alone for two weeks, and you aren't afraid something might happen?"

She was a little calmer, and he could see there was some mockery in what she was saying. She thought of William, of what had just happened, and of what couldn't help but happen over a space of these two weeks.

"It's too funny," she said. "Really, you aren't afraid at all?"

"I'm not afraid of *that*."

And he looked at her pointedly.

"Oh, that's right! I forgot . . ."

The shadow of Alain passed between them. He noticed that she wasn't laughing anymore.

"Hurry up and get undressed, Marcel. There you stand with your arms dangling. It's almost two, and we've had a long hard day . . ."

"Yes—a hard day."

When he lay down beside her and turned out the lamp, he thought she was already asleep. But suddenly she spoke:

"Out of the whole lot of us, she's the only one at peace."

"Who do you mean, dear?"

"Irène, of course!"

"Ah," he groaned, "why are we all so in love with death?"

XXIII

TOTA dressed slowly: William would be late as usual and would not be coming for her before nine. Even though Marcel had been gone for a week, it was the first night they were going to spend together, William having disappeared for two or three days, or, as he put it, having "taken a plunge".

Tota had got along well enough in her solitude. She only knew a few people, and she discouraged advances from strangers—always defiant, bucking, always on the defensive and fearing that people were mocking her accent and her manners.

Above all, she didn't feel the desire to see anybody because nobody here had known them, her and Alain, at La Hume. So who then could have helped her, could have furnished her with points of reference in her search, in this quest that took her across her childhood and adolescence? She didn't go out any more, conjured up the most remote memories, followed down trails wherever they led, interpreted signs. It was not a matter of suffering so much as a matter of fatigue, of exhaustion. She didn't suffer, but she was at the end of her strength. To assure herself of that, all she needed was her reflection in the mirror, these long lines on her face, as after a long march.

But it had been necessary to make a sympathy visit to Hervé. Marcel convinced her by promising her that it was no more than a formality, and that she probably wouldn't be asked in anyway; but to her great surprise, she was introduced into the room of this old woman she knew only slightly, who stayed in bed and appeared very ill. Hervé, seated by her bedside, spied her earthy face with its pure, almost childlike eyes. Marcel made fun of Hervé's love for his mother: he said that types like Hervé always love their mamas dearly. But Tota was moved by the passionate care he was giving to his sick mother, to the point where he had hardly noticed their visitor. The old woman had said to Tota, in a slow voice (as if, perhaps, she had recently had a minor attack), that Irène had always thought very highly of Marcel and spoke of him often. The young woman had responded a bit foolishly, in a tone that tried to be humorous, that Marcel was not worth thinking very highly of. The old sick woman looked at her sadly and replied: "We are all worth a great deal . . ." Then, her eyes closed. Tota, intimidated, and thinking she was asleep, had already tiptoed to the door, when the old woman said in a strong voice: "I will think of you and him . . ."

This promise had displeased Tota: she didn't want anyone occupying themselves with them; she had no need of anyone. In fact, the only person she really needed was Alain. William was the first . . . Tonight, she would not be afraid . . . Yes! She was afraid; but she would let it play itself out; she would not give in to panic tonight. And anyway, William would be coming here, not taking her to his place.

"We'll talk," he had promised, "we'll smoke, we'll drink a bit by your fireplace. Things will happen, or they won't. Don't think about it; close your eyes."

But it was hard not to think about it. She wasn't absolutely sure that this wasn't the least important thing in the world. And then it would be the very best response to the idiotic ideas of Marcel. How strange it is, this unappeasable need to prove to ourselves that a chimera doesn't exist, that it never existed!

William would deliver her from this monotonous search. He would break this chain of images. Was she sure of that? In any case, it was going to happen tonight. Nothing could prevent it; it was inevitable. She couldn't imagine anything that would deter her from making this sorry fall. Why a fall? Just the reverse: she would be fixed; there would be a fixed point in her life. It would at least be pleasant, and maybe delicious. "Yes, but he'll make me suffer—he is sick, after all."

She looked at herself in the mirror, regretting that she had worn the black dress that William liked. She hated black; she had a country girl's taste for lively colors. This black dress made her look skinny . . . She didn't recognize the doorbell. But it was too soon—it must be the postman. The maid was on vacation, so she went to open the door herself—and saw Alain.

Perhaps what surprised her the most was that she wasn't more surprised:

"I felt like I was waiting for you . . ."

She added:

"What a surprise, you coming here today, at this very moment!"

Only then did she see that Alain was wearing black also.

"Father?" she asked.

He nodded. Yesterday, early, their mother had found him groaning on the tiles near the fireplace: he still wanted to burn some letters. He died during the evening, fully conscious to the very end, though he had been unable to speak

"And the money?"

Tota was ashamed to ask this question before every other one. But Alain forced himself to appear not at all shocked: the half-burned letter that their father was still gripping, when they had recovered it, gave them all the facts they needed: the money was safe.

"Well, I'll tell you all about it . . ."

Since she had written him that Marcel had left after the death of his friend Irène, he preferred to come directly to Paris and get her himself.

"But we have scarcely two hours before the train leaves: you've only got time to get changed and pack up your bags . . ."

"Yes," she added, with a sense of having been rescued, "and also to phone someone who was coming to get me here. Go wait in the studio. — What? Is it really worth it to pretend to be suffering? No, Alain, don't frown at me. I'll bet that mama has cried all the tears out of her body."

"She's very upset, and so am I. Go get dressed, you wicked little thing."

"I'm not wicked: I'm sure, once I'm at La Hume, to get emotional. Did you dare enter into his room? I think we'll continue, all our lives, to tiptoe past it, to speak in a whisper, to listen, with his coughing travelling across the ceilings . . ."

When she came back into the studio, dressed for the trip, Alain was sitting on the same chair, his back to the light. She looked at him, and suddenly took him in her arms, kissing him over and over on both cheeks. He kissed her as well.

"Ah!" she exclaimed with a sigh of joy, "that's the best response."

"Response to what?"

"I don't want to tell you; you wouldn't believe me . . . Or maybe it might have the same effect on you too . . . No, no, don't ask me."

She seemed to reflect. Maybe Marcel should come and join them at La Hume?

"How boring! But on the other hand, after having lived with both of us for a couple of days, he'll be cured. He couldn't not be cured."

374-5

"Cured of what?"

She shook her head without responding.

"Another secret?"

"Don't ask me. What happiness to leave with you tonight! If you knew the moment at which you arrived!"

Suddenly she took his head between her hands and turned him toward the light.

"Alain, my darling, something's wrong!"

And as he disengaged himself, laughing weakly:

"Yes! Something's up! What is it?"

He didn't smile; his lips moved slightly, but he said nothing.

"I've got it!" she exclaimed, clapping her hands.

And with that slightly vulgar and complicit air that so many women use when they touch on this subject:

"Love, eh? I'm right, aren't I? Admit it?"

"How stupid you can be, dearest."

"Just like that, you're changed!" she cried. "You're paler, your eyes look bigger . . . Yes or no?" she asked. "Speak up? I won't leave until you speak up. You'll make us miss the train."

She knelt before him as he sat in the chair, and leaned her head against his chest:

"Tell me: is it love?"

He only lowered his eyes.

"Who is it? Do I know her?"

He shook his head.

"When do I get to meet her, your conquest?"

He said nothing, and put a hand over his eyes. He seemed to be in pain.

"Who will you tell, if not me? Alain, are you crying? You're unhappy?"

He assured her that he was happy.

"She doesn't love you?"

"It's time, dearest. You haven't forgotten anything? Tomorrow we'll send a telegram to Marcel."

He was visibly struggling to change the subject. In the car, he asked where Marcel was.

"On a trip with his old flame. Funny, eh? Don't make that face! No! We're going to talk about everything, now, I hope! I'm going to tell you . . ."

He listened to her with profound attention.

376

"Can you believe that he was furious when I wasn't jealous? Wait and see if you think I'm joking. Anyway, even if I had been jealous, I'm absolutely sure nothing is going on between them. He doesn't want a suicide on his conscience: it would trouble his sleep! And then he has this 'prewar' side to him, the 'noble heart' side, as William calls it. I think he's playing to that side in Irène's memory. But it's a major sacrifice to him: it hurt him to leave me . . . For example, if he had foreseen that you would be coming in his absence . . ." She interrupted herself quickly. "No, unrelated point. I don't know why I said that."

The copy of *Parisian Life* that she had bought at the station slipped from her hands. She slept, enveloped in the gray blanket provided by the Orléans train. Her small, deathlike head shook with the jolts on the track. Alain had the feeling of having gone to seek out her body—under so much debris!—and of having carried it in his arms to this car. Where was he going now? He would not run quite so fast, from now on. It was as if Tota had her arms knotted around his neck; and Tota was not alone: many others were grasping at his clothing, and already he trailed a cluster of people behind him like a human bunch of grapes. Impossible to turn back; behind him, all the bridges destroyed; and ahead of him, the fire that he had to cross . . . *Vocation.* It's not for nothing that an adolescent is designated by his name, marked, set apart. Alain, without any mistrust, had made his way back up the river of delights that flowed dully beneath his pure years, and suddenly he found the source: a hill, not very high, a gallows scarcely elevated above the earth, half hidden by this poor eternal eddy of pain, of mockery and of love; and surrounding it, the terrifying indifference of the world (that gesture that lasts down through the centuries: the lance thrust into the heart, thrust by an indifferent hand). He could do nothing. He could look at nothing but the gallows; every response brought him back to the little catechism of children, which for two weeks now the old curé of Sauternes had been making him recite.

This happiness that brought him to the ground one night in La Hume, amid the dusty prairie, and which, later, set him running beneath the chestnut trees on the Champs-Elysées, and which, on the divan in the studio of a Paris apartment, kept him awake in a vigil until the dawn (and, in order to clutch it closely to him, he had lain with his arms crossed across his chest)—this happiness he had, perhaps, lost. At least, he no longer recognized it: someone had dragged it along the open roads and then, suddenly, revealed himself.

"Above all, never say: just this far and no farther . . ."

Tota had buried her face in the dirty pillow, and he could only see her shaven nape. The train's jolts that shook her body reminded him of his previous trip to Paris (only two weeks ago): an interminable journey, in a second-class carriage where, at dinner time, people unwrapped their food from greasy paper. He remembered having formulated, between Chatelle-rault and Poitiers, the question that he later asked his mother. This question had burned within him for so many months; how could he have held it in for so long? How could he have so long vanquished this curiosity that had finally invaded him altogether, possessed him, to the point that he remembered the train moving far too slowly, that he was desperate to reach La Hume, and that he was afraid of dying before learning the answer . . . Then, the old omnibus had left the Cérons station, and scarcely had crossed the Garonne, when without any preparation he asked his mother whether he had been baptized. He expected a yes or no, but he did not expect this frightened deflection of the question:

"Why are you asking me this? You know very well that your father . . ."

He interrupted her impatiently:

"So I wasn't?"

And she, as if to defend herself, and with that servile tone she had learned in the shadow of her husband: "What do you want from me! I have old ideas; I'm from another era. If you don't believe, what difference does it make to you? It doesn't matter, and it doesn't commit you to any-thing. And then bad things can come of it, especially for a girl, from not being baptized. From the moment when I'd had it done for Tota, it was hard to refuse to have it done for you—to refuse the curé of Sauternes, that is, who was very good in those days . . ."

"Then I was also?"

"Don't worry—needless to say, your father knew nothing of it. Nobody knew anything of it: the curé's servant and the sacristan, your godfather and godmother, have all been dead for a long time. There's no trace of it. Everybody knows that what really counts is your First Com-munion, and you never made that. Are you angry?"

He searched for a simple phrase that would reassure his mother and also, without troubling her, tell her the truth. So he said to her quietly, and without seeming to attach any importance to the matter, that on the con-trary, it was sweet to him to know that he belonged to Christ. Was this the first time Alain had pronounced that name aloud? Until he drew his last breath, he would remember the thunder that single syllable made in the old, jolting omnibus on a road in the Entre-Deux-Mers, one night.

Alain recalled that his mother had stared at him narrowly, in the glow of the lantern (which also illuminated the heavy back of the horse, and the makeshift harness). Perhaps she recalled her wedding day, when her husband whispered to her, on the threshold of the church: "Take a good look at this old cavern; you'll never set foot in it again." She had given in on what seemed to her to be the less important point; one could pray just as well at home as in a church; God is everywhere. She had watched over the grain; she had managed her ship well enough; she had accomplished her official duties. And now (which is funny!) the little one interests himself in things she had never spoken about. No doubt about it, he didn't resemble the Forcas family much. On her side of the family, the Brannens side, there had always been religion; herself, at the convent of Loretto, and until her marriage . . . How life's cares had buried all that, covered it all over! Did it really exist?

While the brakes squealed on the descent to La Hume, Alain remembered that she had repeated: "For the doctor to have told me to call you back home, the end must be near. Probably your father will live until spring, but there's also a risk that he may go at any moment; and maybe even at this moment, as I speak." And as the omnibus turned into the avenue, she had looked out to see if there was a light in the sick man's room.

Alain had been struck by this confused feeling of waiting and of hoping, of embarrassment, and of the terror that his mother's words expressed. He had helped her down out of the omnibus. A little lantern, attached to the wall of the entryway, lit up the flagstones, many of which were cracked and uneven. And as soon as the door had opened, they began, instinctively, to keep their voices down. As far back as his memory went, they had always spoken with low voices in that house.

"Wait a minute," she had whispered to him. "I want to ask you: Tota is not ill, is she? Not too tired? You haven't noticed anything?"

He understood that she was thinking of a child. She smiled, thinking of the time perhaps not far off when Tota would come back to La Hume, a baby in her arms. She had never really got close to this violent daughter of hers; but the day she had a baby . . .

"Above all, don't let your father know that you've seen Tota. Be careful: I told him that you went to visit the exposition of mechanical reapers."

Alain's childhood fear came back to him as he ascended the steps behind his mother. The stone steps were slippery with years of use. When they reached the landing, they could see a bright light shining from under one of the doors, through a hole the rats had made. And now the odor of illness dominated everything. Mother and son stood motionless at the door: a large wood fire was burning, lighting the floor, eroded in places, and the mahogany armchairs, but leaving the bed and its alcove in darkness.

"You go in first."

"No, you."

Neither dared enter, until the steady wheezing of the sick man had assured the mother that he was asleep.

"He's sleeping: tomorrow will be a better day," she murmured with deep satisfaction, like a good wife anxious about her husband's ill health.

Alain sat up until dawn beside this stranger, this man who, all his life, had been no part of him . . .

"Is this Angoulême?"

Tota rubbed at the muddy window with her glove.

"Listen, Alain, while you slept I was amusing myself by arranging our life at La Hume. It'll be just as it was before, but without the one who made it so stifling. I'll leave when I've had enough; then I'll come back; we'll travel . . . I doubt that Marcel will be making long stays here . . ."

Her brother listened to her, without saying a word of his own. He thought that in less than a month he would be gone; he didn't yet know where he would go; God knew.

Tota continued, "Oh yes, I forgot about your love affair! I imagine it must have taken place fairly close to our home . . ."

She saw Alain's lips moving, but, in the noise of the train, she could not hear his response:

"Very near—only a stone's throw."[11]

Notes

1. Maurice Barrès (1862-1923) was a major French novelist, journalist, and increasingly rightist and nationalist politician who was a major influence on many in the generation of Hervé and Marcel—and indeed, on Mauriac himself. In 1910, when Mauriac was just twenty-five, Barrès was at the height of his fame, and the older writer took notice of Mauriac's early book of poems, *Les Mains jointes* [Clasped Hands]; for Mauriac, this was a major step in his career, one he wrote about in his 1940 essay, *La Rencontre avec Barrès* [Meeting Barrès]. But as that book makes clear, even in 1910 Mauriac was of two minds about Barrès' politics and theories, and in later years he moved even further away from the elder master. Here, the quaint-sounding phrase, "the studious and romantic lamp," recalls not only what had become the outmoded diction of Barrès, but also the idealistic youth of Marcel and Hervé.

2. Charles Andler, *Nietzsche: Sa vie et sa pensée* [Nietzsche: His Life and Thought] (Paris: Bossard, 1920). Nietzsche's influence on Mauriac and his generation—the generation that experienced World War I—was very great. As a young man, Mauriac was fascinated by him. But in later years, he came to see the influence as negative. Nietzsche the atheist, the philosopher of the will to power, enchanted a disillusioned generation, but Mauriac (like most Catholics) came to see him as a false guide, and a spiritually destructive force.

3. The value of the franc had been steadily decreasing since the Peace of 1919. The franc went from 5.45 to the U.S. dollar in 1919, to 25 to the dollar in 1928, when it was somewhat stabilized by the harsh economic policies of Raymond Poincaré. While this steady erosion in value was disastrous for many, it was an opportunity for those who could afford to play on the stock market—as Marcel has done. For a discussion of economic conditions in France during the period of *What Was Lost*, see

Eugen Weber, *The Hollow Years: France in the 1930s* (New York: Norton, 1994).

4. This is the heroine of Mauriac's most famous novel, *Thérèse Desquey-roux* (1927). She comes from the same part of the country as Alain Forcas, the Southwest, and thus he recognizes the name. Within Mauriac's fictional universe, Alain might well recognize the name for other reasons: Thérèse had been put on trial for the attempted murder of her husband, and people in the vicinity would certainly have heard of the scandal. But Alain is young, relatively innocent, and uninterested in gossip, so her name only has a faint ring for him. On the significance of Thérèse for Mauriac and for *What Was Lost*, see the introduction.

5. Atlas, in Greek mythology, was the Titan who was punished for his rebellion by having to hold up the sky on his shoulders. The metaphorical "Atlases" Mauriac refers to here are the dedicated, semi-reclusive religious, men and women, whose prayers expiate the sins of the rest of humankind. The theme is an important one in the Catholic tradition, and was made explicit in, for example, J. K. Huysmans' autobiographical novel, *En Route* (1895): "in all ages, nuns have offered themselves to heaven as expiatory victims. The lives of saints, both men and women, who desired these sacrifices abound, of those who atoned for the sins of others by sufferings eagerly demanded and patiently borne" (*En Route*, trans. W. Fleming. New York: Hippocrene, 1989, 39). This reference to the idea of expiatory prayer and suffering via the image of Atlas suggests that perhaps we should see other "frail Atlases" in the characters of Irène, Madame de Blénauge, and others in *What Was Lost*. The theme is employed in Mauriac's own earlier works, notably *Préséances* (1921, translated as *Questions of Precedence*) and *Le Baiser au Lépreux* [A Kiss for the Leper] (1922), and is a defining feature of the Catholic novel in general—see, for instance, Evelyn Waugh's *Brideshead Revisited* (1945) and Graham Greene's *The End of the Affair* (1951).

6. Leo Tolstoy's *War and Peace* (1864-1869) and George Eliot's *The Mill on the Floss* (1860) are both examples of the large-scale epic novel favored by previous generations. Mauriac's own works had been lean, spare, focused, and thus in conformity with the new, modern taste. Yet the invocation of these two giant classic novels here may also suggest some parallel between their methods and that of *What Was Lost*, which, like the Tolstoy and Eliot novels, employs sets of characters whose destinies are interlinked, rather than emphasizing a single main character. See the Introduction for a discussion of Mauriac's rethinking of the art of the novel between 1928 and 1930.

7. From Daniel Halévy, *La Vie de Frédéric Nietzsche* [Life of Frederick Nietzsche] (Paris: Calmann-Lévy, 1909), 211. Halévy (1872-1962),

biographer, historian, and art critic, was among the first to introduce Nietzsche and his philosophy to the French.

8. Halévy, 235.

9. From Charles Baudelaire's "Les Phares." The translation here is by Richard Howard, who titles the poem "Guiding Lights" in his translation of *Les Fleurs du mal* (Boston: David R. Godine, 1982), 16-18. The poem is a series of meditations on great artists—Rubens, Leonardo, Rembrandt, etc.—and the last stanza, quoted by Irène, suggests that all the greatest work by the greatest geniuses of the past perhaps amounts to little more than a sob of pain.

10. Dominique Parodi's *Le Problème Moral et la Pensée Contemporaine* [The Moral Problem and Modern Thought] (Paris: Librairie Félix Alcan, 1927) was a collection of his previously published essays on contemporary moral thought. Parodi was a civil servant, Inspecteur Général de l'Instruction Publique at the time, and his book would have struck Irène—and probably any reader enamored of the passionate Nietzsche—as tediously academic. Mauriac's point here is presumably not to ridicule Parodi who, in this book and its sequel, *Les Bases psychologiques de la vie morale* [The Psychological Bases of Moral Life] (Paris: Félix Alcan, 1928), provides a good overview of the pre-existentialist moral theory of the 1920s. Rather, Mauriac seems to be indicating that through her reading, Irène is desperately seeking out spiritual sustenance, and is looking in all the wrong places.

11. The allusion is to the gospel of Luke. On the night He is to be arrested, Jesus takes his disciples to the Mount of Olives to pray. Luke tells us: "When he arrived at the place he said to them, 'Pray that you may not undergo the test.' After withdrawing about a stone's throw from them and kneeling, he prayed, saying, 'Father, if you are willing, take this cup away from me; still, not my will but yours be done'" (Luke 22: 40-42). The reference to the "stone's throw" suggests at once the nearness of the loving Christ, but also the isolation of the suffering Christ. Tota believes Alain is in love with a woman, and he lets her think that for now, but his love is clearly for Christ, and the phrase here shows both Alain's sense of nearness to Him and Alain's own isolation in his newfound religious vocation.

About the Author

François Mauriac, born in Bordeaux in 1885, became one of the greatest novelists of his generation. A series of highly successful novels in the 1920s led to his election to the French Academy in 1933. Mauriac's novels, both those from the 1920s and later, are swiftly paced psychological studies of individuals in crisis; he places these characters within a Catholic framework, so that questions of sin, grace, and redemption are always central. He also wrote reviews, criticism, poetry, plays, and biographies. During World War II he wrote for the French Resistance under the pseudonym "Forez," and after the war he continued to work prolifically both as a novelist and journalist. He was awarded the Nobel Prize for Literature in 1952. He divided his time between Paris and the family home in the countryside near Bordeaux, where most of his novels are set. He died in Paris in 1970.

Raymond N. MacKenzie, the translator, is Professor of English at the University of St. Thomas in St. Paul, Minnesota. He is the author of a biography of the novelist Viola Meynell, and he has published a number of articles on literature, ethics, and publishing history.